NEW RIGHT VS. OLD RIGHT
& OTHER ESSAYS

by

GREG JOHNSON

FOREWORD BY
KEVIN MACDONALD

Counter-Currents Publishing Ltd.
San Francisco
2013

Copyright © 2013 by Greg Johnson
All rights reserved

Foreword © 2014 by Kevin MacDonald

Cover design by Kevin I. Slaughter

Published in the United States by
COUNTER-CURRENTS PUBLISHING LTD.
P.O. Box 22638
San Francisco, CA 94122
USA
http://www.counter-currents.com/

Hardcover ISBN: 978-1-935965-59-6
Paperback ISBN: 978-1-935965-60-2
E-book ISBN: 978-1-935965-61-9

Library of Congress Cataloging-in-Publication Data

Johnson, Greg, 1971-
 [Essays. Selections]
 New right vs. old right & other essays / by Greg Johnson : foreword by Kevin MacDonald.
   1 online resource.
 Includes bibliographical references and index.
 Description based on print version record and CIP data provided by publisher; resource not viewed.
  ISBN 978-1-935965-61-9 (epub) -- ISBN 978-1-935965-59-6 (hardcover : alk. paper)
 1. Conservatism--Philosophy. 2. Conservatism--United States. 3. Right and left (Political science)--United States. 4. Fascism. 5. National socialism. 6. Jewish nationalism. 7. White nationalism--United States.
 I. Title. II. Title: New right versus old right and other essays.

JC573
320.52--dc23

2013024587

Contents

Foreword by Kevin MacDonald ❖ iii

1. Introduction ❖ xiii

Politics & Metapolitics

2. New Right vs. Old Right ❖ 1
3. Hegemony ❖ 10
4. Metapolitics & Occult Warfare ❖ 18
5. Theory & Practice ❖ 35
6. Reflections on Carl Schmitt's *The Concept of the Political* ❖ 38
7. The Relevance of Philosophy to Political Change ❖ 45
8. The Moral Factor ❖ 56
9. The Psychology of Conversion ❖ 70

Disputed Questions

10. Our Fault? ❖ 76
11. The Burden of Hitler ❖ 85
12. Dealing with the Holocaust ❖ 92
13. White Nationalism & Jewish Nationalism ❖ 108
14. The Christian Question in White Nationalism ❖ 116
15. Racial Civil Religion ❖ 119
16. That Old-Time Liberalism ❖ 124
17. The Woman Question in White Nationalism ❖ 128
18. Notes on Populism, Elitism, & Democracy ❖ 135
19. The Perils of Positive Thinking ❖ 144
20. The Politics of Resentment ❖ 149
21. "Worse is Better" ❖ 154

Building a Movement

22. Learning from the Left ❖ 158
23. Explicit White Nationalism ❖ 163

24. Secret Agents ❖ 169
25. The Psychology of Apostasy ❖ 173
26. First, Do No Harm ❖ 181

Distractions & Dead Ends

27. White Nationalists & the Political "Mainstream" ❖ 185
28. Why Conservatives STILL Can't Win ❖ 191
29. Status Competition, Jews, & Racialist Mainstreaming ❖ 197
30. The Laugh Test ❖ 204
31. Premature Populism ❖ 209
32. On Violence ❖ 215

Index ❖ 225

About the Author ❖ 230

Foreword

Kevin MacDonald

Perhaps it's best to start off with what *New Right vs. Old Right* is not. Greg Johnson does not assail his readers with statistics to prove the Jewish role in the decline and impending fall of whites in America and elsewhere. He does not discuss the corruption of the media and the academic world and how they got that way. He does not discuss data on race differences in IQ and criminality to explain the behavior of non-white America. He doesn't aim to refute the current mantra that race is nothing more than a social construct designed to provide white people with unearned privilege.

Those intellectual battles are over, and we have won, although the mainstream media and academic world continue to promulgate cultural Marxist blather as if it were a set of truths set in stone. The starting point for *NRvOR* is that the media, the academic world, and the political process are hopelessly corrupt. So where do we go from here?

Greg Johnson's basic point is that we must work to create a metapolitics of explicit white identity—that is, a movement that will develop "the intellectual and cultural foundations for effective White Nationalist politics in North America, so that we can ultimately create a white homeland or homelands on this continent."

Greg is one of the reasons why I think this is a feasible project. A very great reason for optimism is that there are so many intelligent, well-spoken people who "get it"—who understand that whites around the world are in decline and that there will be dire consequences if whites are unable to establish white homelands. People like Greg Johnson are part of a hugely important trend. I have recently met a great many young, intelligent, well-educated, and well-spoken people at conferences dedicated to activism on behalf of the interests of white America— the exact opposite of the image of uneducated, violent males sporting swastikas and missing a couple of teeth that has been so carefully crafted by our hostile elites.

Despite growing up with a constant barrage of multicultural, anti-white propaganda beginning in elementary school, these individuals understand that at this point America is an unfolding disaster as whites are increasingly displaced throughout the economic and political spectrum. They are acutely aware that whites are a minority of births in America and that whites will be a minority within their lifetimes—a minority with diminished prospects and increasingly victimized by the non-white majority, many of whom retain historical grudges against white America. It is very likely that the America of the future will be beset with chronic conflict among different racial/ethnic groups. The idea that America or the West can avoid such conflicts as their societies become ever more factionalized is magical and utopian.

The goal, therefore, is not, a "supremacism" that is in any way invidious. Rather, "the best way to ensure peace and good will among peoples and preserve human racial, cultural, and religious diversity is to give each distinct group a homeland where it can live and develop according to its own distinct nature and destiny."

This is an attitude that seems to me to be pervasive in the white advocacy movement. It at once defuses a very effective bit of rhetoric of the Left—repeated with predictable regularity by organizations like the Southern Poverty Law Center. We are white advocates, people who, as Greg phrases it in several places following Michael Polignano, "take our own side" in issues of racial/ethnic conflict. And in taking our own side, we are doing exactly what racial/ethnic groups have done from time immemorial. No one accuses the Koreans of "Korean supremacism" for adopting policies aimed at retaining Korean demographic and cultural predominance. And imagine the horror by Western elites at a proposal to flood African countries with whites so that native Africans cease to be a political majority.

Make no mistake about it. The policies that are making whites minorities in lands they have dominated for hundreds or (in the case of Europe) thousands of years are not driven by utopian dreams of a raceless future, except among gullible, intimidated whites. The non-whites who are so enthusiastically embracing the decline of white political and cultural power are driven by hatred toward whites as a people and as a culture. This is a major theme of my writing on Jewish influence, and apparent as well in a host of non-white intellectuals and activists.

Greg Johnson received his Ph.D. in philosophy, and it shows. His forte is the well-developed argument presented in a lucid, easily understood style. There will be no complaints about this book being filled with turgid prose. And I can't find any major disagreements.

I was particularly struck by several points. For example, unlike the European New Right, Greg is an advocate of white racial nationalism:

> insofar as the breakdown of European national identities and the blending of European stocks in our North American context forces us (1) to give greater place to biological race and other deep roots of common European identity, and (2) to put greater emphasis on the Jewish question, given the role of American Jewry in promoting anti-white policies both in the United States and in white countries worldwide.

Right. As a biologist, there is always the tendency to see matters like race as a decontextualized matter. DNA, after all, is DNA. But American whites are indeed a very intermixed lot — a successful example of a European melting pot. In effect, we have created a new biological reality not present in any European country.

Nevertheless, we must remember that Europeans are in general closely related biologically, particularly in the north and east of Europe, as recent data continue to show. Indeed,

> typical pairs of individuals drawn from across Europe have a good chance of sharing long stretches of [identical genes] by descent, even when they are separated by thousands of kilometers. We can furthermore conclude that

pairs of individuals across Europe are reasonably likely to share common genetic ancestors within the last 1,000 years, and are certain to share many within the last 2,500 years.[1]

The white race is indeed a biological as well as a cultural reality. This biological reality forms a powerful basis for a scientifically based understanding of a commonality of interests wherever whites are living, whether in Europe or in the European diaspora.

And, yes, although the organized Jewish community has pursued the same set of policies favoring displacement-level immigration and multiculturalism throughout the West, Jewish influence varies in different Western societies. This brings up the need for developing a good model of cultural diffusion within the West. For example, academic culture is self-consciously international. If indeed the main impetus for the leftward shift is Jewish involvement in the Left beginning in the United States with the movements described in *The Culture of Critique*, it is not at all surprising that this culture spread to other areas with less Jewish influence given the pre-eminence of the U.S. in the post-World War II Western world. An aspiring academic in, say, Norway or Finland, who subscribes to a White Nationalist worldview would find himself ostracized from international academic societies, while countrymen who subscribed to the reigning cultural Marxism would find international recognition.

The same phenomenon occurs in the political realm, as, for example, when Austrian politician Jörg Haider joined a coalition government in 2000. This resulted in huge international pressure, with EU member states refusing to cooperate with the Austrian government and Israel withdrawing its ambassador. The assault on the Golden Dawn party in Greece is a more recent

---

[1] Ralph Peter and Graham Coop, "The Geography of Recent Genetic Ancestry across Europe," *PLOS Biology*, vol. 11, no. 5 (May 7, 2013): e1001555. doi:10.1371/journal.pbio.100155

http://www.plosbiology.org/article/fetchObject.action?uri=info%3Adoi%2F10.1371%2Fjournal.pbio.1001555&representation=PDF

example. Any Western government that opposed continued immigration and multiculturalism would be subjected to similar pressures.

The culture of Western suicide exists throughout the white world, and dominating the most powerful country in the West goes a very long way to dominating the entire Western world, particularly given the fact that Jews often control media even in countries with very tiny Jewish populations, as with the Bonnier family in Norway and Sweden.

Greg does not shy away from discussing difficult issues having to do with National Socialism, supporting the ideal of an organic, hierarchical, meritocratic society dedicated to advancing the interests of whites and rejecting "*party politics, totalitarianism, terrorism, imperialism, and genocide.*"

I agree entirely. It's a very good strategy to confront such issues head-on rather than to leave them to be discussed solely by our enemies. It's the same with the holocaust. The holocaust is simply not important for white advocacy, and whatever happened is not the responsibility of any living whites; it's something that must be simply "stepped over," to use Jonathan Bowden's felicitous phrase. Even if the holocaust were proved to have never occurred to the satisfaction of one and all, there is more than enough resentment by Jews about their past in Europe and the United States to fuel the hostility toward the West that has been such a prominent feature of the organized Jewish community and so many influential Jewish individuals. The reality of Jews as a hostile elite aiming to displace white elites throughout the West would not change at all.

I should think that it would be uncontroversial that the white advocacy movement must be metapolitical, since there is a crying need to build up a self-confident, prideful culture than can eventually become mainstream. Greg's argument that it is premature to pursue nationalist party politics — that at this point the money can be better used in education and organizing — will be more controversial. The question is whether these are really incompatible goals and, as Greg rightly notes, "We share the same broad aims, but we differ as to the best means of achieving them. We need to acknowledge these differences frankly, then divide our camp and pursue our common aims by the various paths that seem best to us." Different ways should be attempted in the hope that eventually something will work. In the meantime, we must be as inclusive as possible.

In fact, nationalist parties have made substantial headway in Europe, and many observers are expecting a significant representation of nationalist parties to result from the 2014 European Parliament elections. With increasing success, the messages of these parties have inevitably become more widely known. Significantly, these parties have not developed with an explicitly pro-white or pro-ethnic nationalism agenda, but have rather attempted to stay under the radar of political correctness on race and on Jewish influence, basing themselves on an implicit ethnic nationalism that opposes immigration and multiculturalism for a whole host of reasons apart from the danger of ethnic swamping that is in fact lurking in the background. Not surprisingly, these messages are often most effective with the white working class, the group that has suffered the most from the immigration tsunami.

Indeed, I believe that model of change that I think most probable is that the revolution will begin in Europe with the success of one of these parties, particularly if it occurs in a pivotal country like France where there is a clear possibility that the Front National will obtain power, and in a context where other nationalist parties have substantial representation in other areas of Europe so that an effective countermovement of isolation and ostracism cannot develop. I think we are rapidly approaching such a situation now. Compared to America, Europe has the advantage of very ancient cultures and identities that are mortally endangered by this new dispensation. Once such a party gains power, then more explicit messages of ethnic and racial interests may become more acceptable, paving the way for more the dissemination of a theoretical framework based explicitly on ethnic interests.

I worry that in the absence of near-term political goals, a purely metapolitical movement is in danger of being a detached inward-looking, even self-serving elite. For one thing, the Left is completely in control of the academic scene and very actively—

indeed passionately—polices any deviation from political correctness. This is quite unlike the situation in American universities where Franz Boas was able to control academic anthropology by the early 20th century, and several of the New York Intellectuals obtained positions at elite universities well before 1960. This is a very formidable barrier to the spread of an elite culture of white identity given the close relationship between universities and intellectual life in the West. There was no complaint from the academic world when the 1965 immigration law opened up immigration to the United States to all peoples of the world. Indeed, in several Western countries, Australia comes to mind, the movement to open up immigration to non-whites originated in the universities.

Even in America, with so many barriers against us, political action inside or outside the context of the electoral process could be a positive force for change. Americans need to see noisy, intelligent, attractive, committed white people marching in the street with signs opposed to immigration, multiculturalism, and the strident ethnic politics of other groups; there is a need for a steady drumbeat of political advertising where pro-white themes, whether explicitly white or not, are repeated over and over to the point that they become part of the furniture of life even if winning elections remains a distant goal.

Such movements may be particularly important for whites with less education who may be turned off by an elite culture of white identity. The white working class in fact has been the prime loser in the cultural changes promoted by our hostile elites. A great many of them are angry and, with less to lose than so many well-educated whites, they are an important natural constituency.

In any case, I wholeheartedly agree that we have to be open to a diversity of approaches.

Greg's essay, "The Moral Factor," raises the important issue of moral motivation which I think is an aspect of Western uniqueness. One does not see Chinese people agonizing over the fact that the Han Chinese greatly expanded their territory at the expense of other peoples. Nor does one see the Bantu peoples of Africa worrying about the ethics of displacing other African peoples as they spread far and wide from their homeland in Central Africa, including into South Africa where their treatment at the hands of white South Africans became Exhibit A for white evil during the apartheid era; nor do the Bantu-speaking peoples agonize about the widespread practice of slavery in Africa. Arabs do not apologize about their conquests in the name of Islam or their centuries-old role in slavery and the slave trade. As Greg notes, the Spaniards have apologized for the *Reconquista* that expelled the Muslims from Spain, but there are no apologies from the Muslims for the *Conquista*.

Whites are the only people to abolish slavery, and a great many of the activists and the fundamental popular sentiments so crucial in the ultimate victory over slavery were motivated by moral idealism, including especially empathy for slaves.[2] They did so despite very real costs to many individuals and to society as a whole, and all this occurred before the rise of the Jewish hostile elite. Indeed, this unique characteristic of whites is exploited by Jewish intellectuals for their own hateful ends. My basic theory is that this is a holdover of Northern European hunter-gatherer culture, where one's status in a group is based on reputation for moral behavior (honesty, fair dealing) rather than on kinship relations—an aspect of Western individualism.

So I agree that "even if White Nationalism is politically meaningful, people will resist it if they think it is immoral. But they will move heaven and earth to establish white homelands if they think it is the right thing to do." We must win the moral battle. The problem is that "our people overwhelmingly believe that our cause is unjust." And yet, the moral argument for white survival is obvious and compelling. Fundamentally, our basic survival as a people and as a culture are threatened. As Greg notes, "the present system is not merely anti-white, it is genocidally anti-white."

That's enough for me to mark the present system as utterly

---

[2] Kevin MacDonald, "Empathy and Moral Universalism as Components of White Pathology: The Movement to Abolish Slavery in England," *The Occidental Quarterly*, vol. 13, no. 2 (Summer 2013), pp. 39–63.

depraved morally. It is profoundly immoral to inflict multiculturalism upon the white populations of the West, given that ethnic conflict is absolutely predictable, based upon everything we know of the bloody history of ethnically divided societies. This is especially the case given that support for multiculturalism and support for their own demographic and political eclipse have never been majority views among whites. Whether in Australia or New Zealand, North America or Europe—in every case throughout the West, immigration and multi-culturalism have been projects of media, academic, and political elites. These changes have been top-down, not at all bottom-up.

We must pay more attention to the morality of infringing upon the legitimate rights and interests of the white majority. Everyone has rights and everyone has interests. The interests and rights of whites as a majority are no less morally legitimate than those of any other group. Whites must jettison the ideal of moral universalism and ask what is good for the future of whites.

On the basis of this collection of essays, Greg Johnson has a compelling vision of the impending disaster facing the people and culture of the West and what we can do about it right now. It is presented in a highly readable, well-argued manner that at once shows the power and confidence of the developing metapolitical culture of a Western renaissance. I wholeheartedly recommend it.

January 15, 2014

Kevin MacDonald, Professor of Psychology at California State University—Long Beach, is the author of *A People That Shall Dwell Alone: Judaism as a Group Evolutionary Strategy* (1994), *Separation and Its Discontents: Toward an Evolutionary Theory of Anti-Semitism* (1998), and *The Culture of Critique: An Evolutionary Analysis of Jewish Involvement in Twentieth-Century Intellectual and Political Movements* (1998), as well as *Cultural Insurrections: Essays on Western Civilization, Jewish Influence, and Anti-Semitism* (2007).

INTRODUCTION*

This book was written in urgency out of a sense of danger. Europeans, my people, both in our mother continent and scattered around the globe, now live under a cultural, political, and economic system that has set our race on the path to cultural decadence and demographic decline. If these trends are not reversed, whites will disappear as a distinct race. The incomparable light we bring to the world will be extinguished, and the greatness of our achievements will be preserved only in fragments, like the scraps of literature, shards of pottery, and shattered artworks that survived the wreck of pagan antiquity.

To stop this, we need to become conscious of our identity and interests and regain control of our politics, culture, and destiny. But this will require more than just a political movement. The purpose of these essays is to promote a North American New Right, which I understand as a specifically metapolitical movement which aims to lay the intellectual and cultural foundations for effective White Nationalist politics in North America, so that we can ultimately create a white homeland or homelands on this continent. We also hope to learn from and contribute to the similar struggles of European peoples around the globe.

Although I make my views and preferences clear, the purpose of these essays is less to present my own worldview than to argue for the necessity of a metapolitical approach to White Nationalism. I see the North American New Right as an inherently pluralistic movement. I recognize that one can arrive at the same political conclusions from a number of different intellectual starting points. I also recognize that my own views can and will be developed and improved, both by myself and others. Thus I

---

*Some of this Introduction is freely adapted from my Editorial "Toward a North American New Right," in *North American New Right*, vol. 1, ed. Greg Johnson (San Francisco: Counter-Currents, 2012). Other parts come from my "Frequently Asked Questions," Part 1, which can be found at http://www.counter-currents.com/2012/06/frequently-asked-questions-part-1/

focus more on raising metapolitical questions than on answering them. I also discuss how a metapolitical movement can be organized, how it can interface with political parties and the culture at large, and how it differs from other approaches to White Nationalism.

In this brief introduction, I wish to define three basic concepts that appear again and again throughout the book: *metapolitics*, *ethnonationalism*, and *White Nationalism*.

Political change does not just happen. It has necessary causes and conditions. *Metapolitics* refers to the non-political preconditions of political change. These conditions fall into two broad categories: (1) education and (2) community organizing. Education refers to the creation and propagation of a worldview, an intellectual case for a new political order. Community organizing refers to the creation of an actual, real-world community that lives according to our worldview in the present day and serves as the vanguard and nucleus of a new political order to come.

Three basic metapolitical questions need to be answered if we are to make a coherent and persuasive case for White Nationalism: *identity* (who are we, and who isn't us?), *morality* (what are our duties to ourselves, our race and subracial groups, and other races?), and *practicality* (how can we actually create the White Republic?).

Ethnonationalism is the idea that every distinct ethnic group should enjoy political sovereignty and an ethnically homogeneous homeland or homelands. The opposing view is multiculturalism, which holds that multiple ethnic groups should share the same homelands and governments.

Unfortunately, ethnic, racial, and cultural diversity inevitably lead to friction, which can either wear away distinct identities or spark hatred, conflict, and violence. Therefore, the best way to ensure peace and good will among peoples and preserve human racial, cultural, and religious diversity is to give each distinct group a homeland where it can live and develop according to its own distinct nature and destiny.

White Nationalism is a political philosophy that seeks to define national identity in racial rather than religious, cultural, or creedal terms. White Nationalism makes the most sense in the context of European colonial societies like the United States and Canada, Australia and New Zealand, or Argentina and Uruguay, in which older white ethnic identities have been undermined through the blending of distinct European immigrant stocks, creating an ever more blended, generic white identity.

White Nationalism also makes sense in the context of competition from other races, which tend to see themselves and whites in simple racial terms. Even whites who do not see themselves merely as whites may be forced to do so as racial conflict increases, simply because their enemies will see and treat them as generically white.

In Europe, where old national and regional identities remain robust, generic whiteness and White Nationalism, if adopted as one's *primary* identity and political philosophy, would actually promote the breakdown of distinct identities and the homogenization of Europe. However, a sense of European identity can still supervene upon more compact national and regional identities.

This wider sense of European identity can actually work to preserve particular identities in two important ways. First, it can help to prevent conflict among European peoples. Second, it can help European peoples to unite in the face of non-white immigration, which is primarily organized under the banner of Islam.

The message of the North American New Right, if boiled down to a simple mantra, is this: whites are a distinct ethnic group with distinct interests. We live in a world in which there are real ethnic conflicts. It is right for whites to take our own side in these ethnic conflicts. Multicultural, multiracial societies make ethnic conflict and hatred inevitable. Ethnic conflict can best be ended by the creation of ethnically homogeneous homelands for all peoples. Thus it is an existential imperative—a matter of life and death—for whites to create or preserve ethnically homogeneous homelands.

All of these essays have been previously published at Counter-Currents/*North American New Right*, under my editorship, or at *The Occidental Observer*, under the editorship of Kevin MacDonald. I wish to thank Dr. MacDonald for allowing the latter pieces to be reprinted here.

I wish to give special thanks to Michael Polignano, the co-founder of Counter-Currents Publishing and *North American New Right*, without whom this book, and so much more, would have been impossible. I also wish to thank Kevin MacDonald for his Foreword and Kerry Bolton, Jack Donovan, and Ted Sallis for their promotional blurbs, Matthew Peters for his careful proofreading, and Kevin Slaughter for his excellent design work. I wish to thank Collin Cleary, F. Roger Devlin, Gregory Hood, Michael O'Meara, Matt Parrott, Ted Sallis, Trainspotter, and many others who cannot be named for improving or even inspiring these essays through conversations and comments. Finally, I wish to thank the readers, authors, and donors of Counter-Currents/*North American New Right* for their indispensable support.

Although Alain de Benoist, Guillaume Faye, and other thinkers of the European New Right—and beyond them, the great minds of the European philosophical tradition—have influenced and inspired me, the most proximate and powerful influence on this book is Jonathan Bowden, who helped me find my voice. Thus I dedicate it to his memory.

Greg Johnson
San Francisco
December 29, 2013

NEW RIGHT VS. OLD RIGHT

What is "new" about the North American New Right, and how does it relate to the "Old Right"?

Before I can answer that, I need to clarify what the Old Right and the New Right have in common and what differentiates them from today's phony Right: namely the present-day center-Right parties and all forms of classical liberalism.

The true Right, in both its Old and New versions, is founded on the rejection of human *equality* as a fact and as a norm. The true Right embraces the idea that mankind is and ought to be unequal, i.e., differentiated. Men are different from women. Adults are different from children. The wise are different from the foolish, the smart from the stupid, the strong from the weak, the beautiful from the ugly. We are differentiated by race, history, language, religion, nation, tribe, and culture. These differences matter, and because they matter, all of life is governed by real hierarchies of fact and value, not by the chimera of equality.

The true Right rejects egalitarianism root and branch.

The true Right has three species: traditional society, the Old Right, and the New Right.

Every traditional society known to man is inegalitarian. All forms of traditional society have been destroyed—or are in the process of being destroyed—by modern, egalitarian, mass society.

For our purposes, the Old Right means Fascism, National Socialism, and other national-populist movements, which are the pre-eminent attempts to restore traditional hierarchical social forms within the context of modernity.[1] Fascism and National Socialism were not merely reactionary, rearguard resistances to

---

[1] Thus I am not referring to the American "Old Right" of the 1930s to the 1960s, which opposed the New Deal and American entry into World War II. Nor am I referring to the "Old Right" of the pre-Thatcherite Conservative Party in the United Kingdom.

modern egalitarianism by partisans of corrupt hierarchies. They represented a genuinely revolutionary impetus to restore vital, archaic, hierarchical values within the context of modern science, technology, and mass society.

The New Right and the Old Right share the same goal: a society that is not just hierarchical but also *organic*, a body politic, a racially and culturally homogeneous people, a people that is one in blood and spirit, a people that is politically organized and sovereign and thus in control of its own destiny.

Our ideal is *a hierarchical society free of exploitation and injustice* because the sole justification of political inequality is the common good of the body politic, not the factional good of the ruling stratum.

So how does the New Right differ from Fascism and National Socialism? This is a vital question, because of the intense stigmas attached to these movements since the Second World War. *The North American New Right, like the European New Right, is founded on the rejection of Fascist and National Socialist party politics, totalitarianism, terrorism, imperialism, and genocide.*

The North American New Right is a new movement. We do not have any thinkers of the caliber of Alain de Benoist, Guillaume Faye, and many others. We are deeply indebted to the decades of work they have done. But since North America differs from Europe, our approach differs as well, in three important ways.

First, because of the blending of European stocks and breakdown of more compact European national identities in North America, we are forced to stress the deeper roots of common European identity, including racial identity.

Second, because of the leading role of the organized Jewish community in engineering the destruction of European peoples, and because the United States is the citadel of Jewish power in the world today, the North American New Right must deal straightforwardly with the Jewish question.

Third, the North American New Right cultivates a much more frank and direct critical engagement with Fascism and National Socialism. The European New Right tends to focus on the fringes of the National Socialist and Fascist milieu, which has produced enormous intellectual dividends, particularly with the study of the Conservative Revolutionary movement. The North American New Right, however, takes full advantage of our First Amendment protections. But our willingness to go where there be dragons means that we need to clarify our precise relationship to the Old Right.

Again: *The North American New Right is founded on the rejection of Fascist and National Socialist party politics, totalitarianism, terrorism, imperialism, and genocide.*

We believe that racial and cultural diversity within the same society inevitably leads to hatred and violence, and that nationalism is the most practical way to ensure peace between peoples.

We believe that *all* peoples should have sovereign homelands where they can live according to their own lights, free from the interference of other peoples.

We believe that such a world can be achieved through gradual and humane programs of territorial partition and population transfer.

We believe that these aims can come about by changing people's consciousness, i.e., by persuading enough people in positions of influence that *everyone* has a stake in ethnonationalism.

The promotion of political change through the transformation of consciousness and culture is what we call *metapolitics*.

Metapolitics refers to what must come before the foundation of a new political order. Metapolitics breaks down into two basic activities. First, there is *education*: articulating and communicating forms of White Nationalism tailored to the interests and outlooks of the full array of white constituencies. This includes not just ivory tower theorizing but also artistic expression, topical cultural and political commentary, and the whole range of media by which they are communicated. Second, there is *community organizing*, meaning the cultivation of real-world communities that live according to our vision in the present and may serve as the seeds of a New Order to come.

The primary metapolitical project of the North American New Right is to challenge and replace the hegemony of anti-white ideas throughout our culture and political system. The entire cultural and political mainstream — including every shade of the "respectable" political spectrum—treats white racial consciousness and white self-assertion as evil.

Our goal is to critique and destroy this consensus and make white racial consciousness and self-assertion hegemonic instead, so that no matter what political party wins office, white interests will be secured. Our goal is a pluralistic white society in which there is disagreement and debate about a whole range of issues. But white survival will not be among them.

There are systematic analogies between the Old Right and the Old Left, and between the New Right and the New Left.

The Old Right and Old Left had widely divergent aims, but shared common means: hierarchical, ideological political parties organized for both electioneering and armed struggle; one-party police states led by dictators; the elimination of opposition through censorship, imprisonment, terror, and outright murder, sometimes on a mind-boggling industrial scale.

Yes, in the case of classical National Socialism, revisionists argue that many of these atrocities are exaggerated or made up out of whole cloth. But revisionism about the Second World War is really beside the point, because the terroristic, imperialistic, genocidal impulse exists in National Socialism *today*. For instance, latter-day National Socialist William Pierce routinely pooh-poohed the holocaust. But he was willing to countenance *real* terrorism, imperialism, and genocide on a scale that would dwarf anything in the 20th century. That spirit is what we reject.

Yes, there were degrees of totalitarianism. The Communist abolition of private property entailed a far greater disruption of and intrusion into private life than Fascism or National Socialism, which merely sought to harmonize private property and private enterprise with the common good whenever they conflicted. Fortunately, hard totalitarianism—even the softest version of hard totalitarianism—is neither desirable nor necessary to secure the existence of our people, so we reject it.

It is instructive to look at how the New Left has handled the mind-boggling atrocities of the Old Left. The best New Leftists do not deny them. They do not minimize them. They do not pin their hopes on "Gulag revisionism" or rehabilitating the reputation of Pol Pot. They simply disown the atrocities. They step over them and keep moving toward their goals.

This is exactly what we propose to do. We are too busy resisting our own genocide to tie ourselves to defending the mistakes and excesses of the Old Right. They are simply not our problem. To borrow a phrase from Jonathan Bowden, "We've stepped over that."[2] Our enemies keep throwing it down in our path, and we just keep stepping over it.

The New Left retained the values and ultimate goals of the Old Left. They also retained elements of their philosophical framework. They then set about spreading their ideas throughout the culture by means of propaganda and institutional subversion. And they won. Aside from Cuba and North Korea, orthodox Communism is dead. Capitalism seems everywhere triumphant. And yet in the realm of culture, Leftist values are completely hegemonic. The Left lost the Cold War, but they won the peace.

(Since in the West, both the Old Left and the New Left functioned primarily as a vehicle for Jewish ethnic interests, it would be more precise to say that Jewish values are hegemonic throughout the culture, even on the mainstream Right.)

The New Left and New Right have widely divergent aims, but very similar means, namely the pursuit of political change through transforming ideas and culture, aiming at the establishment of intellectual and cultural hegemony.

The New Right rejects the totalitarianism, terrorism, imperialism, and genocide of the Old Right.

But we do not reject their political model: the ethnically and culturally homogeneous, hierarchically organized, organic society. We want a world in which *every* distinct people has such a homeland, including the Jews.

Nor do we reject the theoretical frameworks of Fascism and National Socialism, which today are more relevant and better-grounded in science and history than ever before.

Nor do we reject such figures as Hitler and Mussolini. Objectivity requires that we recognize their virtues as well as their flaws. We have much to learn from them. We will never repudi-

---

[2] http://www.counter-currents.com/2012/05/revisionism/

ate awakened white people just to curry favor with the bourgeoisie.

I have received some gentle ribbing about including Hitler and Mussolini among the birthdays we commemorate at the Counter-Currents/*North American New Right* website, as it smacks of the totalitarian cult of personality. But as an editor, I find that birthdays are ideal, regularly occurring occasions to discuss important figures. They also produce spikes in search engine traffic, which we want to capture. Besides, we commemorate many birthdays, and it would be craven to discuss people like Ezra Pound or Knut Hamsun but ignore the people they were imprisoned for following. So we will keep commemorating their birthdays until, eventually, everybody does.

One of the main motives of the New Left's move from politics to culture was disappointment with the proletariat, which was so effectively mobilized by Fascism and National Socialism, not to mention the centrist regimes of the Cold War era.

The New Left believed they represented the interests of the workers, but their approach was entirely elitist. They focused their attention on influencing the college-educated middle and professional classes, because these people have disproportionate influence on the rest of society, particularly through education, the media, and popular culture.

Likewise, the New Right represents the interests of all whites, but when it comes to social change, we need to adopt a resolutely elitist strategy. We need to recognize that, culturally and politically speaking, some whites matter more than others. History is not made by the masses. It is made *out of* the masses. It is made by elites *molding the masses*. Thus we need to direct our message to the educated, urban middle and professional classes and above.

There is no shortage of Old Right-style groups with populist messages targeting working-class and rural constituencies. But we need to go beyond them if we are going to win.

The North American New Right is an intellectual *movement*, not a fixed doctrine. The goals are fixed. The basic intellectual strategy is fixed. But everything else is in movement: usually toward our goals, but sometimes just whirling around the dance floor for the sheer joy of it (which, in a subtler way, also moves toward our goals).

There is a wide array of different and often incompatible intellectual traditions within the New Right. We have followers of the Traditionalism of Julius Evola and René Guénon as well as other thinkers who emphasize a metaphysics of eternal form. We have followers of non-Traditionalist, flux and history-oriented philosophers like Nietzsche, Spengler, and Heidegger. We have believers in decline and believers in Promethean progressivism. We have Darwinian biologists and scientific materialists squared off against metaphysical dualists. We have atheists, and we have representatives of all schools of religion, Christian and pagan, Eastern and Western.

We need this kind of diversity, because our goal is to foster versions of White Nationalism that appeal to all existing white constituencies. We can speak to multitudes because we contain multitudes.

How does the North American New Right relate to Old Right-style groups in North America and around the globe? And how do we relate to various democratic nationalist parties in America and Europe?

Alex Kurtagić has recently argued that democratic party politics can perform the metapolitical functions of education and community organizing, thus there is no fundamental contradiction between metapolitics and party politics.[3] Of course political campaigning involves education and community organizing, but these are merely the by-products of pursuing office. And that goal means that all educational and organizing efforts must be dominated by the election cycle and the political issues of the day.

That is fine, if one's real goal is to win office. But outside of proportional representation systems, seeking office is pretty much futile. So if one's real goal is education and organizing, then political campaigning is merely a distraction. So why not focus all one's energy into educational and organizing efforts,

---

[3] http://www.theoccidentalobserver.net/2012/04/the-role-of-party-politics-in-the-culture-war/

and determine the agenda ourselves, rather than let electoral politics determine it for us?

Why not take all the money spent on purely political activities — voter registration drives, campaign travel, campaign literature — and channel it into education and organizing?

David Duke, for example, has been doing enormously important work with his writings, speeches, and videos. Most of that work would come to a stop if he were to make another futile and expensive run for office.

Intellectually, we need to draw a sharp, clear line between New Right metapolitics and all forms of nationalist party politics. We share the same broad aims, but we differ as to the best means of achieving them. We need to acknowledge these differences frankly, then divide our camp and pursue our common aims by the various paths that seem best to us.

I do not wish to spend time criticizing and attacking other sincere white advocates, competing for turf and followers or squabbling over dimes. In the end, the only valid argument for or against an approach is to look at its results. I want to win support by doing good work, not denigrating the work of others.

Even though one can draw a sharp *intellectual* line between New Right metapolitics and nationalist party politics, no wall separates us in the real world. The North American New Right is not a political party or a party-like intellectual sect. We are an informal network that can overlap and penetrate all social institutions, including parties. I maintain contacts with people all over the globe who are involved in various political parties. They know where I stand. Where we disagree, we agree to disagree.

Speaking personally, however, I wish that a wall could be erected in some cases, for if there are only six degrees of social separation between me and Barack Obama, there are far fewer degrees of separation between me and the next Anders Behring Breivik. And, for me, that is just too close for comfort. *I do not want anything to do with gun-toting armies of one.* (The only gun I want to own is one of Charles Krafft's porcelain ones.)

You see, I *really believe* that what I am doing is right and important. Too right and too important to expose to the risk of grown men dressing up as Knights Templar or Storm Troopers and playing with real guns. I have nothing against guns or gun-owners as such. But the Old Right model attracts unstable, violence-prone people, which just makes our job harder.

But since I can't build a movement—even a metapolitical movement—by being a hermit, the best I can do is draw clear *intellectual* lines of demarcation: again, *the North American New Right is founded on the rejection of Fascist and National Socialist party politics, totalitarianism, terrorism, imperialism, and genocide.*[4]

Cynics have accused the New Left of being nothing but a dishonest marketing ploy. Of course, there is no point in trying to convince cynics, who know *a priori* that the truth is always more sordid than it seems. But the New Left actually delivered on its promises: Marxism without totalitarianism, without terror, without camps.

Of course we all know that the present regime is a form of soft totalitarianism which is enacting the genocide of the white race in slow motion. But the point is that this regime was not imposed upon our people through a violent revolution. They accepted it because of the transformation of their consciousness. They can be saved the same way.

Counter-Currents/*North American New Right*,
May 11, 2012

---

[4] Breivik is a complex case, because he emerged from the Counter-Jihad movement, a Jewish-dominated false opposition to the Islamic colonization of Europe. But we still share his basic concerns and his goal of Europe for Europeans, even though we reject his actions and much of his analytical framework. See my article, "Breivik: A Strange New Respect," http://www.counter-currents.com/2012/05/breivik-a-strange-new-respect/

Hegemony

In September of 2001, just after the September 11 terrorist attacks, I flew to Paris to attend the Front National's Fête des Bleu-blanc-rouge, a political rally and fair attended by tens of thousands of French nationalists, plus well-wishers from around the world. Before the event began, I attended an impromptu meeting of Anglophone nationalists from the United States, Canada, and Great Britain.

When the topic of 9/11 came up, there was a very instructive disagreement. The Americans wanted to emphasize the role of Jewish domination of American foreign policy in causing 9/11. England, however, has a much larger Muslim population per capita than the US, and many of the Englishmen present had witnessed the jubilation of Muslims at the attacks. So they emphasized the problem with Muslim immigration.

Of course, they were both right. The 9/11 attacks could not have happened without Jewish domination or Muslim immigration. As I listened to the discussion becoming more and more heated, it dawned on me that no matter what side one takes on the question, "Do we blame the Jews or the Muslims?" white people cannot really lose, since we want to free ourselves of *both* Jews and Muslims.

Framing the Argument

I had always thought of politics as a matter of winning arguments, i.e., being on the prevailing side in debates about political issues. But it occurred to me that there is a power greater than that of winning an argument. That is the power to *frame* an argument, to set the parameters of debate, so that one always wins, no matter what the outcome. It is a case of saying, "Heads I win, tails you lose."

A couple of years later, Mike Polignano and I went to a movie in Berkeley. Before the trailers for upcoming films, they showed advertisements. One ad featured a contest between Coke and Diet Coke. I smiled and remarked, "That is a contest that the

Coca-Cola Corporation cannot lose."

Getting people to debate questions like, "Do we blame the Muslims or the Jews?" is a form of political control. Once the public argues within these parameters, we don't need to worry about the outcome. Whites really cannot lose.

Or, to be precise, the only way we could lose is by failing to understand the nature of the question, taking one side too seriously, and developing hard feelings toward our "opponents."

To avoid that outcome, one must not only *frame* the question. One also needs to *control* both sides of the debate. One must not just *script* political theater. One must also *stage* it. But one needs to make sure that the actors don't take their roles too seriously. This is Nerfball, not hardball. Stage fighting, not real fighting. One guy takes a swing, the other jerks his head back, and the sound effects guy creates a smack. It just has to *look* real to the people in the audience. The ring announcers and talking heads do the rest, selling people on the idea that what they are seeing is a real contest.

Controlling the political realm by framing and stage-managing political debate is a form of what is called "hegemony."

HEGEMONY

"Hegemony," from the Greek *hegemonia*, means leadership, domination, rule. But it is not just any kind of rule. For the ancient Greeks, hegemony referred to imperial or federal leadership, in which the *hegemon* rules over other states with regard to foreign and military affairs but leaves domestic matters in their hands. For the man in the street, therefore, hegemony appears as a distant, indirect, mediated, "soft" form of domination—although, of course, *hegemons* had the power to make war on recalcitrant followers.

Hegemony can also take a cultural form, ruling over the political realm by shaping the values and ideas that set the parameters and goals of specifically political activity, including debate. In other words, cultural hegemony is a matter of "metapolitics." Thus hegemony is a key concept for the metapolitical project of the North American New Right.

If political power ultimately comes from the barrel of a gun, metapolitics determines who aims the gun, at whom it is aimed, and why. If political power is "hard" power, because it ultimately reduces to force, metapolitical hegemony is "soft" power that ultimately reduces to persuasion. (Persuasion is a matter of rhetoric, which involves but cannot be reduced to rational argument.)

JEWISH HEGEMONY

Cultural hegemony is the secret of the soft form of Jewish totalitarianism, "liberal democracy," that won out against the hard form, namely Communism. In the West, our masters discovered that they could maintain total power on all the issues that concern them while leaving the illusion of freedom of choice. How? Simply by making sure that all options were Jew-safe and Jew-approved.

In Genesis 32, we read that Jacob, who had robbed his brother Esau of his birthright, was frightened to learn that Esau and 400 men were approaching his camp. So Jacob divided his camp in two, reasoning that if one group were attacked, the other would survive. Furthermore, Jacob sent part of his camp to Esau's camp, while he remained behind. These followers of Jacob came bearing gifts for Esau, but they could of course also act as spies to help Jacob, and even if Jacob's people were attacked and destroyed, some of them would survive in Esau's camp.

This bit of Unholy Scripture is a model of Jewish hegemony to this day. In the early 20th century, Jews were overwhelmingly political Leftists and supported the Leninist model of hard totalitarianism. But once their golem Stalin turned on them, many Jews began to re-evaluate Communism as a tool of Jewish ethnic interests. Thus, to hedge their bets, a series of Jewish Communist "defectors" (defectors from Communism, but not from the Jewish community) joined the American conservative movement and quickly moved into positions that allowed them to redefine conservatism after World War II.

For instance, two Jewish ex-Communists, Frank Meyer and Eugene Lyons, were among the surprising number of Jews who influenced the founding of William F. Buckley's *National Review*.[1]

By far the biggest influx of Jewish defectors, however, were the neoconservatives, most of whom came from the Zionist wing of the Trotskyite movement, i.e., the most ethnocentrically Jewish wing of the most ethnically Jewish faction of the Communist movement.[2]

Now that Jewish intellectual movements have redefined American conservatism to accord with Jewish interests on all important issues, it really doesn't matter *all that much* to the Jewish community whether Republicans or Democrats win elections. Yes, most Jews still *prefer* Democrats to Republicans. Yes, some of them still act like every Republican is an existential threat. Some of them even believe it. (But Jews face every issue as if their very survival depends upon it. It is a form of delusion and hysteria that has served them well.) But the truth is: from a Jewish point of view, both major parties are the same on all essential issues, and any differences between them do not make a difference for Jewish survival. That is real power, total power, yet "soft" power.

As a corollary, Jewish hegemony means that, from a White Nationalist point of view, both major parties are the same on all essential issues as well: they are opposed to our racial survival and flourishing. All the differences between them make no difference to us on the most important, existential issue.

Of course Jewish hegemony extends well beyond two-party politics into all realms of culture — education, religion, the arts, literature, pop culture, economics, etc. — ensuring that whites are distracted with an endless array of options, as long as they are *trivial* options that do not threaten Jewish hegemony. This

---

[1] On the Jewish founders of *National Review*, see George H. Nash, "Forgotten Godfathers: Premature Jewish Conservatives and the Rise of *National Review*," *American Jewish History*, vol. 87, nos. 2 & 3 (June–September 1999), pp. 123–57.

[2] On neoconservatism, see Kevin MacDonald's essays "Neoconservatism as a Jewish Movement" and "Neoconservative Portraits" in his *Cultural Insurrections: Essays on Western Civilization, Jewish Influence, and Anti-Semitism* (Atlanta: The Occidental Press, 2007).

is what we celebrate as "freedom."

But freedom does not consist in the multiplication of trivial options. Freedom means being able to choose *momentous* options. And the most momentous option for whites is to choose to get off the road to extinction and back on the road to godhood.

That is a choice denied us by Jewish hegemony. Being "free" under Jewish hegemony is nothing more than being happy slaves. For whites, Jewish freedom means being entertained right up to the point that we cease to exist as a people. If we are to survive, therefore, we must break Jewish hegemony.

WHITE NATIONALIST POLITICS

How can whites in North America regain control of our destiny? This is the question of how we organize what we call — out of a hope that springs eternal — the White Nationalist "movement."

The most popular movement model has been the political party, which comes in two colors, the democratic (such as the American Nazi Party, the Populist Party, the American Third Position, etc.) and the revolutionary (the National Alliance, the Northwest Front), i.e., those who seek to come to power within the system and those who seek to overturn the system. Of course, there is no contradiction to pursuing both aims. The NSDAP and Communist parties worldwide have done both. But still these are different aims which require different kinds of organizations. Thus every party will tend toward one option or another.

Ultimately, we will have to gain political power, and keep it. Thus I believe that whites need political organizations and political experience. But I have no illusions that we are going to vote our way off the endangered species list. Nor do I think that White Nationalists will be able to launch a revolution or a war of secession against the system as it stands today. So what can we do in the meantime?

Furthermore, political parties, whether revolutionary or democratic, are not for everyone. Some people don't "qualify" for membership. Others don't like being part of hierarchical groups with ideological orthodoxies, not to mention the church-like interpersonal "drama" that comes with such groups. What can these people do for our cause?

Finally, the White Nationalist revolutionary fantasy literature of William Pierce and Harold Covington does not sit well with most Americans, who do not relish the idea of Bolshevik-like revolutionary sects seizing power, establishing a one-party state, shooting everyone who opposes them, and dinning propaganda into the heads of the rest.[3] The Jews abandoned Bolshevism to pursue "soft" hegemony. Couldn't some White Nationalists do the same?

WHITE NATIONALIST HEGEMONY

It is too soon for White Nationalist politics. So in the meantime, we need to focus on metapolitics, which will lay the foundations for the pursuit of political power. Metapolitics has two elements: (1) *propaganda*, i.e., articulating and communicating our message, and (2) *community organizing*, i.e., creating a community that lives according to our philosophy today and will serve as the nucleus of the new political order we seek to build tomorrow.

What should be our message? Among other things, that whites are a distinct ethnic group with distinct interests. That we live in a world in which there are real ethnic conflicts. That it is right for whites to take our own side in these ethnic conflicts. That multicultural, multiracial societies make ethnic conflict and hatred inevitable. That ethnic conflict can best be ended by the creation of ethnically homogeneous homelands for all peoples. That it is an existential imperative—a matter of life and death—for whites to create or preserve ethnically homogeneous homelands for ourselves by any means necessary.

Our goal should not be merely to make this the common sense of the political Right, but the common sense of the whole political spectrum—of the whole culture—so that no matter what political party wins election, our people will never again

---

[3] Personally, I find Covington's novels tremendously useful and entertaining. Pierce's novels are useful as well.

have to fear for our survival. We do not need to move people in the right direction along the political spectrum. We need to move the whole spectrum in the *white* direction.

Our goal need not be a Right-wing, one-party state, but a pluralistic society in which we are still arguing about feminism, abortion, environmentalism, etc. But the arguments will all be among white people, and no white group will be able to ally itself with non-whites to gain the upper hand against other members of our extended racial family.

That is real power, total power, but "soft" power: white cultural and political hegemony. And there is nothing sinister about it. It is what existed in America before the rise of today's Jewish hegemony.

Yes, white hegemony would quietly restrict our options and frame debates to ensure racially healthy outcomes. But most of us accept limitations on our choices to attain greater goods, such as the preservation of endangered species. Well, whites are the most important endangered species of all. We want a society in which you can choose anything you want, as long as it does not imperil the long-term existence of our race.

DIVIDED WE WIN

How can White Nationalists pursue this kind of hegemony? We too need to divide our camp and go forth to colonize every shade of the political spectrum. We need to find ways to address our message to every white group and subgroup, for all whites have racial interests.

Old-school white advocates tend to be captives of political "apparatus" thinking. They believe that the struggle is entirely political, and that we will win only when our political team beats the enemy political team. But before we can engage the enemy, we must build up our political apparatus. We must unify our camp.

This naturally leads one to think that the very existence of multiple organizations and approaches to white advocacy is an impediment to our cause, a weakness in the movement that must be overcome. Thus all too often, the first order of action is not to attack the enemy, but to attack other white advocacy groups in the hope that one can discredit their leaders, smash their organizations, pull away their members and donors, and unite them behind one leader.

The value of the metapolitical path to white hegemony is that it makes a virtue out of necessity, namely the existence of multiple groups and approaches (including political apparatuses). This kind of diversity will always be with us, and combating it is a criminal waste of scarce resources that could be used to attack the enemy. Besides, the best way to attract followers is to attack the enemy effectively, not people who are more or less on our side.

To my mind, a diverse array of White Nationalist groups and approaches can strengthen our cause in two ways. First, even if there is "one right way" to save our race, it has not been discovered yet, and it is more likely to come to light if people experiment with different approaches. Second, we whites are a diverse people, and our movement needs to craft messages that resonate with the full range of white constituencies. The more approaches to white advocacy our movement can embrace, the more white constituencies we can address.

They key to making diversity within our movement work for us is to create discreet channels for communication and coordination among different camps of white advocates. Such back-channel coordination will maximize our impact and minimize destructive infighting and "friendly fire" incidents.

Counter-Currents/*North American New Right*,
August 20, 2011

METAPOLITICS
& OCCULT WARFARE

In 1897, Robert Lewis Dabney prophesied the triumph of women's suffrage based on his estimate of the history and character of the only force opposed to it, Northern conservatism:

> This is a party which never conserves anything. Its history has been that it demurs to each aggression of the progressive party, and aims to save its credit by a respectable amount of growling, but always acquiesces at last in the innovation. What was the resisted novelty of yesterday is today one of the accepted principles of conservatism; it is now conservative only in affecting to resist the next innovation, which will tomorrow be forced upon its timidity and will be succeeded by some third revolution; to be denounced and then adopted in its turn. American conservatism is merely the shadow that follows Radicalism as it moves forward towards perdition. It remains behind it, but never retards it, and always advances near its leader.

The political hegemony of the Left was and is based largely on the intellectual hegemony of Leftist ideas, chiefly freedom, equality, and progress. Today's phony Right shares the Left's basic worldview, but not their clarity of vision, singularity of purpose, and moral idealism. Rightists are merely tepid or retarded Leftists, who lag behind their brighter classmates. Yet the superior Leftists always bring them round in the end. In every battle between Left and Right, the Left can count on a fifth column inside every Rightist, namely his own deepest moral convictions. If one begins with Leftist premises, sooner or later, one will draw Leftist conclusions and put them into practice.

But politics is not merely a matter of intellectual influence and persuasion. It is not just about changing minds, but changing the world. And that requires organized, concerted, purposeful action. Thus politics is also about vectors of control, chains of command, leaders and followers.

Samuel Francis explained the leftward drift of contemporary politics in terms of leadership. On the Left, the leadership is always to the Left of its constituency, moving them toward ever more radical positions. Furthermore, on the Right, the leadership is also to the Left of its constituency. Thus politics moves steadily to the Left, because the Left's radical vanguard extends its influence through the whole political spectrum and pulls it along behind.

The Right follows the Left, just as train cars follow the engine. The Leftist cars are at the front of the train and the Rightist cars at the rear, thus they reach the destination later, but in no sense do they have an independent course or motive power. There is just one engine, and the people in the engine determine the direction of the train. The people in charge of the various cars may wear uniforms and carry themselves with an air of authority. But they are just conductors and ticket punchers, along for the ride with the rest of us.

How has the Left attained such power? And can it be attained by the Right and used in reverse? The answers are to be found in the Traditionalist school of René Guénon and Julius Evola.

There is no question that technology, science, and medicine are making remarkable advances. But from a White Nationalist point of view, everything is getting worse politically, culturally, and racially. This is why so many White Nationalists are attracted to Traditionalism, which explains contemporary events in terms of the myth that history moves in cycles—beginning with a Golden Age then declining through Silver, Bronze, and Iron (or Dark) Ages, until a new Golden Age dawns.

But Guénon and Evola did not regard historical decline as a disembodied force. They thought it was produced by concrete, embodied groups of historical agents. Although human agency plays a large role in history, however, most human beings are not historical agents. They are the objects, not the subjects of history. Historical agency is the preserve of tiny elites, vanguards that extend lines of influence and control throughout the entire culture, pulling it ever deeper into decadence. The vast majority of mankind is merely along for the ride.

Guénon and Evola discuss these historical elites under the rubric of "occult war." It is "occult" merely in the sense of "hidden." In Evola's words, it is "a battle that is waged imperceptibly by the forces of global subversion, with means and in circumstances ignored by current historiography."[1] Evola also writes that the occult dimension of history "should not be diluted in the fog of abstract philosophical or sociological concepts, but rather should be thought of as a 'backstage' dimension where specific 'intelligences' are at work" (*Men Among the Ruins*, p. 236).

Evola does add, ominously, that these occult forces "cannot be reduced to what is merely human" (*Men Among the Ruins*, p. 235). But occult war is not *necessarily* connected with the occult in the usual sense of the word, i.e., mysticism and magic, although the two senses do overlap in such groups as the Freemasons.

How does occult warfare produce political and historical change? According to Evola:

> The deeper causes of history ... operate prevalently through what can be called "imponderable factors," to use an image borrowed from natural science. These causes are responsible for almost undetectable ideological, social, and political changes, which eventually produce remarkable effects: they are like the first cracks in a layer of snow that eventually produce an avalanche. These causes almost never act in a direct manner, but instead bestow to some existing process an adequate *direction* that leads to the designated goal. (*Men Among the Ruins*, p. 237)

As Evola describes it, occult warfare is essentially identical to *metapolitics*.

Metapolitics deals with the underlying causes and conditions

---

[1] Julius Evola, *Men Among the Ruins: Post-War Reflections of a Radical Traditionalist*, trans. Guido Stucco, ed. Michael Moynihan (Rochester, Vt.: Inner Traditions, 2002), p. 235.

of political change. Metapolitics operates on two levels: *intellectual* and *organizational*. Metapolitical *ideas* include moral systems, religions, collective identities (tribal, national, racial), and assumptions about what is politically possible. Metapolitical *organizations* propagate metapolitical ideas, bridging the gap between theory and practice. Examples of metapolitical movements include the European New Right and the North American New Right.

Small metapolitical changes can lead to vast political transformations over time. For instance, the values articulated in the Sermon on the Mount eventually overthrew the whole ancient world. But since metapolitical causes are often remote from political effects, and since metapolitical causes are often abstract and esoteric ideas entertained by only a few, metapolitics is invisible to most people, who focus only on the concrete and immediate. Metapolitics is, therefore, "occult" in the literal sense of the word, i.e., "hidden." But it is often hidden in plain view and need take no special precautions to conceal itself from the public eye.

The concept of occult warfare is the Traditionalist contribution to what is generally derided as "conspiracy theories," including both history and speculation regarding "secret societies." This truly is hazardous territory.

Not a day goes by when my colleagues and I do not conspire together to advance the agenda of the North American New Right. And not a day goes by when our enemies do not conspire to advance their agenda. Yet if you raise the topic of conspiracy, most people are trained to roll their eyes. They do this because they are told that it is what smart people do. Many of them also have direct experience of preposterous conspiracy theories advanced by fevered, aggressive kooks. There is no question that most conspiracy theories are cranky and false, many of them ridiculously so. But what better way to conceal real conspiracies from serious, sober inquiry than promulgating fake ones that taint any discussion of conspiracy with an air of madness?

Evola, however, is "careful to prevent valid insights from generating into fantasies and superstitions," including a paranoid tendency "to see an occult background everywhere and at all costs" (*Men Among the Ruins*, p. 238). He treats all assumptions about occult warfare as mere "working hypotheses" put forth to integrate and explain empirical data. He claims that when a phenomenon cannot be entirely explained by known causes, one is entitled to conclude that unknown causes exist and to speculate about their nature.

I would like to add that some of these unknown causes might merely be random factors, since there is no reason to assume that all historical events are the product of conscious intentions (open or occult). Accidents do happen in history. But when one observes human affairs moving steadily in one direction, one is entitled to conclude that this is no accident and that conscious design is at work. And if the conscious designs of the obvious agents do not suffice to explain historical trends, then we are entitled to posit hidden agents and designs at work.

Among the testimonies that Evola considers are Benjamin Disraeli's claims that, "The world is governed by people entirely different from the ones imagine by those who are unable to see behind the scenes," and:

> The public does not realize that in all the conflicts within nations and in the conflicts between nations there are, besides the people apparently responsible for them, hidden agitators who with their selfish plans make these conflicts unavoidable. . . . Everything that happens in the confused evolution of peoples is secretly prepared in order to ensure the dominion of certain people: it is these people, known and unknown, that we must find behind every public event. (*Men Among the Ruins*, pp. 238–39)

Evola also treats the *Protocols of the Learned Elders of Zion* as evidence of occult warfare. Evola recognizes that the *Protocols* are not actual protocols but rather a literary presentation of a secret agenda for world domination. But in his view, the veracity of the *Protocols* cannot be proved or disproved by tracing their *origins*. Instead, their truth is proven by their *correspondence* to actual events. Thus, "The value of the document as a working hypothesis is undeniable: it presents the various aspect of global subversion (among them, some aspects that were destined to be outlined and accomplished only many years after the publication of the *Protocols*) in terms of a whole, in which they find their sufficient reason and logical combination" (*Men Among the Ruins*, p. 240).

Guénon and Evola believe that the occult war is carried on by secret initiatic societies. Just as Tradition is propagated through initiatic societies, the Counter-Tradition is propagated through counter-initiatic societies, which are profane images of genuine initiatic orders teaching inverted doctrines that promote decadence and decline.

The secret initiatic society is the ideal vehicle for both Tradition and Counter-Tradition, for three basic reasons.

First, both Tradition and subversion are based upon bodies of eternal principles that must be propagated over time through a process of initiation, i.e., the communication of doctrines from teacher to student in a hierarchical course of study, in which lower degrees lay the foundations for higher ones.

This, of course, describes any educational process, even the most trivial. But only an organization whose teachings evoke the utmost piety, and whose process of initiation evokes the utmost solemnity, can hope to persist through the ages. Thus the foundation of its doctrine must be eternal truths — persistence in time being the consequence of pursuing eternal truths and living in accordance with them.

Second, both Tradition and subversion are not merely matters of theory. They also involve action: actions that embrace the globe, span the ages, and determine the destinies of nations, civilizations, and races; plans of action that unfold over generations, centuries, even millennia. No organization can hope to motivate generations to toil in the pursuit of aims that will never come to fruition in their lifetimes unless it can mobilize the highest form of impersonal idealism. But the highest form of idealism is only evoked by the highest good, which again requires a foundation in eternal truths.

Third, an organization that perpetuates itself over millennia and acts on a global scale, for good or evil, is bound to make enemies. Thus to persist, it must be secret. Secrecy also serves another purpose, allowing initiates to penetrate and influence, for good or evil, other organizations that would resist them if their competing loyalties were known. A third purpose of secrecy is that it allows an organization to survive changes of regimes, even the fall of whole civilizations. For a secret society may penetrate all of the institutions of a given society, but it should also depend on none of them. Its substance should lie within itself, ultimately grounded in its orientation to the eternal, the most substantial thing of all.

Archimedes claimed that he needed only two things to move the world: a lever and a place to stand. The place to stand cannot move, but it allows one to move other things. To move the world, one must have a place to stand outside the world. To move all of history, one needs a place to stand outside history: a secret society that does not move with history, because its foundations are above history and above politics, in a doctrine that does not change because it is based on the eternal.

If one is to move history, rather than be moved by it, one must be an unmoving axis around which all other things revolve. One must be like Aristotle's god, the Unmoved Mover, who does not move because he is complete and self-contained (substance itself), but who sets the rest of the world in motion, because all things seek to imitate his aloof self-sufficiency. One must be like the Taoist Sage Emperor, who acts without acting, simply by incarnating the unchanging principle of order around which all other beings arrange themselves.

One can hypothesize the presence of an initiatic Traditional body at work wherever one finds a social order that persists over a long period of time: ancient Egypt, Mesopotamia, Persia, India, China, Japan, Rome, Byzantium, the Catholic Church, and the Old Regimes of Europe.

One can hypothesize the presence of an initiatic Counter-Traditional body at work wherever a steady trend toward disorder persists. In the case of the rise of modernity, many different groups and interests were united in working to overthrow the old order: Protestants, neo-pagans, natural scientists, rationalist and empiricist philosophers, capitalists, and political liberals were among the first wave. Subsequent waves included Jews, socialists, anarchists, and Communists. But since the Second World War, the Jewish element of subversion has become hegemonic.

If an initiatic secret society grounded in the eternal is the place where one stands, what is the lever? What are the means by which one moves history? The short answer is: by any means necessary. If the metaphysical foundations and practical aims of a secret order are as fixed and unchanging as Being itself, the means by which it seeks to influence and direct history should be as manifold and shifting as the historical flux. Absolute dogmatism about foundations and aims can be wedded to absolute pragmatism about means. Truth and order may employ lies and chaos. Good may be pursued by any means, including evil ones, provided that they really are means. If the ends do not justify the means, nothing will. All of these techniques, however, fall under two basic headings: the spreading of ideas and the infiltration and subversion of institutions.

In *Men Among the Ruins*, Evola develops a number of René Guénon's ideas on the tools of occult warfare (pp. 244-51).

First, the promulgation of materialistic and positivistic prejudices about historical causation blinds the intelligent to the occult dimension of history.

Second, to prevent those who reject materialism from finding the truth, false spiritual or idealist conceptions of history (e.g., Hegel, Bergson) are promulgated.

Third, when the effects of subversion begin to show up on the material plane and provoke a reaction in the name of ideals drawn from the traditional past, the agents of subversion promulgate counterfeit or distorted versions of these ideas, so that "reaction is contained, deviated, or even led in the opposite direction" (*Men Among the Ruins*, p. 245).

Fourth, since "the basis of the order to be destroyed consist[s] in the supernatural element—that is, in the spirit—conceived not as a philosophical abstraction or as an element of faith, but as a superior reality, as a reference point for the integration of everything that is human" (*Men Among the Ruins*, p. 245), all genuine spiritual longings must be channeled into inverted forms of spirituality directed toward the aims of the Counter-Tradition.

Fifth, to weaken, derail, and destroy any genuine opposition that might remain, the enemy encourages them to attack those who share the same principles and to adopt the principles of their enemies. An example of the first tactic is promotes infighting among the resistance: "thus, they attempt in every possible way to cause any higher idea to give in to the tyranny of individual interests or proselytizing, prideful, and power-hungry tendencies" (*Men Among the Ruins*, p. 247). An example of the second tactic is to encourage the opposition to embrace the principles of the enemy in order to gain momentary rhetorical or political advantages. A good contemporary example is the tendency of White Nationalists to appeal to forms of moral universalism that undermine all nationalism simply to score cheap points against Zionism.[2] Evola stresses that "unconditioned loyalty to an idea"—as opposed to the egotism that leads to infighting or the pragmatism that leads one to adopt the enemy's idea—"is the only possible protection from occult war" (*Men Among the Ruins*, p. 247).

Sixth, if the forces of subversion are in danger of being unmasked and punished, they will deflect public anger onto scapegoats. Evola actually suggests that the *Protocols* might be an attempt to make Freemasons and Jews into scapegoats for a much deeper conspiracy (*Men Among the Ruins*, p. 248). Evola would probably not entertain such thoughts today, since the specifically Jewish nature of the ruling powers was not so apparent in 1953 when *Men Among the Ruins* was first published.

Seventh, when subversion progresses far enough to provoke a reaction, this reaction can be diverted from the pursuit of a healthy new society based on eternal truths toward a return to an older form of society in which the sickness is merely not so advanced. In America today, this is manifested in reactionary nostalgia for the 1980s or the 1950s or the 19th century or the Founding Era. Of course, if we could return to the 1950s, our descendants would be coping with the same problems 60 years later.

---

[2] See "White Nationalism and Jewish Nationalism," chapter 13 below.

Eighth, all principles or institutions may be undermined if people confuse them with their representatives. All representatives are inevitably imperfect, but when these imperfections come to light, the agents of subversion argue that it is the institution or principle that must be replaced, not their fallible representatives.

Ninth, Evola claims that one of the principal tools of subversion is to infiltrate Traditional organizations and replace their leadership, in order to destroy the organization outright or to use it to further the ends of subversion. Evola claims that Freemasonry was originally a vehicle of genuine Tradition, but it was infiltrated and taken over by partisans of the Counter-Tradition (*Men Among the Ruins*, pp. 250–51).

If the dominant current of decline is, to one extent or another, actually created, sustained, and guided by occult warfare, is it possible to use the same means to reverse decline? No — and yes.

Traditionalists do not think it is possible to replace decline with "progress," i.e., progress toward the realization of Golden Age ideals, since they believe that decline is the dominant current of time. One declines *from* the Golden Age; one does not progress *toward* it. But at the end of the Dark Age, a new Golden Age will dawn, so although one cannot *progress* toward a Golden Age, one can *decline* toward it; one can slide into it. Thus, from this perspective, further decline can actually be seen as a kind of progress, for things cannot get better until decline has run its course.

But this is no argument for quietism, for inaction, for just waiting for an impersonal historical destiny to do our work for us. For, as we have seen, historical destiny is not impersonal. It works through concrete individuals and groups who have a place to stand and a lever to move the human world. In *The Crisis of the Modern World*,[3] Guénon writes:

> . . . the characteristic features of this epoch are in actual fact those which the traditional doctrines have from all

---

[3] René Guénon, *The Crisis of the Modern World*, trans. Arthur Osborne (Ghent, N.Y.: Sophia Perennis et Universalis, 1996).

time indicated for the cyclic period to which it corresponds [namely the Dark Age or Kali Yuga]. . . . what is anomaly and disorder from a certain point of view is nevertheless a necessary element of a vaster order and an inevitable consequence of the laws which govern the development of all manifestation. However, let it be said at once, this is no reason for consenting to submit passively to the disorder and obscurity which seem momentarily to triumph, for, were it so, we should have nothing better to do than keep silence [which Guénon did not do]; on the contrary, it is a reason for striving to the utmost to prepare the way out of this "dark age," for there are many signs that its end is already near, if not imminent. (*Crisis*, p. 9)

Guénon does not merely claim that we ought to resist the Dark Age, but that *resistance already exists*. He offers a metaphysical argument for this claim:

This [resistance] also is part of the appointed order of things, for equilibrium is the result of the simultaneous action of two contrary tendencies; if one or the other could cease to act entirely, equilibrium would never be restored, and the world itself would disappear; but this supposition has no possibility of realization, for the two terms of an opposition have no meaning apart from one another, and whatever the appearances, one may be sure, that all partial and transitory disequilibriums contribute in the end toward realizing the total equilibrium. (*Crisis*, p. 9)

Guénon's point is that all realities are comprised of opposed forces in equilibrium. Today, Dark Age currents are dominant. But that does not mean that Golden Age counter-currents are entirely absent, for if they were absent, the world would collapse into total chaos, rather than display the evil and inverted order that exists today. (If chaos reigned, one would expect the good guys to win once in a while.) Thus a Golden Age counter-current must exist and exert a countervailing influence to the Dark Age, but in a hidden and recessive manner. Furthermore, as with the forces of subversion, this Golden Age counter-current does not exist merely as a disembodied tendency. It is the work of concrete individuals and groups.

In the final chapter of *The Crisis of the Modern World*, Guénon further discusses this counter-current. He claims that, "the modern world would cease to exist at once if men understood what it really is, since its existence, like that of ignorance and all that implies limitation, is purely negative: it exits only through negation of the traditional and superhuman truth" (*Crisis*, p. 157).

Such truth cannot be understood by the vast majority, but this is not necessary, since "it would be enough if there were a numerically small but powerfully established elect to guide the masses, who would obey their suggestions without suspecting their existence or having any idea of their means of action . . ." (*Crisis*, p. 157). Clearly, this elect must operate at least in part through dissimulation, as do the initiates of the Counter-Tradition.

Guénon discusses how such a Traditionalist elect might work to end the Kali Yuga. First, he emphasizes that there cannot be any absolute discontinuity between the Kali Yuga and the coming Golden Age, meaning that they exist within the same causal nexus, so that things we do now will affect the Golden Age to come. A Traditionalist elect with the knowledge and the power to end the Kali Yuga, "could so prepare the change that it would take place in the most favorable conditions possible, and the disturbances that must inevitably accompany it would in this way be reduced to a minimum." But, even if that proved impossible, the Traditionalist elect could perform "another yet more important task, that of helping to preserve the elements which must survive from the present world to be used in building up the one to follow" (*Crisis*, p. 158).

Along the way, Guénon drops a bombshell in question form: "is it still possible for this elect to be effectively established in the West?" (*Crisis*, p. 157) — implying that the elect does not exist in the West. He goes on to explain that such Traditionalist elites do, however, still exist in the East, safeguarding the "ark" of Tradition (*Crisis*, p. 159). He also speculates on how a Western elect might be reconstituted, either by finding and reviving a living remnant of Tradition in the West, which Guénon thinks unlikely, or by Westerners becoming initiates of Eastern masters. The latter path was, for instance, taken by Savitri Devi, probably under Guénon's influence:

> I embraced Hinduism because it was the only religion in the world that is compatible with National Socialism. And the dream of my life is to integrate Hitlerism into the old Aryan tradition, to show that it is really a resurgence of the original Tradition. It's not Indian, not European, but Indo-European. It comes from back to those days when the Aryans were one people near the North Pole. The Hyperborean Tradition.[4]

I do not know if a Traditionalist elect has emerged in the West since 1927, when Guénon published *The Crisis of the Modern World*, but if Guénon is right, we can rest assured that Eastern masters (a kind of League of Shadows, perhaps) are waging the occult war on our behalf, otherwise the Dark Age—which is not chaos but a kind of negative order—would have given way to complete chaos long ago.

There is no "vast Right-wing conspiracy," but perhaps there should be. I am sure that by now some of you are thinking, "Let's start a Traditionalist secret society of our own and wage occult war against the modern world! That which is falling should also be pushed." Secret societies are staples of the Anglo-American political imagination, so it is no surprise that the idea recurs regularly among White Nationalists.

To cite just two examples of many: when I met Wilmot Robertson on March 3, 2001, his one piece of advice for advancing our cause in North America was to create some sort of secret society. On May 17, 1955, in a private letter, Anthony M. Ludovici also recommended the creation of such a society, despite his bad experiences with the English Mistery and the English Array in the 1930s.[5]

---

[4] Savitri Devi, *And Time Rolls On: The Savitri Devi Interviews*, ed. R. G. Fowler (Atlanta: Black Sun Publications, 2006), p. 117.

[5] http://www.anthonymludovici.com/antisemi.htm

I think, however, that creating secret societies is a needless distraction for White Nationalists, for several reasons.

First, if Guénon is right, such a secret order already exists. But they don't have a P.O. Box or a Facebook page. You can't join them by sending in a check. *They* have to come to you. So the only thing you can do is *focus on making yourself worthy of being chosen by such an elite group*. That way, you hedge your bets. If such a society really does exist, you might well be asked to join, and if Guénon and Evola are just having us on, you have still made yourself worthy of such an elite, and that's the most important thing in the end.

Second, I have heard of many secret societies, which means that they have not remained secret. And once the existence of such a group is known, it can only add to one of the greatest problems with the White Nationalist subculture: lack of trust, including outright paranoia.

This climate is exploited and exacerbated by our enemies, but they are not the sole cause of it. I think that White Nationalists have a strong innate predisposition to paranoia. Ethnocentrism, like most psychological traits, tends to be distributed on a bell curve. It stands to reason that White Nationalists would tend to be more ethnocentric than average, which is my experience. High ethnocentrism, however, seems to be correlated with an inability to trust fellow whites as well.

There is a simple explanation for this: with whites, low ethnocentrism is the norm, so when a white manifests high ethnocentrism, he is likely to be met with disapproval from other whites, which will tend to alienate him from his people. (For Jews, high ethnocentrism is the norm. Thus when a Jew acts ethnocentrically, other Jews are likely to approve of it, which reinforces both ethnocentrism and a sense of belonging to the Jewish community.)

But the ability to trust strangers—which involves being willing to take a certain amount of risk—is one of the conditions for the rise of large-scale, complex social institutions. Otherwise, you are only able to cooperate with the small number of people whom you know. Since highly ethnocentric whites tend not to trust their fellows, this makes them less capable of forming effective organizations and movements. The enemy, apparently, understands this, thus they do everything they can to stoke discord and paranoia. Talk of secret societies simply adds suspicion and resentment to an already poisoned atmosphere.

(Personally, I am predisposed to low levels of ethnocentrism and high levels of trust toward strangers. I arrived at my nationalist convictions not by instinct, but by much thought and experience, and although my willingness to trust strangers has allowed me to expand and create organizations, I have been repeatedly burned by crooks, cranks, and crazies.)

Third, despite every precaution, secret societies can be subverted. All hierarchical organizations are vulnerable to subversion at the top, which allows a few well-placed conspirators to put vast numbers of people to work in good faith promoting evil ends. This is particularly true of secret societies, in which rank and file members often do not even know the identity of their leaders, much less their true loyalties and agendas.

Furthermore, although secret societies may be difficult to subvert, the very secrecy that protects them makes them high-value targets for subversion. Sometimes the best way to keep your secrets is not to make a great show of concealing them, lest you attract prying eyes. This is why secret societies deny that they are secret. (The standard Masonic boilerplate is to claim they are merely "discreet.") Thus if you want to keep your identity and involvement in White Nationalism secret, *never* join a secret society. Because, chances are, the enemy already joined it long ago. "Open conspiracies" entail no such risks and cannot be so easily subverted.

Fourth, although people can usually accomplish more by cooperating than by going it alone, a higher than average number of White Nationalists, particularly our most original thinkers and committed doers, are not "organization men" but people who accomplish more working alone or in informal, non-hierarchical networks rather than in structured, hierarchical organizations. Such people tend to chafe against the fraternal chumminess, cliques, pecking orders, and secret handshakes that come with all hierarchical groups, even those devoted to the most exalted aims. Organizations, by their very nature, create interpersonal drama, which individualistic types despise. Sometimes the quickest way to destroy cooperation among a group of White Nationalists is to propose that they agree on something as simple as a name.

Since we need to mobilize all the talent we can, we must give the square pegs the freedom they need to work and create. So what good is an elite organization whose structure and ethos are incompatible with the personality profiles of many of the best people in our cause? We need to accept the fact that today's White Nationalist movement might work best on the model of a Montessori school, not a Hitler Youth rally.

Fifth, it is possible to learn and apply the most essential principles and techniques of occult warfare without duplicating their organizational matrix. One can access Traditional wisdom outside an initiatic organizational framework. Indeed, most people who call themselves Traditionalists today have not undergone a process of initiation in some sort of secret order. Instead, we largely work alone, reading the increasingly abundant and easily accessible corpus of Traditionalist literature (no secrets these!). Then we try to apply the insights we glean to our lives. And if we really believe that these ideas can change the world, then we should not keep them secret but spread them as widely as possible to encourage others in our cause to adopt them as well.

The North American New Right adopts three basic principles of occult warfare. First, we lay our foundations in the eternal, because only such foundations can evoke the highest impersonal idealism and the utmost seriousness, and maintain them over generations of struggle. Second, our foundations and aims—a White Republic or Republics in North America—are fixed and non-negotiable, in order to provide a firm place for us to stand while we rearrange the rest of the world to suit us. Third, the lever by which we will move the world is the pursuit of intellectual and cultural hegemony.

From the fixed center of our doctrine and aims, we send out lines of influence in all directions, deconstructing the hegemonic anti-white ideas and constructing our counter-hegemony in the form of pro-white outlooks tailored to all existing white ethnic and interest groups, propagated through all possible media. Our aim is a pluralistic society in which all shades of opinion, realms of culture, and political options are compatible with white survival and flourishing—a society in which white degradation, dispossession, and extinction are off the menu.

The *Protocols* are a literary presentation of the guiding intelligence of an alien race, a race that believes itself destined for world domination, which it pursues through occult warfare against European man and all the other peoples of the world. They promised themselves the world, and they are delivering on it. It is evil, of course, but even an evil destiny mobilizes and empowers a people. To survive, one must aim at more than mere survival. To secure one's future, one must envision what it will be like. Other things being equal, peoples who lack a sense of destiny tend to become the playthings of peoples who have them.

Whites desperately need to recapture our sense of an exalted, cosmic destiny. We are the people who care for the welfare of the world, for the preservation of what is true, beautiful, and good. We must secure biological and cultural diversity. We must lay the foundations for the outward, cosmic expansion and upward evolution of our race. And, since as far as we know, mankind is the only intelligent race in the universe, our evolution can be viewed as the evolution of the cosmos as a whole.

We must also evolve the guiding intelligence necessary to fulfill this destiny. It is worth exploring whether such an intelligence needs to be embodied in a hierarchical occult order, or if it can inhere in a decentralized, resilient metapolitical network.

Counter-Currents/*North American New Right*,
December 10–13, 2012

THEORY & PRACTICE

To achieve our political aims, the North American New Right must understand the proper relationship of social theory to social change, metapolitics to politics, theory to practice. We must avoid drifting either into inactive intellectualism or unintelligent and thus possibly counterproductive activism.

Guillaume Faye's *Archeofuturism*[1] offers many important lessons for our project. Chapter 1, "An Assessment of the *Nouvelle Droite*," is Faye's settling of accounts with the French New Right. In the late 1970s and early 1980s, Faye was among their leading thinkers and polemicists before quitting in disillusionment. After twelve years, he returned to the battle of ideas with *Archeofuturism* (1998), which begins with an explanation of his departure and return.

In the 1970s and 1980s, the *Nouvelle Droite*, led by Alain de Benoist, was a highly visible and influential intellectual movement. It published books and periodicals like *Nouvelle École* and *Éléments*; it sponsored lectures, conferences, and debates; it engaged the intellectual and cultural mainstreams. The *Nouvelle Droite* did more than receive mainstream press coverage, it often set the terms of debates to which the mainstream responded.

The *Nouvelle Droite* was deep; it was highbrow; it was radical; it was relevant; and, above all, it was exciting. It was based on the axiom that ideas shape the world. Bad ideas are destroying it, and only better ideas will save it. It had the right ideas, and it was increasingly influential. Its metapolitical strategy was a "Gramscianism" of the Right, i.e., an attempt to shape the ideas and ultimately the actions of the elites—academics, journalists, businessmen, politicians, etc.—as envisioned in the writings of Italian Marxist Antonio Gramsci.

However, according to Faye, as the 1980s came to a close, the *Nouvelle Droite* became less influential: "Regrettably, it has

---

[1] Guillaume Faye, *Archeofuturism: European Visions of the Post-Catastrophic Age*, trans. Sergio Knipe (London: Arktos, 2010).

turned into an ideological ghetto. It no longer sees itself as a powerhouse for the diffusion of energies with the ultimate aim of acquiring *power*, but rather as a publishing enterprise that also organizes conferences but has limited ambitions" (pp. 24–25). The causes of this decline were based partly on objective conditions, partly on the movement's own weaknesses.

Whether fair to the *Nouvelle Droite* or not, two of Faye's criticisms contain universal truths that seem particularly relevant to our project in North America.

1. The rise of the Front National of Jean-Marie Le Pen caused a decline in the visibility and influence of the *Nouvelle Droite*, whereas one might have expected the Front National's good fortunes to magnify those of the *Nouvelle Droite*. After all, the two movements share much in common, and there can be little doubt that the *Nouvelle Droite* influenced the Front National and brought new people into its orbit.

Faye laments the "airlocks" sealing off different circles of the French Right. In particular, he claims that the *Nouvelle Droite* never engaged the Front National, because its members fundamentally misunderstood Gramsci, whose cultural battle was organically connected with the economic and political struggle of the Italian Communist Party.

The *Nouvelle Droite*, however, treated the battle as entirely cultural and intellectual. Thus they were not really Gramscians. They were actually followers of Augustin Cochin's theory of the role of intellectual salons in paving the way for the French Revolution.[2] Unlike the men of the old regime, however, we do not enjoy the luxury of ignoring party and electoral politics.

The North American New Right aims to change the political landscape. To do that, we must influence people who have power, or who can attain it. That means we must engage organized political parties and movements. No, in the end, white people are not going to vote ourselves out of the present mess. But we are not in the endgame yet, and it may still be possible to influ-

---

[2] On Cochin, see F. Roger Devlin, "From Salon to Guillotine: Augustin Cochin's *Organizing the Revolution*," *The Occidental Quarterly*, vol. 8, no. 2 (Summer 2008), pp. 63–90.

ence policy through the existing system. Moreover, parties do not exist merely for the sake of elections. They provide a nucleus for the new order they advocate. Finally, there are other ways to attain power besides elections. Just look at the Bolsheviks.

We know that the present system is unsustainable, and although we cannot predict when and how it will collapse, we know that collapse will come. It is far more likely that whites can turn that collapse to our benefit if we already have functioning political organizations that aim at becoming the nucleus of a new society. Yet we will not have such political organizations unless we engage the presently existing political institutions, corrupt, sclerotic, and boring though they may be.

2. Even though the *Nouvelle Droite* did not engage with organized politics, it was organized according to "an outdated 'apparatus logic' of the type to be found in political parties, which was not appropriate for a movement and school of thought... which led cadres to flee on account of 'problems with the apparatus'" (p. 27). By an "apparatus logic," Faye seems to mean a hierarchical organization in which an intellectual and editorial "party line" is promulgated.

Although Faye does not say so, the inability of the *Nouvelle Droite* to interface with the Front National may in fact be based on the fact that they shared the same structure and thus naturally perceived each other as rivals promulgating slightly different "party lines" and competing for the adherence of the same constituency. If this is true, then the North American New Right can avoid this problem by configuring itself not as a hierarchical apparatus with a party line but as a lateral network that cultivates dialogue on a common set of questions from various viewpoints and that can overlap and interface with any number of hierarchical organizations without competing with them.

Counter-Currents/*North American New Right*,
September 30, 2010

REFLECTIONS ON CARL SCHMITT'S
The Concept of the Political

"Can we all get along?" —Rodney King

Carl Schmitt's short book *The Concept of the Political* (1932) is one of the most important works of 20th-century political philosophy.[1]

The aim of *The Concept of the Political* is the defense of politics from utopian aspirations to abolish politics. Anti-political utopianism includes all forms of liberalism as well as international socialism, global capitalism, anarchism, and pacifism: in short, all social philosophies that aim at a universal order in which conflict is abolished.

In ordinary speech, of course, liberalism, international socialism, etc. are political movements, not anti-political ones. So it is clear that Schmitt is using "political" in a particular way. For Schmitt, the political is founded on the distinction between friend and enemy. Utopianism is anti-political insofar as it attempts to abolish that distinction, to root out all enmity and conflict in the world.

Schmitt's defense of the political is not a defense of enmity and conflict as *good* things. Schmitt fully recognizes their destructiveness and the necessity of managing and mitigating them. But Schmitt believes that enmity is best controlled by adopting a *realistic* understanding of its nature. So Schmitt does not defend conflict, but *realism* about conflict. Indeed, Schmitt believes that the best way to contain conflict is first to abandon all unrealistic notions that one can do away with it entirely.

Furthermore, Schmitt believes that utopian attempts to completely abolish conflict actually increase its scope and in-

---

[1] Carl Schmitt, *The Concept of the Political*, trans. George Schwab (Chicago: University of Chicago Press, 2007).

tensity. There is no war more universal in scope and fanatical in prosecution than wars to end all war and establish perpetual peace.

Us & Them

What does the distinction between friend and enemy mean?

First, for Schmitt, the distinction between friend and enemy is *collective*. He is talking about "us vs. them" not "one individual vs. another."

Schmitt introduces the Latin distinction between *hostis* (a collective or public enemy, the root of "hostile") and *inimicus* (an individual and private adversary, the root of "inimical"). The political is founded on the distinction between friend (those on one's side) and *hostis* (those on the other side). Private adversaries are not public enemies.

Second, the distinction between friend and enemy is *polemical*. The friend/enemy distinction is always connected with the abiding potential for violence. One does not need to *actually* fight one's enemy, but the *potential* must always be there. The sole purpose of politics is not group conflict; the sole content of politics is not group conflict; but the abiding *possibility* of group conflict is what creates the political dimension of human social existence.

Third, the distinction between friend and enemy is *existentially serious*. Violent conflict is more serious than other forms of conflict, because when things get violent *people die*.

Fourth, the distinction between friend and enemy is *not reducible to any other distinction*. For instance, it is not reducible to the distinction between good and evil. The "good guys" are just as much enemies to the "bad guys" as the "bad guys" are enemies to the "good guys." Enmity is relative, but morality — we hope — is not.

Fifth, although the friend/enemy distinction is not reducible to other distinctions and differences — religious, economic, philosophical, etc. — *all differences can become political* if they generate the friend/enemy opposition.

In sum, the ultimate root of the political is the capacity of human groups to take their differences so seriously that they will kill or die for them.

It is important to note that Schmitt's concept of the political does not apply to ordinary domestic politics. The rivalries of politicians and parties, provided they stay within legal parameters, do not constitute enmity in Schmitt's sense. Schmitt's notion of politics applies primarily to foreign relations—the relations between sovereign states and peoples—rather than domestic relations within a society. The only time when domestic relations become political in Schmitt's sense is during a revolution or a civil war.

Sovereignty

If the political arises from the abiding possibility of collective life or death conflict, the political rules over all other areas of social life because of its existential seriousness, the fact that it has recourse to the ultimate sanction.

For Schmitt, political sovereignty is the power to determine the enemy and declare war. The sovereign is the person who makes that decision.

If a sovereign declares an enemy, and individuals or groups within his society reject that declaration, the society is in a state of undeclared civil war or revolution. To refuse the sovereign's choice of enemy is one step away from the sovereign act of choosing one's own enemies. Thus Schmitt's analysis supports the saying that, "War is when the government tells you who the bad guy is. Revolution is when you decide that for yourself."

Philosophical Parallels

The root of the political as Schmitt understands it is what Plato and Aristotle call "*thumos*," the middle part of the soul that is neither theoretical reason nor physical desire, but is rather the capacity for passionate attachment. *Thumos* is the root of the political because it is the source of attachments to (1) *groups*, and politics is collective, and (2) *life-transcending and life-negating values*, i.e., things that are worth killing and dying for, like the defense of personal or collective honor, one's culture or way of life, religious and philosophical convictions, etc. Such values make possible mortal conflict between groups.

The abolition of the political, therefore, requires the abolition of the human capacity for passionate, existentially serious, life and death attachments. The apolitical man is, therefore, the apathetic man, the man who lacks commitment and intensity. He is what Nietzsche called "the Last Man," the man for whom there is nothing higher than himself, nothing that might require that he risk the continuation of his physical existence. The apolitical utopia is a spiritual "boneless chicken ranch" of doped-up, dumbed-down, self-absorbed producer-consumers.

Schmitt's notion of the political is consistent with Hegel's notion of history. For Hegel, history is a record of individual and collective struggles to the death over images or interpretations of who we are. These interpretations consist of the whole realm of culture: worldviews and the ways of life that are their concrete manifestations.

There are, of course, many interpretations of who we are. But there is only one truth, and according to Hegel the truth is that man is free. Just as philosophical dialectic works through a plurality of conflicting viewpoints to get to the one truth, so the dialectic of history is a war of conflicting worldviews and ways of life that will come to an end when the correct worldview and way of life are established. The concept of human freedom must become concretely realized in a way of life that recognizes freedom. Then history as Hegel understands it—and politics as Schmitt understands it—will come to an end.

Hegel's notion of the ideal post-historical state is pretty much everything a 20th- (or 21st-) century fascist could desire. But later interpreters of Hegel like Alexandre Kojève and his follower Francis Fukuyama interpret the end of history as a "universal homogeneous state" that sounds a lot like the globalist utopianism that Schmitt wished to combat.

WHY THE POLITICAL CANNOT BE ABOLISHED

If the political is rooted in human nature, then it cannot be abolished. Even if the entire planet could be turned into a boneless chicken ranch, all it would take is two serious men to start politics—and history—all over again.

But the utopians will never even get that far. Politics cannot be abolished by universal declarations of peace, love, and tolerance, for such attempts to transcend politics actually just reinstitute it on another plane. After all, utopian peace- and lovemongers have enemies too, namely "haters" like us.

Thus the abolition of politics is really only the abolition of *honesty* about politics. But dishonesty is the least of the utopians' vices. For in the name of peace and love, they persecute us with a fanaticism and wanton destructiveness that make good, old-fashioned war seem wholesome by comparison.

Two peoples occupying adjacent valleys might, for strategic reasons, covet the high ground between them. This may lead to conflict. But such conflicts have finite, definable aims. Thus they tend to be limited in scope and duration. And since it is a mere conflict of interest—in which both sides, really, are right—rather than a moral or religious crusade between good and evil, light and darkness, ultimately both sides can strike a deal with each other to cease hostilities.

But when war is wedded to a universalist utopianism—global Communism or democracy, the end of "terror," or, more risibly, "evil"—it becomes universal in scope and endless in duration. It is universal, because it proposes to represent all of humanity. It is endless, of course, because it is a war with human nature itself.

Furthermore, when war is declared in the name of "humanity," its prosecution becomes maximally inhuman, since anything is fair against the enemies of humanity, who deserve nothing short of unconditional surrender or annihilation, since one cannot strike a bargain with evil incarnate. The road to Dresden, Hiroshima, and Nagasaki was paved with love: universalistic, utopian, humanistic, liberal love.

LIBERALISM

Liberalism seeks to reduce the friend/enemy distinction to differences of opinion or economic interests. The liberal utopia is one in which all disputes can be resolved bloodlessly by reasoning or bargaining. But the opposition between liberalism and anti-liberalism cannot be resolved by liberal means. It is perforce political. Liberal anti-politics cannot triumph, therefore, without the political elimination of anti-liberalism.

The abolition of the political requires *the abolition of all differences*, so there is nothing to fight over, or *the abolition of all seriousness*, so that differences make no difference. The abolition of difference is accomplished by violence and cultural assimilation. The abolition of seriousness is accomplished by the promotion of spiritual apathy through consumerism and indoctrination in relativism, individualism, tolerance, and diversity worship—the multi-cult.

Violence, of course, is generally associated with frankly totalitarian forms of anti-political utopianism like Communism, but the Second World War shows that liberal universalists are as capable of violence as Communists. They are just less capable of honesty.

Liberalism, however, generally prefers to kill us softly. The old-fashioned version of liberalism prefers the soft dissolution of differences through cultural assimilation, but that preference was reversed when the unassimilable Jewish minority rose to power in the United States, at which time multiculturalism and diversity became the watchwords, and the potential conflicts between different groups were to be managed through spiritual corruption. Today's liberals make a fetish of the preservation of pluralism and diversity, *as long as none of it is taken seriously*.

Multicultural utopianism is doomed, because multiculturalism is very successful at increasing diversity, but, in the long run, it cannot manage the conflicts that come with it.

The drug of consumerism cannot be relied upon because economic crises cannot be eliminated. Furthermore, there are absolute ecological limits to the globalization of consumerism.

As for the drugs of relativism, individualism, tolerance, and the multi-cult: only whites are susceptible to their effects, and since these ideas systematically disadvantage whites in ethnic competition, ultimately those whites who accept them will be destroyed (which is the point, really) and those whites who survive will reject them. Then whites will start taking our own side, ethnic competition will get political, and, one way or another, racially and ethnically homogeneous states will emerge.

LESSONS FOR WHITE NATIONALISTS

To become a White Nationalist is to choose one's friends and one's enemies for oneself. To choose new friends means to choose a new nation. Our nation is our race. Our enemies are the enemies of our race, of whatever race they may be. By choosing our friends and enemies for ourselves, White Nationalists have constituted ourselves as a sovereign people—a sovereign people that does not have a sovereign homeland, yet—and rejected the sovereignty of those who rule us. This puts us in an implicitly revolutionary position *vis-à-vis* all existing regimes.

The conservatives among us do not see it yet. They still wish to cling to America's corpse and suckle from her poisoned teat. But the enemy understands us better than some of us understand ourselves. We may not wish to choose an enemy, but sometimes the enemy chooses us. Thus "mainstreamers" will be denied entry and forced to choose either to abandon White Nationalism or to explicitly embrace its revolutionary destiny.

It may be too late for mainstream politics, but it is still too early for White Nationalist politics. We simply do not have the power to win a political struggle. We lack manpower, money, and leadership. But the present system, like all things old and dissolute, will pass. And our community, like all things young and healthy, will grow in size and strength. Thus today our task is metapolitical: to raise consciousness and cultivate the community from which our kingdom—or republic—will come.

When that day comes, Carl Schmitt will be numbered among our spiritual Founding Fathers.

Counter-Currents/*North American New Right*,
February 24, 2011

THE RELEVANCE OF PHILOSOPHY TO POLITICAL CHANGE*

The title of this essay is somewhat misleading, since I am going to argue that philosophy is relevant to all human endeavors, not just politics. Philosophy is not just metapolitical, but meta-everything.[1] But I know you are interested in political change, so that was my hook to get you reading. Furthermore, I will argue that philosophy is more than just relevant to life, but of paramount importance.

Philosophy is the pursuit of wisdom, and wisdom is necessary for success in every realm of life, including politics. Wisdom, I will argue, is unconditionally good. You can never be too wise. All the other goods we pursue, however, are good for us only on the condition that they are used wisely. Thus we need to pursue wisdom as well, so that all of our other pursuits add up to a good life, which is what all of us ultimately want.

THE QUEST FOR THE GOOD LIFE

The first premise of my argument is: "All human beings are pursuing the good life, as we see it."

When people are given choices, they choose the option that seems *better* to them at the time. Even if they have to choose between evils, they choose what appears at the time to be the *lesser* of two evils. This preference for the apparent good throughout the course of one's life is what I mean by "pursuing

---

* The most recent incarnation of this essay was a talk in Seattle on October 14, 2012. I wish to thank everyone who was present for a stimulating discussion. The original incarnation was the opening lecture of undergraduate Introduction to Philosophy classes that I taught in the 1990s.

[1] Philosophy is an important part of metapolitics, but it is not the whole of metapolitics, which encompasses other intellectual disciplines as well as the media for their propagation and the communities that they engender.

the good life as we see it."

The phrase "as we see it" is important, because it indicates that my premise is first and foremost a *psychological* claim about the choice of *apparent* goods. We choose what seems best to us at the time, even if we later learn that we were calamitously mistaken.

The use of the phrase "as we see it" does not, however, imply that all goods are subjective, i.e., that are no objective goods.

A subjective good is something that is good *because we want it*. An objective good is something that is *good in and of itself*. It is, therefore, something that we *should* want, whether we want it or not.

A common synonym for the claim that values are subjective is *relativism*. A common synonym for the idea of objective values is *absolutism*. No objectivist or absolutist seriously argues that *all* goods are objective or absolute. But there are subjectivists who maintain that *all* goods are subjective or relative.

AGAINST RELATIVISM

There is a simple argument for the existence of objective goods, hence the falsehood of complete subjectivism. All human beings are pursuing the good life as we see it. Yet most people are not happy with their lives. Moral subjectivism or relativism cannot explain this fact.

The moral relativist basically claims that the good life is whatever we define it to be. But if I get to define the good life for myself, I have no excuse for not *having* a good life. Moral relativism is basically the view that, in the game of life, we get to make up the rules as we go along. But if you get to make up the rules, you have no excuse if you do not win. Even if you suffer terrible misfortune, the relativist would claim that it is within your power simply to define it as good.

So why, if we are all pursuing the good life as we see it, are so many of us unhappy with our lives? The best explanation is that there are *objective* conditions for a good life, and many of us do not meet them.

There are two basic ways that we can fail to meet these conditions. First, there are factors that are outside of our control, which I will call *fortune*, good or ill. Second, there are factors that are in our control, such as our thoughts and actions. Even the most intrepid pursuit of the good life will fail if we lack good fortune or if we think or act wrongly.

Another term that is often used as a synonym for the good life is "happiness." There are two senses of happiness: subjective and objective. Subjective happiness is a feeling, namely *feeling well*. Objective happiness is a state of being, namely *being well* or *well-being*. The good life can be identified with happiness in the sense of well-being. And, ideally, well-being should be crowned with happiness in the subjective sense.

Everybody would rather feel happy than unhappy. But subjective happiness is not the highest good. Sometimes people have better things to do with their lives. Life often forces us to choose between subjective happiness and greater goods. Some people, for instance, choose duty over happiness. They would rather *be* noble than *feel* good. But in such cases, one can say that people are sacrificing subjective *happiness* to objective *well-being*.

CONDITIONAL VS. UNCONDITIONAL GOODS

The second premise of my argument is a distinction between conditional and unconditional goods:

Conditional goods are those things that are good under some conditions and bad under other conditions.

Unconditional goods are those things that are good under any condition, goods that can never become detrimental.

Conditional goods can become bad due to circumstances, e.g., the wrong time, the wrong place, the wrong degree, or the wrong priority or balance in relation to other goods. Too much of a good thing can be a bad thing. But you can never have too much of an unconditional good. They are good regardless of time, place, degree, and other circumstances.

THE COMPONENTS OF A GOOD LIFE

To enjoy a good life, we must gain and keep the particular goods that are components of a good life. These components include, from the most basic to the more rarefied:

- food
- water
- shelter
- exercise
- sleep
- security
- health, physical and mental
- beauty
- material goods
- family
- friends
- sex
- entertainment
- self-respect
- the respect of one's peers
- achievement
- knowledge
- intelligence

Are these goods conditional or unconditional? I wish to argue that they are all conditional, because it is possible to imagine situations in which they can become bad. One can have too much water, too much food, too much exercise, too much rest, too much sex, too much entertainment, etc. One can be too rich and too good-looking.

Can one be too healthy? Perhaps not, as physical and spiritual health are core components of well-being. But one can, at least, be too *concerned* with one's health, to the point that one neglects other goods.

One can surely have too much self-esteem; one can be too popular; one can be too focused on achievement. One can also know too damn much or be too damn smart for one's own good.

Even though the components of a good life can sometimes be bad, the good life itself is always and unconditionally good. The great problem of the good life, therefore, is *how to create an unconditional good out of conditional goods, how to pursue the unconditional good by conditionally good means.*

There are no circumstances under which we would not want to live a good life. But not every life is a good life. Life as such is not unconditionally good. Only a good life is. Thus if a particular life is not worth continuing, ending it is not a rejection of the value of the good life but rather an affirmation of it. The good life, in short, can also include a good death.

GETTING THE COMPONENTS OF A GOOD LIFE

There are two basic sources of the components of a good life: *fortune* and *work*. Fortune is capricious and unfair. Some people are born healthy, beautiful, intelligent, and talented. Some are born to wealth and privilege. Some have happy, loving families. Some are born in civilized, peaceful, prosperous societies. The rest fall along every gradation to the opposite extremes. Work is one of the ways that we try to correct the inequities of fortune.

Both fortune and work are themselves conditional goods. One can be too lucky, since misfortune is one of the ways we build strength and character—although if one is really lucky, one's weakness will never be tested. And one can work too much or give work too much importance in one's life.

THE QUESTION OF USE

Work and fortune are the two ways that we come to possess goods. But to live well, it is not enough merely to *possess* goods. We also have to *use* them. And since conditional goods can also turn bad, it is not enough merely to use them. We have to use them *well*; we have to make *right use of all things*.

Wisdom is the ability to make right use of all things. The opposite of wisdom is folly, a penchant for making bad use of all things.

Without wisdom, none of the things we possess are necessarily good for us. Fortune showers gifts upon some people: health, beauty, status, wealth, etc. But if one lacks wisdom, the greater the gifts, the greater one's potential for disaster. A classic example is Diana, Princess of Wales, who had every advantage of fortune, yet she still failed to lead a good life, largely because she made foolish choices. Great gifts combined with great folly lead to terrible consequences. In fact, foolish people are better off with fewer gifts, since they have fewer ways of harming themselves and others.

With wisdom, however, you can live a good and happy life, even if fortune deals you few advantages and many disadvantages. Fate deals us all a hand. Some get good cards and some get bad ones. But people who play good hands foolishly can end up losing, while people who play bad hands wisely can win. Thus wisdom is a great equalizer. Wisdom allows us to push back against bad fortune and create our own good luck.

Conditional goods contribute to a good life *only if they are used wisely*. Without wisdom, none of the conditional goods accrued by good fortune or hard work will necessarily add up to a happy life. Wisdom is the *sine qua non* of a good life — the essential condition without which it cannot exist.

Thus wisdom, like the good life itself, is an unconditional good. There are no conditions under which one is better off being foolish than wise. One can be too rich, smart, or beautiful for one's own good. But one can never be too wise for one's own good. Wisdom is aligned unswervingly with the good life. It never strays from the good, and because it never loses sight of the good, it can direct all other things toward the good. Thus wisdom is the most important component of the good life, second in importance only to the good life itself.

If we are serious about the good life, then the pursuit of wisdom, namely philosophy, should be our first and foremost concern, prior even to the pursuit of conditional goods. For the more goods we accumulate without the wisdom to use them, the greater the danger to our well-being.

Is Wisdom *Always* Necessary for the Good Life?

I have argued that wisdom is necessary for the good life. But is it *always* necessary? Is it at least *possible* that a person who is indifferent to wisdom, even a complete fool, might still lead a good life? The world is filled with happy-go-lucky people who give no thought to tomorrow; people who trust in the kindness of strangers, God, or Mother Nature; people whose retirement plans consist of winning the lottery; stoners who think "it's all good," etc.

It is at least conceivable that some of these people really

could luck out. Not only could fortune deal them certain gifts, but it could do so at the right time, in the right place, and in the right degree, so they are never challenged to make right use of anything. This lucky streak could, moreover, continue their whole lives long. It is, of course, not very likely.

Enjoying the good life through sheer luck could be called a fool's paradise. But only a fool would count on it. The beginning of wisdom is to decide not to depend on luck but instead to create some of one's own. (Even Forrest Gump did not depend entirely on good luck. He also had the good sense to listen to what his momma said.)

IS WISDOM *SUFFICIENT* FOR THE GOOD LIFE?

The idea that wisdom alone is sufficient for a good life is equivalent to the claim that the good life depends entirely on things that we can control, thus we can lead good lives without the goods of fortune, indeed in the midst of the greatest misfortune. The Roman Stoics Seneca and Epictetus argued that wisdom is sufficient for the good life, thus the wise man is immune to misfortune.

Although this in not the place to argue the point, I believe the Stoic view is appealing but false. I follow Aristotle, who claims that the good life requires more than just virtue. It also requires external goods, which we must obtain through fortune and work. External goods, however, are not entirely under our control. Thus the good life is not immune to misfortune.

If forced to choose between external goods and the goods of the soul, we should always choose the goods of the soul. But then we are no longer talking about the good life but merely the least bad life. Socrates argued that a righteous man who was persecuted, condemned, and martyred by society is better off than a corrupt man who enjoys all the gifts of good fortune. But that is not the same thing as saying that a virtuous man on the rack is living a good life.

THEORETICAL VS. PRACTICAL WISDOM

The kind of wisdom I am discussing is usually called *moral* or *practical* wisdom, as distinguished from *theoretical* wisdom.

Philosophy is often divided into five fields: *metaphysics*, which deals with being and man's place in the cosmos, including such topics as the existence of a God or gods and the freedom and immortality of the soul; *epistemology*, which deals with knowledge and truth; *aesthetics*, which deals with the beautiful; *ethics* or *moral philosophy*, which deals with the good life; and *political philosophy*, which deals with the good life together. Moral and political philosophy cannot really be separated, since man is a social animal, thus the good life is pursued in society, and it must be pursued collectively as well as individually.

Metaphysics, epistemology, and aesthetics are the theoretical branches of philosophy. Their discoveries are not, in themselves, practical, but they are certainly *relevant* to practical philosophy.

For instance, metaphysical debates about whether the soul is mortal or immortal, whether a God or gods exist, whether we are free or determined, etc. all have implications for moral philosophy.

Epistemological debates on faith and reason, reason and sense experience, science and common sense, etc. all have practical implications. Every serious inquiry, moreover, uses the tools of logic.

Even aesthetics has practical implications. Aesthetics deals with beauty as such, not just art, and beauty often serves as a guide to determining what is real, true, and good. Furthermore, the appreciation of beauty, which can be systematically cultivated, is one of the components of the good life.

Thus even if practical wisdom is our primary concern, theoretical wisdom is not *merely* theoretical.

Does theoretical wisdom have to be subordinated to practical wisdom? To answer this, we have to ask if theoretical wisdom is unconditionally good. Are metaphysical, epistemological, and aesthetic speculation good under every condition? I would argue that they are not. Even true theories can be bad if pursued in excess or without regard to context and consequences. Thus theoretical wisdom must be guided by practical wisdom, even as practical wisdom is informed by theoretical wisdom.

But this does not imply that all theoretical activity must be bent toward producing practical effects. Beautiful and useless things—pursued as ends in themselves—are part of every good life, whether they are games, hobbies, adventures, exploration, aesthetic experience, scientific investigation, or metaphysical speculation.

Not everything that is *consistent* with the good life has to produce good *effects*. Indeed, some things that we pursue as ends in themselves are actual components of the good life, which is also an end in itself. Thus they do not need to produce good effects to contribute to the good life; they have a closer relationship to the good life than cause and effect, because they are already parts of the good life.

PRACTICAL WISDOM VS. PRACTICAL KNOWLEDGE

Theory is about understanding the world. Practice is about changing it. What is the difference, then, between practical wisdom and practical knowledge, such as arts and technical skills?

Both practical knowledge and practical wisdom are about changing the world. Both cannot be reduced to statements of fact or abstract principles and rules. Both involve the perception of unique, concrete, changing situations and insight into the applicability of facts and abstract principles to concrete circumstances.

The crucial difference is that practical knowledge is *morally neutral*, thus it can be used for good or evil ends, whereas practical wisdom is always directed at the good and is thus *intrinsically moral*.

For example, surgeons make the best torturers, because the same skills that can relieve pain can also be used to inflict it. The difference between a surgeon and a torturer is not, therefore, a matter of knowledge but of ethics, of moral wisdom which ensures that *right use* is made of knowledge. (A profession is a combination of a body of morally neutral theoretical and practical knowledge with a supervening ethical code that applies that knowledge to good ends.)

CONCLUSIONS

I have argued that all human beings are pursuing the good life, which is unconditionally good. But the main components of the good life are good *for us* only on the condition that they are used wisely. Thus wisdom is the most important component of the good life, because without it, all the gifts of fortune and the products of our hard work can turn against us and become sources of misery rather than well-being. Wisdom, however, is unconditionally good, just like the good life itself, so it will never turn on you.

Philosophy, which is the pursuit of wisdom, is the most important activity for anyone who is serious about the good life. Philosophy is the only discipline that aims at attaining unconditionally good things: wisdom and the good life itself.

Keep this in mind when you are weighing your options: Philosophy first—or biology? Philosophy—or a trip to the gym? Philosophy—or television? Philosophy—or overtime at work?

In each case, philosophy should come first, because knowledge of biology, fitness, relaxation, and money are all good things, but they are not unconditionally good things. And they can actually be as treacherous as rattlesnakes unless you are able to use them wisely.

If philosophy is of paramount importance for all of life, then *a fortiori* it is of paramount importance for political change as well. Metapolitics is not entirely a matter of philosophy, but the core metapolitical questions about morality, destiny, and political institutions are philosophical.

Thus if you are serious about pursuing the good life not just for yourself, but for our people as a whole, wisdom is an unconditional good, and philosophy is an indispensable study.

WHERE TO START

This essay is based on the first lecture (conducted as a Socratic discussion) that I would give in undergraduate Introduction to Philosophy classes. I had a whole course of study mapped out to follow it. But where should my readers start? The answer is with Socrates.

The central argument of this essay comes from Socrates. In

Plato's dialogue *Euthydemus*, Socrates accepts the challenge of persuading the dumbest jock in the gym, Clinias, of the importance of studying philosophy (278d–282d). If the argument worked on Clinias, then surely it has worked on you.[2]

> Counter-Currents/*North American New Right*,
> December 27, 2012

---

[2] There is no substitute for reading Plato's dialogues and other Socratic writings, but just as one needs swimming lessons before jumping in the deep end, so one needs some basic background before studying Socrates. I would recommend beginning with A. E. Taylor's *Socrates: The Man and His Thought* (Garden City, N.Y.: Doubleday, 1953), the work of an honest, unpretentious, old-school English philosopher. For a more subtle but still highly accessible discussion of Socrates, see Leo Strauss's lecture course, "The Problem of Socrates: Five Lectures," in Leo Strauss, *The Rebirth of Classical Political Rationalism: An Introduction to the Thought of Leo Strauss*, ed. Thomas L. Pangle (Chicago: University of Chicago Press, 1989). Strauss, of course, is a treacherous figure with his own agenda, so use him wisely, i.e., as a point of departure, and don't get lost in his intellectual labyrinth.

THE MORAL FACTOR

> "Man does *not* strive for happiness, only the Englishman does." —Nietzsche

The central questions of metapolitics deal with *identity*, *morality*, and *possibility*.

As Carl Schmitt argues, the political is based on the distinction between us and them. The question of identity is: Who are we? And: Who are we not? Specifically, White Nationalism requires an answer to the question: Who is white, and who is not?

The moral question is: What is the right thing to do? Is creating a white homeland a moral thing to do? Even if White Nationalism is politically meaningful, people will resist it if they think it is immoral. But they will move heaven and earth to establish white homelands if they think it is the right thing to do.

But moral idealism is not enough. For politics is the art of the possible. Thus we need to know not just that White Nationalism is morally right, but also that it is politically possible. Is the global, multicultural, multiracial utopia being proffered even possible? Is a world without important differences—and thus without enmity—possible? And, if that world is an illusion, what of the alternative? Are ethnically homogeneous homelands possible? And if they are, is it possible for our people to regain control of our destiny and establish such homelands?

AGAINST POLITICAL CYNICISM

One of the most pervasive anti-metapolitical attitudes is what I call *political cynicism*. Political cynics hold that morality is, in fact, irrelevant to politics, meaning that considerations of right and wrong do not enter into political decision-making on the part of rulers or the people who are ruled. On this view, the powerful make laws solely on the basis of self-interest, and the weak comply solely on the basis of self-interest. Political behavior can, in short, be understood solely in terms of calculations based on carrots and sticks, i.e., greed and fear.

Political cynicism implies that all talk of morality is just a mask for more sordid motives. For instance, powerful people promote multiculturalism because it is in their interest, and powerless people go along with them out of fear of the consequences of non-compliance. All talk of white guilt, the evils of racism, and the moral imperative for whites to give way to non-whites is just window-dressing that plays no actual role in decision-making.

Political cynicism has practical implications. If morality is bunk and politics is all about money and power, then we should dispense with moral arguments and focus entirely on pursuing money and power. These views lead some White Nationalists to place their hopes in investment schemes and political electioneering. Others, like the Order, stockpiled weapons and robbed armored cars. But the reason they have made little headway is not merely that the enemy has more money and power, but that our people overwhelmingly believe that our cause is unjust, which increases the scope and intensity of resistance to us.

One cannot deny the power of greed and fear in politics. Nor can one deny that politics requires money and power. What I deny is that they are the *only* factors, that politics can be *reduced* to them, and that morality is not a factor as well. The purpose of this essay is to argue that morality—by which I mean people's *opinions* of what is right and wrong—is a political factor as well. Beyond that, I will argue that morality can be a decisive and dominant factor, capable of trumping cynical power politics, of triumphing over greed and fear.

I will argue, furthermore, that although White Nationalism is widely thought to be immoral, actually our cause is good and the enemy's cause is evil. Moreover, we have the means to persuade people that White Nationalism—indeed, ethnonationalism for everyone—is noble and good. We cannot compete with the enemy in terms of money and power. But we can compete morally. If we can persuade enough of the people who hold the guns and checkbooks that we are *right*, we can win. Political cynicism, then, is the rankest folly. The cynics urge us to ignore the moral factor—where we are strongest and our enemy is weakest—and focus entirely on power politics—where we are weakest and our enemy is strongest.

SAVING THE APPEARANCES

The first problem with political cynicism is that it does not explain everything about politics. If one thinks that morality plays no role in politics—that morality is merely a matter of *appearances*, as opposed to the sordid *reality* of power politics—one still needs to *explain* the appearances. If morality plays no role in politics, why do people persist in *thinking* that it does? Why do politicians feel the need to trot out moral arguments? If political morality is a sham, why is it so widespread and deemed so important?

If politics is all about power rather than morality, why do dictatorships, in which individuals have little or no political power, devote immense expenditures to education and propaganda to convince the populace that their rule is fundamentally moral? If politics is entirely about power, wouldn't one expect the states that have the most power over their populaces to invest the least in moral propaganda?

The cynics can't argue that moral appeals are merely meaningless residues of the past, for that would imply that there was a time when morality *did* matter to politics. But if moral considerations truly *never did matter*, wouldn't moral appeals have disappeared long ago?

Furthermore, even if there are no moral truths, just opinions—even if morality is just a matter of passionately held falsehoods—*opinion is the lifeblood of politics*. Even totalitarian regimes recognize this, which is why they seek to mold public opinion. Politics would only reduce to money and power if everyone *thinks* it does. Morality matters to politics, simply because people *think* it does.

The same sort of cynicism that dismisses all morality as mere falsehood could, and often does, say the same thing about religion. Even if one thinks that a particular religion is true, one must logically conclude that the rest are false. Even if one thinks that all religions are true in some Traditionalist sense, one has to grant that their exoteric doctrinal and devotional differences exist on the level of opinion. But whether one thinks that religion is entirely a matter of opinion or just mostly a matter of opinion, one cannot deny that it *matters* politically. And if religion—whether true or false—matters to politics, then so does morality. Indeed, although rational and secular moral systems are possible, most existing moral codes are derived from religious revelation.

In short: if morality plays no role in politics, the cynics must still explain why people *think* it does. And if people *think* that morality plays a role in politics, then it *does* play a role in politics, because politics is largely a matter of opinion.

BOURGEOIS MAN & PLATONIC PSYCHOLOGY

The second and deeper problem with political cynicism is that the "amoral" model of human behavior it puts forward is actually the product of a particular moral code. Man is not "by nature" a selfish calculating creature moved by greed and fear. That's just bourgeois man. Bourgeois behavior has always been possible for human beings, but it was not considered normal, much less ideal, until the rise of modern liberalism.

I believe that we can best understand bourgeois man by looking backward to Plato's *Republic*. At the core of the *Republic* is a systematic analogy between the structure of the city and of the individual soul. Socrates analyzes the soul into three parts: reason, spirit, and desire.

Desire is directed toward the necessities of life: food, shelter, sex, and—above all—self-preservation. Since we share these desires with other animals, we can call them "creature comforts."

Spirit (*thumos*) does not refer to anything ethereal or ghostly. It is more akin to "team spirit." Spiritedness is "love of one's own," but it is not merely selfishness, for what one regards as one's own can extend beyond one's person and possessions to one's family, one's community, one's homeland, one's race, etc. A particularly broadened spiritedness can lead the individual to sacrifice his life to preserve a greater good with which he identifies.

Spiritedness is very much connected with one's sense of honor, which is offended when others deny our worth or the worth of the things we love. Furthermore, because spiritedness involves passionate attachment to one's own and a willingness to fight for its honor and interests, it is the basis of political life. Like Carl Schmitt, Plato and Aristotle believed that politics necessarily involves the distinction between us and them and the potential for enmity, which arise from the spirited part of the soul.

Reason for Plato is not just a morally neutral calculative or technological faculty, which deliberates about the right means to attain any given end. Reason is also a moral faculty which can discover the nature of the good and establish the *proper goals* of human action.

Conflict & Order in the Soul & Society

It is possible for the different parts of the soul to be in conflict with one another.

Desire vs. Reason: On a hot day, one's desires might urge you to drink a cold beer. But one's reason might resist the temptation because one has a drinking problem.

Desire vs. Spiritedness: One might resist the desire to drink beer because giving into temptation is incompatible with one's sense of honor.

Reason vs. Spiritedness: If one is insulted by a much larger man, spiritedness may desire to fight, but reason may resist on the grounds that victory would be impossible or too costly. (If valor has two parts—spiritedness and reason—*discretion*, i.e., reason, is the better part.)

If the different parts of the soul can come into conflict, then there are three basic types of men—rational, spirited, and desiring—based on which part of the soul tends to win out. This is the sense in which the soul is like society: it can be hierarchical; different parts can rule over one another. Man's most fundamental freedom is his choice of masters. We can choose to be ruled by our reason, our spiritedness, or our desires.

As with an individual, a society as a whole can be ruled by its rational, spirited, or desiring parts.

In the *Republic*, Socrates calls the city ruled by reason "*kallipolis*" — the fine or beautiful city. But we have no name for a rational form of government, because it does not exist (yet). But we approximate to it by designing impartial deliberative procedures to make decisions and create and apply laws.

A society ruled by spiritedness is a warrior aristocracy.

A society ruled by desire is an oligarchy, if power is in the hands of the rich, and a democracy, if it falls into the hands of the poor.

BOURGEOIS MAN & SOCIETY

I use the term *bourgeois* to refer to oligarchical and democratic man alike. The bourgeois type is ruled by his desires. His spiritedness is constricted to the hard nub of self-love, or love of one's self-image (vanity), and sublimated into competition for money and the status symbols money can buy. His reason is merely a technical faculty for calculating how to pursue pleasures and avoid pains. His desires basically boil down to greed and fear. His highest value is a life of comfort and security. His greatest fear is a violent death.

Bourgeois man is the source of political cynicism, for he eliminates moral considerations from politics and seeks to reduce it entirely to a calculus of greed and fear. But that itself is a *moral decision*: the rejection of one model of the good life for another. Bourgeois man is himself a *moral type*. He thinks that bourgeois society is fundamentally *good*. When forced to defend it in moral terms, he lifts his head and squeals about such notions as individual rights, the sacrosanct freedom of the individual, and the moral equality and dignity of man. Then he puts his snout back in the slop.

If all men were bourgeois men, then resistance to the system would be futile, because nobody is easier to rule than a man whose highest value is a long and comfortable life and whose greatest fear is a violent death. If a man values wealth more than honor or community or principle, he can be bought. If a man fears death more than slavery, he can be enslaved. Indeed,

Bourgeois man does not need to be seized violently and sold into slavery. He will *sell himself* into slavery. Bourgeois man is a natural slave, whether he wears chains or a three-piece suit.

ALTERNATIVES TO BOURGEOIS MAN

Fortunately, not all men are of the bourgeois type. In terms of Plato's psychology, the alternatives to desire-driven bourgeois man are men who are ruled by reason and by spiritedness, i.e., intellectuals and warriors. If bourgeois man corresponds to the Hindu Vaishya (merchant) and Sudra (laboring) castes, then the man ruled by reason is the Brahmin, and the spirited man is the Kshatriya.

The intellectual's highest values are the true, the good, and the beautiful. He hates the dishonest, sordid, and ugly more than death itself. Thus he is willing to die for matters of principle. The warrior's highest value is honor, and he fears dishonor more than death itself. Thus warriors are willing to die over matters of honor. If intellectuals and warriors can conquer the fear of death over matters of principle and honor, then they can conquer all lesser fears as well.

This makes intellectuals and warriors much harder to rule than bourgeois types. Thus the leadership of any effective revolutionary movement needs to be composed of intellectuals and warriors rather than bourgeois producer-consumers. Specifically, they need to be intellectuals and warriors *by nature*, in terms of their deepest values and moral psychology, not merely in terms of their professions. There are businessmen and bricklayers who are warriors and intellectuals *by nature*.

Intellectuals come in two kinds: those who are interested in pure theory and those who have practical commitments and aims. According to Cicero's *Tusculan Disputations*:

> When Pythagoras was once asked who philosophers were, he replied that life seemed to him to resemble the games in the Olympic festival: some men sought glory, others to buy and sell at the games, and some men had come neither for gain nor applause, but for the sake of the spectacle and to understand what was done and how

it was done. In the same way, in life, some are slaves of ambition or money, but others are interested in understanding life itself. These give themselves the name of philosophers (lovers of wisdom), and they value the contemplation and discovery of nature beyond all other pursuits. (V, III, 8)

Here we have the three Platonic types: the spirited men competing for honor, the appetitive men hawking sausages, and the intellectual men watching from the stands. Pythagoras's point is that the pure intellectual is a spectator not a participant in the great game of life, including politics.

Pure theorists, however, do not make revolutions. Thus in the metapolitical context, intellectual and warrior types may be distinct, but they should not be separate. Each type needs the other. Thus they should work together and strive to embody one another's virtues.

Intellectuals naturally love ideas. To prevent them from becoming unmoored among abstractions, they need to remind themselves of the concrete groups to which they belong and for which they are fighting.

Warrior types are naturally attached to concrete groups and predisposed to take offense and fight over matters of honor. But intellectual discretion is the better part of valor: one has to know who one's friends are, who one's enemies are, and when and how to fight effectively.

A Moral Case for White Nationalism

Offering a moral case for White Nationalism combines the virtues of the intellectual and the warrior, because it is an intellectual defense for loving one's own people and fighting for them. This is not the place to set forth an ethical theory. But I will at least sketch a few of its desirable elements in broad strokes.

1. Objectivity

I believe that moral theories and moral judgments can be founded on facts and supported by reason. Thus they can be true if they meet objective criteria—or false if they do not measure up.

2. Biological Foundations

Following Plato and Aristotle, I believe that an objective morality can be founded in human nature, specifically an account of human self-actualization. Since man is both an individual and a social being, objective morality deals with both individual and collective self-actualization.

3. Universality

If moral and political right and wrong are based on human nature, what are the ethical implications of the diversity of human nature? Namely, the differences between men, women, and children, and the differences between the races and subraces of mankind? At minimum, we can say that there will be some universal moral principles, in view of our common humanity. For our purposes, two universal principles stand out.

First, it is natural, normal, and good for all people to love one's own—to be partial to people and places that are close to you—to have stronger or weaker obligations based on proximity or distance (including genetic distance) from one's self. These spirited attachments—suitably refined and enlightened by the intellect—are the proper basis of political nationalism.

Second, the group has metaphysical and moral priority over the individual. The preservation of the group is more important than the preservation of the individual, because the individual is an offshoot of his people, and, when his finite existence is over, he lives on through his people. Thus, when faced with the choice of sacrificing oneself for the good of one's people or living on at their expense, one should choose self-sacrifice for the greater good. This is the foundation of effective White Nationalist politics, since men who are willing to make sacrifices—and even court death—for their people are far harder for the system to cow and control than bourgeois types, who value their own lives and comfort over the existence of their people.

4. Objective Pluralism

To the extent that there is a common human nature, there are universal moral principles. To the extent that human nature is diversified by age, sex, and race, we should expect variations and particularities among moral principles.

First of all, we would expect universal principles to be applied differently in different cases. For instance, it makes sense that self-sacrifice for the group should fall more to males than females, since individual males are more expendable from a reproductive point of view. Furthermore, although it makes sense for the young and strong to fight, it also make sense that self-sacrifice among males should fall more to older males, since they have less life ahead of them anyway, and to males who have reproduced rather than those who have not.

Second, we should expect different particular rights and duties for men, women, and children. Furthermore, when we look at the fine-grained norms of social life, we should expect these to vary between races and subraces, for if their natures are truly different, then the conditions of their actualization will be different as well.

But this does not imply moral relativism if that means that the right way of life is merely a matter of subjective choice. Instead, what we have here is a completely *objective* form of relativism, in the same way that the most comfortable pair of shoes varies from foot to foot, but in completely objective ways.

The objective pluralism of some moral principles means that there is not a "one-size-fits-all" way of life for all peoples. It implies that any attempt to create a one-size-fits-all system will be about as comfortable and elegant as one-size-fits-all shoes and clothes. Objective moral pluralism is thus one of the foundations of political pluralism—including ethnonationalism—whereas one-world globalism is the political equivalent of outfitting the world in totalitarian boiler suits and flip flops.

5. Reciprocity

The Golden Rule of "Do unto others as you would have others do unto you" counsels taking a certain moral risk in behaving toward others not as they are *actually* behaving toward you, but as you would *like* them to. This sort of risk is necessary to expand one's moral community, and it is richly rewarded when one's moral dealings are reciprocated in kind.

But because morality is about self-actualization, individual and collective, one should not allow one's moral risks to turn into moral exploitation and parasitism. Nothing is more obscene than exploiting people through their virtues. Thus, at a certain point, it is necessary to demand reciprocity as a condition for further dealings. Since white dispossession involves a host of non-reciprocal moral demands—for instance, only white countries are under the alleged moral obligation to destroy themselves through immigration—simply demanding moral reciprocity would bring many of our problems to a screaming halt.

MORAL SERIOUSNESS

> "This ain't no party. This ain't no disco.
> This ain't no foolin' around."
> —Talking Heads, "Life During Wartime"

I have been involved with the White Nationalist scene since the year 2000. My experience has been overwhelmingly positive, but not entirely so. The hardest thing to take has not been the crooks and crazies, but the pervasive lack of *moral seriousness*, even among the best-informed and most principled White Nationalists. I know people who sincerely believe that our race is being subjected to an intentional policy of genocide engineered by the organized Jewish community. Yet when faced with a horror of this magnitude, they lead lives of consummate vanity, silliness, and self-indulgence.

I am convinced that more people will get involved with our cause if we follow two rules: (1) each person gets to determine his own level of explicitness and involvement, and (2) the rest of us have to respect those decisions. But our cause will never move forward unless we can also persuade people to (1) do everything they can within their own individually determined comfort zones, and (2) expand their comfort zones, so they are willing to take greater risks for the cause. But to do that, we need to grapple with the issue of moral seriousness.

I know White Nationalists who would run down the street in broad daylight shouting "thief!" at the top of their lungs if their car were being stolen. But when confronted with the theft of our whole civilization and the very future of our race, they merely mutter euphemisms in the shadows.

I know White Nationalists who are fully apprised of the gravity of the Jewish problem, who have seen the Jewish takeover and subversion of one Right-wing institution after another, and yet still think that they can somehow "use" Jews.

I know White Nationalists who are fully aware of the corruption of the political establishment yet still get caught up in election campaigns. I know outright National Socialists who have donated far more to Republicans than they have to the movement.

I know White Nationalists who spend $50,000 a year on drinks and lap dances—or $30,000 a year dining out—or $25,000 a year on their wardrobes—or $100,000 on a wedding, yet bitterly complain about the lack of progress in the movement.

I know White Nationalists who tithe significant portions of their income to churches which pursue anti-white policies, yet never consider regular donations to the pro-white cause.

I know people with convictions to the right of Hitler who argue that we should never claim that we are fighting *for* the white race or *against* Jewish power, but who still think that *somehow* our people will want to follow us rather than 10,000 other race-blind, Jew-friendly conservative groups.

I know White Nationalists who believe that our race is being exterminated, yet insist that our enemies "know not what they do," that they are deceiving themselves, that they are fundamentally people of good will, and that this is all some sort of ghastly misunderstanding.

I know White Nationalists who would never admit to hating anyone or anything, even the vulture gnawing at their entrails.

None of them are being forced to behave this way. All of them are operating within their self-defined comfort zones. All of them could do more, even within their comfort zones. So why do they fail to comport themselves with the urgency and moral seriousness called for by the destruction of everything we hold dear?

I want to suggest two explanations. First, deep in their hearts, they don't believe that we can win, so they aren't really trying. Second, and more importantly, they are still wedded to the bourgeois model of life.

People display their true priorities when facing death.

The true intellectual values truth more than life itself. Socrates is a hero to intellectuals because when forced to choose between giving up philosophy or death, he chose death. Most intellectuals do not face that choice, but if they do, they hope they are capable of heroism too, for nothing reveals fidelity to truth more clearly than a martyr's death.

The true warrior values honor more than life itself. Leonidas and the 300 are heroes to warriors because when faced with death or dishonor, they preferred death. Again, not every warrior faces the choice so starkly, but if he does, he hopes he will choose a glorious death, for nothing reveals fidelity to honor more clearly than a heroic death.

Bourgeois man values nothing higher than life itself. He fears nothing more than a violent death. Therefore, there is no form of heroic death that demonstrates true fidelity to bourgeois values. The true intellectual dies a martyr. The true warrior dies on the battlefield. The true bourgeois looks forward to a comfortable retirement and dying in bed.

Yes, countless American soldiers have died fighting for "freedom," "democracy," and college money. But they have been suckered out of their lives by men who think there is nothing worth dying for, so that the bourgeoisie can make money, play golf, and die in bed.

You only have one death. Thus even people who would glory in heroic martyrdom have to choose their battles wisely and make their deaths count. Yes, you have to pace yourself. Yes, you have to save yourself. Yes, you can't live as if every day were your last.

But these truisms easily serve as rationalizations for cowardice. Because, at a certain point, you have to ask what you are saving yourself for. You can't take it with you. And ultimately, accomplishments do not come from saving ourselves but from *spending* ourselves. What we do not give, will be taken by death in the end.

Yet the whole bourgeois dream is premised on evading this simple, grim reality. Bourgeois man seeks eternal springtime and perpetual peace, a "happily ever after" on sunlit putting greens, free of tragic choices and tragic grandeur, free of ideals that can pierce his heart and shed his blood.

But you can't overthrow a system you are invested in. You can't challenge the rulers of this world and count on reaching retirement age. You can't do battle with Sauron while playing it safe. In the face of world-annihilating evil, we can no longer afford to be such men.

Counter-Currents/*North American New Right*,
December 4 & 5, 2013

The Psychology of Conversion

How do we convert people to White Nationalism? To answer that question, we have to ask ourselves how we were converted, then do the same for others. The most natural method of conversion is to share the information that converted us: information on biological race differences, the problems of diversity, systematic anti-white discrimination and vilification, the peril of whites being demographically swamped by fast-breeding non-whites, and the role of the organized Jewish community in creating this situation and preventing our people from solving these problems.

When you view conversion as a matter of information, the task seems rather clear-cut. But it also seems rather overwhelming and hopeless. For although the internet has been a great boon to our cause, there is simply no way that we can compete with the system in terms of ability to access and indoctrinate the minds of our people. Once our cause is framed as a race with the system to deliver information, we can only despair or take refuge in fantasies of leveling the playing field through collapse or finding a pro-white billionaire who will buy us a television network or a movie studio.

I want to suggest, however, that the process of conversion is both more complex and more hopeful than simply delivering information to people.

In *The Varieties of Religious Experience*, William James devotes two chapters to the psychology of religious conversion. In these chapters, he quotes extensively from autobiographical accounts of religious conversions (all of them to Christianity). What is striking about these narratives is that the conversions did not take place through the acquisition of new information or even a new worldview. In all cases, it is clear that the converts *already* believed in God, sin, and redemption through Jesus Christ *before* their conversions.

Thus conversion was not a matter of changing their beliefs, but instead a matter of changing the relative *importance* of their beliefs. James distinguishes between the center and the margins of our interests. At the center of our interests are "hot and vital" matters from which "personal desire and volition make their sallies." They are the "centers of our dynamic energy . . ."[1] They are the things that *matter*, the things that cause us to *act*.

James also claims that our beliefs naturally cluster together into different "systems" of ideas. As our interests shift, some systems become the focus of our attention, glowing with heat and vital interest, while others become cool and marginal. According to James, when one's "focus of excitement and heat . . . come[s] to lie permanently within a certain system . . . we call it a *conversion*, especially if it be by crisis, or sudden" (p. 217).

James wishes to reserve the word conversion for religious transformations, but one can speak of political conversions as well. "To say that a man is 'converted' means . . . that religious ideas, previously peripheral in his consciousness, now take a central place, and that religious aims form the habitual center of his energy" (p. 218). When a new system of ideas becomes the permanent core of one's life, "everything has to re-crystallize about it" (p. 218).

James' account of conversion has important implications for White Nationalism.

First is the sobering realization that informing our people is not enough if the information remains peripheral to the active centers of their lives. If the information is not important enough to act on, then nothing will change.

Second, the key to White Nationalist conversion is ultimately moral. It is a matter of values. The key is not to inform, but to make information *matter*, to make it of central and supreme importance, so that competing values no longer have the power to inhibit us from acting upon it.

Unfortunately for us, James claims that psychology can only describe the process of conversion, but it cannot account for all

---

[1] William James, *The Varieties of Religious Experience* (New York: Modern Library, 1994), p. 217.

the details of *how* and *why* these changes take place. Indeed, he says that not even converts themselves are fully aware of all the factors at work.

James' account of conversion applies quite well to my case, although I don't know if I am typical or not. I did not become a White Nationalist through the educational efforts of the movement. I was aware of racial differences, the negative effects of diversity, anti-white discrimination, white demographic peril, and even the Jewish problem through mainstream sources and personal experiences long before I encountered the movement. Most of the information I received about these matters was, of course, selected to confirm establishment biases and freighted with negative value judgments. But nevertheless, I was aware of every element of my present worldview by the time I was 16.

Only three things were lacking.

First, I needed to put the information together and draw the proper conclusions. And even that was pretty much sketched out too, for hadn't I been informed a thousand times already that white racial awareness is a slippery slope to National Socialism?

Second, I was inhibited from drawing these conclusions by the extreme moral stigmas attached to them and by the extremely negative images I had been sold of advocates of such ideas. I simply could not be one of *those people*, those vicious, moronic brutes.

In my case, the moral stigma was far less forbidding, because I had never been an egalitarian or felt the least shred of unearned guilt. But even though I was capable of disbelieving in Christianity, equality, and white guilt, I still accepted that no decent, intelligent, cultured person today could believe anything remotely like White Nationalism. (That only changed in 2000, when I met my first actual White Nationalist.)

Beyond the moral stigmas attached to ethnocentrism, I also ascribed undue value to freedom, individualism, and capitalism and assumed that such European values were universal and would be reciprocated by all peoples.

I sought out information from the movement only *after* my inhibitions had melted away, only *after* I finally drew the conclusions *from what I already knew* about our race's terrible plight and what must be done to reverse it.

I believed everything that White Nationalists believed, and I became quite well-informed rather quickly. But not even that was enough to convert me to White Nationalism, for one more factor stood in the way.

I was still not a real White Nationalist, because my beliefs were essentially a private hobby, an intensely interesting sideline to my life, but nothing more. The core of my interest was still philosophy, and my goal was to pursue an academic career.

The reasons why my White Nationalist beliefs were marginal are complex. Part of the matter, surely, is the fact that they came later than my other convictions. But another part of it is that I believed that White Nationalism ultimately *didn't matter*. Specifically, I believed that there was nothing I could do—nothing *anyone* could do—to reverse our race's decline.

But I did not despair, because I also believed that the current system was unsustainable, thus it will eventually perish from its internal corruptions and contradictions. And since it seemed unlikely that the system would outlast our race, I believed that after "the collapse" our people would have a fighting chance. Until then, however, nothing could be done. So my primary energies were focused elsewhere, where I felt I could make a difference.

My real conversion to White Nationalism came together in the fall of 2001. The reasons are complex as well.

One factor was 9/11, which led me to make my first public statements on the Jewish problem, because I came to believe that real headway was now possible. Another formative experience was my visit to Paris to attend the Front National's Fête des Bleu-blanc-rouge. It was intoxicating to be among thousands of like-minded people. We cannot win as isolated individuals. But there in Paris was concrete, palpable, visceral proof that white people could join together to accomplish great things.

There were other galvanizing events as well, but when I think them through, they all lead back to the dawning conviction that *I* could do something, because *we* could do something. Even if you believe that something can be done, you will not act if you feel that you are alone, since individuals cannot change the course of history by themselves. We know that if we declare ourselves openly, there will be opposition. Thus it makes sense to be cautious until you know that others will stand with you. And for all the flaws of "the movement," then and now, I became convinced that enough White Nationalists are capable of courage, loyalty, and solidarity that we can change the course of history, just like other intellectual movements have done. We really can save the world.

Another crucial realization was that there is no contradiction between activism and belief in larger historical forces that constrain our ability, individually or collectively, to change the world. The solution lies in the teaching of the Bhagavad-Gita: that each individual should do his duty, regardless of the consequences. We know the right thing to do, but we do not know the consequences of doing the right thing. Thus one should act according to knowledge of duty, not conjectures about consequences. One should do one's duty to the utmost and let the gods sort out the results. And I believed that my duty was to fight. That is the ethic of a movement that can save the world.

Once these ideas crystallized, everything else fell by the way. Pursuing an academic career seemed particularly absurd. I couldn't do it. Not even as a racket.

I wish to close with a heartening suggestion. Maybe we can worry less about informing out people, because (1) they are better informed than we think, and (2) the system is educating them better than we ever can.

One reason I found 9/11 tremendously encouraging is that is showed Americans to be far better informed about the Jewish problem than I had expected. A few days after the attacks, NBC and Reuters released poll data indicating that two-thirds of the public believed that the terrorist attacks happened because the United States was too close to Israel. In the years since, direct experience has only deepened my conviction that our people are much more aware of White Nationalist concerns than some might think. If you create a safe and sympathetic environment, then listen, it is astonishing what you will hear. And like me, most of these people have been first exposed to these ideas by the system, not the movement.

Some of us despair because we will never be able to compete with the system's diversity propaganda. But don't White Nationalists believe that exposure to diversity inevitably creates ethnic hatred and conflict? If so, then by forcing diversity upon whites, the system is doing our work for us. And the propaganda is only getting more intense. I grew up in an overwhelmingly white community. My education was virtually untouched by political correctness. I was immune to white guilt. But still, I was past 30 when I finally arrived at White Nationalism. Today, I know fully conscious, well-informed White Nationalist teenagers. Most of their education came from the system. The movement just provided the finishing touches.

I believe that America today is very much like Eastern Europe in the 1980s: a totalitarian system committed publicly to another version of the lie of egalitarianism. Like Communism, the American system is becoming increasingly hollow and brittle as more whites decide, in the privacy of their own minds, that equality is a lie, diversity is a plague, and the system is stacked against them. But they do not act on these convictions because they think that they are basically alone. If they slip, they know they will be persecuted, and nobody will come to their defense. (Nobody but *those people*.) But if the system's ability to stifle dissent wavers long enough for people to realize that they are not alone, then things can change very quickly. And such changes hinge on moral factors, not information.

I am not denigrating movement efforts to educate the public. But information alone cannot produce conversion. Thus no question is more important for White Nationalists to crack than the psychology of conversion. I would be particularly interested to hear Kevin MacDonald's thoughts on the matter, but all of us need to reflect on our own intellectual journeys. Our goal should be to develop a whole array of techniques to convert passive believers into active fighters. Information is the kindling, conversion the spark that will set the world ablaze.

Counter-Currents/*North American New Right*,
December 18, 2013

OUR FAULT?

The existing American system has driven white birth rates below replacement level while flooding the country with fast-breeding non-white immigrants, both legal and illegal; it promotes racial integration, miscegenation, anti-white discrimination, multiculturalism, and diversity worship; it denigrates white achievements and pathologizes white pride and ethnocentrism while stoking non-white resentment, entitlement, and truculence; and it apparently has no brakes.

If these conditions persist, our race will become extinct. And since genocide is defined not merely as killing a people outright, but also as creating conditions inimical to their long-term survival, the present system is not merely anti-white, it is genocidally anti-white.

A common claim among racially conscious conservatives and White Nationalists is that this slow-motion anti-white genocide is "our fault," sometimes even "all our fault." To give just two recent examples, Patrick Buchanan entitled his latest book on the decline of white America *Suicide of a Superpower*. Alex Kurtagić, speaking at the 2012 *American Renaissance* conference, said, "Western man has brought catastrophe on himself. . . . Western man has become his own worst enemy, opening his borders to the rest of the world and thus 'sponsoring his own decline.'" (For other examples, see Tanstaafl's discussions of the "suicide meme" at *Age of Treason*.[1])

1. The claim that white dispossession is *entirely* our fault is absurd on the face of it, since it denies that other groups exercise any agency and bear any responsibility at all. It exculpates the non-whites flooding into white lands, driving us from our homes, destroying our cultures, and crowding out our posterity.

But it is more than absurd. It is repugnant. It implies that white victims of non-white rapists, robbers, and killers are re-

---

[1] http://age-of-treason.blogspot.com/search/label/suicide%20meme

sponsible for their plight, but their assailants are not. It implies that Christopher Newsom and Channon Christian were responsible for their own torture and murder at the hands of a gang of blacks, not the blacks themselves.

Whites, however, find such grandiose claims irresistible, for even when we flagellate ourselves for being responsible for all the evils in the world, we secretly revel in the fact that we are the masters of the world, the only people who matter, the only people who make history.

But in the end, when push comes to shove, people who believe themselves guilty for all the evil in the world will give way before the force of people who believe themselves morally righteous. White guilt is promoted to ease the way to white dispossession and white genocide.

2. Whenever you hear talk about what "we" are doing to "ourselves," you should be suspicious. For collectives do not act. Individuals and small, like-minded elites act in their names. In every society, there are those who rule and those who are ruled. There are those who do things, and those who have things done to them.

Thus "America" is not committing suicide. Some Americans are destroying the country for the rest of us, because it is to their advantage. And if one looks at those who are promoting and profiting from America's decline, Jews are massively overrepresented among them, although there are white culprits as well.

3. Before we weigh the sense in which whites are responsible for our own predicament, we have to state clearly that 90% of the time, the claim that it is "our fault" is not being advanced as a serious, sincere proposition. Thus one would be a fool to analyze it as such. Most of the time, the claim that white dispossession is "our fault" really means one thing: that it is *not* the fault of the organized Jewish community. The primary purpose of blaming whites is merely to avoid blaming Jews. Questions of plausibility aside, one could just as well blame God, witches, or space aliens, so long as attention is directed away from the Jews.

Buchanan, for example, knows that many of the destructive policies that he chronicles in his book were pushed by the organized Jewish community in order to enhance their power at the expense of whites. But Buchanan has chosen to play by Semitically correct rules, so he treats the Jews as part of "us" and then claims that "we" are doing it to ourselves. Whatever Kurtagić actually thinks is going on, he had to blame whites, for *American Renaissance* forbids White Nationalists from criticizing Jews (while sponsoring Jews to criticize White Nationalism).

So nine times out of ten, when somebody claims white dispossession is "our fault," this is a dishonest attempt to avoid talking about the Jewish question. Of course the motives, and thus the blameworthiness, of these lies vary. Some are told by sincere white advocates playing an angle. Others are told by Jews hoping to prevent whites from effectively resisting genocide.

4. Some white advocates argue that not all of us should talk about the Jewish problem. Education takes place in stages. One does not study geometry before arithmetic. Before one can understand the Jewish role in the race problem, one first has to understand that there is a race problem at all. First we must learn the facts. Then we can get to the explanation. Furthermore, people have been so brainwashed by racial egalitarianism that it is very difficult to get them to think critically about race. The job is even harder if one throws the Jewish question into the mix, given the six million ways our people have been brainwashed about Jews—from the churches, the schools, the mass media, and popular culture.

This argument has merit, but it does not justify *lying* about the "suicide" of the West. It is one thing to focus on educating our people about the race problem and leaving the Jewish question to someone else. It is quite another thing to cover for the Jews by claiming that they are white like us and that we are the cause of our own dispossession.

If one wishes to focus on the race question alone, then how should one answer when the Jewish question is raised? An honest answer is simply to point out that there is a debate within the white advocate community about the Jewish role in white dispossession. This answer takes no side but conceals no truths either. It does not amount to complicity with and covering for Jewish subversion. One should state it flatly and then get back on message.

5. Now that we have dealt with the dishonest use of the "our fault" meme, we can deal with the actual question: To what extent is white dispossession our fault? I believe that white dispossession is, *to some extent*, our own fault. Thus white dispossession is *not entirely* the fault of the Jews. The Jews could not have done this to us without white collaboration.

6. But we have to analyze what is meant by "fault" here. In the minimum sense, being at fault refers to being a causal factor in one's own downfall. The strongest sense of "fault" is specifically *moral* culpability. Moral culpability is relative to two factors: power and knowledge. The more power one has to promote or halt white dispossession, the more responsibility one has. The more knowledge one has of white dispossession, the more responsibility one has.

The fact that many whites think that it is *moral* to promote the destruction of their own people is no excuse. They know very well that they are harming people, evading reality, and telling lies, even if they think that it is justified by their ultimate ends.

There is also a sense in which moral ignorance should never be treated as an excuse, for above any particular moral imperative is *the moral imperative to know the truth about right and wrong*. We ought to know what we ought to do. People who labor under false moral systems *ought to know better*. We all ought to know better, because we all ought to do right.

One can also be at fault in a morally innocent way. One can, for instance, have the best of intentions but still contribute to evil because one is enmeshed in a system that transforms good intentions and deeds into evil results. But once one becomes aware of how one's decent acts are perverted to serve evil ends, one is responsible to change the system that makes one complicit in evil.

It may be impossible to unplug completely from an evil system. Or even if it is possible, it may render one completely incapable of changing the system. One might have to withdraw from society completely and live under a bridge. But if everyone who became aware of the evils of our system simply dropped out to save his own soul from further culpability, *the system would only be strengthened*. But the highest imperative is not to maintain the goodness of one's own soul. The highest imperative is to fight evil. Thus one should stay plugged into the system, regardless of the personal costs, and do everything one can to change it. And provided that one *actually is* working to change it, one incurs no more bad karma.

The weakest sense of "fault" is simply a *vulnerability*, an Achilles heel. Everybody has weaknesses. They are not immoral *per se*. But how one deals with one's weaknesses is a moral issue. Specifically, if one is aware of one's weaknesses and how they can be used by others to further evil ends, one has the responsibility to stop it.

7. The guiltiest whites are the powerful politicians, businessmen, and intellectuals who handed control of our destiny over to Jews. Somewhat less guilty are powerful whites who are products of the current system and who work with non-whites to promote anti-white policies: affirmative action, racial integration, non-white immigration, multiculturalism, globalization, miscegenation, white guilt, etc. These people deserve punishment.

8. Of course, crimes of commission are worse than the crimes of omission. But the fact remains that powerful whites who simply do nothing to halt white dispossession are more culpable than powerless ones.

9. For people in power, ignorance of how long-term trends affect their people is no excuse, because part of their responsibility is to know about such things. They ought to know better.

10. Most whites are relatively powerless. We are merely along for the ride. But most powerless whites still share the universalistic, altruistic, anti-ethnocentric values of the whites who are actively selling us out. Many others share the cynical,

selfish, individualistic, devil-take-the-hindmost values of those who actively betray us merely for money and power.

White traitors would be far fewer if their actions were viewed as evil by the majority of the white community. Thus all whites who share the values that promote white genocide also share a small degree of complicity.

11. But what of whites who reject white genocide and the values that promote it? One cannot redeem oneself merely by rejecting deadly ideas, for if one stands by and does nothing to stop them, one is still *a bit* culpable for the outcome.

12. Worse still are those who know full well the perils that our race faces and decide to "do something," but then do something counterproductive. It is better to do nothing, than to do something counterproductive. Of course serious men disagree about what is productive. But there are better and worse ways to conduct disputes. And the deeper problem is that we lack serious men to begin with. But if one grasps the full peril of the situation, there is simply no margin for buffoonery.

13. Since all whites at one time or another fall into the above categories, *we are all – to widely varying degrees – culpable for our racial decline. All* whites bear *some* responsibility, although whites as a whole do not bear *full* responsibility.

But once one understands one's mistakes and learns how to avoid them in the future, there is no point in dwelling on the past. Our goal as White Nationalists should be to bear *no further culpability* for our ongoing genocide. And the way to do that is: (1) to understand the problem to its roots, (2) to reject all the causes of our predicament, and (3) to actively work for our race's salvation. Until you do that, you remain part of the problem.

There are different ways to work for our race's salvation. You decide your own level of explicitness and involvement, and the rest of us will accept that. But whatever you do, make sure that it counts, then do it to be best of one's ability. You must do your duty, and your first duty is to determine what that duty is.

14. But it is not just the case that whites, individually, are more or less culpable in our own genocide. For genocide is not just a matter of individuals. It is also a matter of the system. The liberal, democratic, capitalist system alone is conducive to white genocide, even without Jewish involvement.

Jewish power and influence have a long history. But present-day Jewish hegemony is a relatively recent phenomenon. It was certainly well advanced when the Jewish cabal around Woodrow Wilson delivered the United States into World War I. Yet the Jewish lobby was defeated in 1924 by immigration restrictionists. But beginning with the presidency of Franklin Delano Roosevelt, Jewish hegemony was firmly established, and Jews have moved from victory to victory.

It is fair to say that Jews are the primary architects, organizers, defenders, and beneficiaries of this anti-white genocidal system. But if Jews built the superstructure, whites laid the foundations long before the rise of Jewish hegemony.

White capitalists promoted wave after wave of immigration of increasingly heterogeneous white and non-white stocks in order to gain advantages over the native-born working class. (The vast majority of American Jews came here as immigrants, drawn by the anti-national, anti-racial logic of capitalism.)

White businessmen bought black slaves and hired Chinese coolies rather than pay white workers living wages. (The fact that Jews were among the sellers of slaves is immaterial. They could not have sold them if nobody was buying.)

The white universalism, egalitarianism, and racial altruism that sustain the system are entirely alien to Judaism. Their roots lie in Greek natural law philosophy, Christianity, and Enlightenment liberalism. These values led Americans to fight a bloody and devastating civil war largely over black slavery long before the rise of Jewish hegemony.

As Patrick Buchanan points out in *Suicide of a Superpower*, the materialistic values of liberal democracy have led to declining fertility in every First World country, including Israel and Asian countries, which lack hostile Jewish elites. If you combine this system with the racial egalitarianism and altruism and non-white immigration that existed in America before Jewish hegemony, one arrives at pretty much the same system that is killing us today. In other words, the present American system could conceivably have developed along essentially the same lines, *even if Jews had never set foot on our shores.*

This means that if the Jews suddenly departed tomorrow, but the capitalist system and universalist, egalitarian values remained in place, our race would still be on the path to extinction. Thus we need to do more than merely separate ourselves from other races. We also need to get to the deepest roots of the problem: the moral, political, and economic weaknesses that Jews are exploiting so effectively.

15. We are not, however, entitled to ignore reality just because it *could* have been different. And the reality we face is the rule of a hostile Jewish elite promoting genocide against whites. Jews are not the only members of our ruling coalition, but they are the senior partners who determine the overall direction of the system and have subordinated it to their ethnic interests. All other groups in the ruling coalition—environmentalists, labor unions, feminists, homosexuals—have to take a back seat when their interests conflict with the Jewish agenda of white genocide.

16. Furthermore, Jews are the primary guardians of the present system. Even if one wishes to criticize and change this system without mentioning Jews, as soon as one presents a credible challenge, one will find oneself opposed by Jews acting as Jews to secure their collective interests. Sometimes we do not get to choose our enemy because our enemy chooses us. Ultimately, there is no way for whites to regain control of our destiny without explicitly naming and fighting Jewish power. As Alex Linder said, there's no way out but through the Jews.

17. Assigning blame to whites does not in any way lessen Jewish culpability. If I foolishly walk into a black neighborhood and get murdered, my folly does not lessen the assailant's guilt. It does not transform homicide into suicide and absolve the killer of his crime. Likewise, due to white weaknesses, follies, and vices, the organized Jewish community is now committing genocide against our race. But that does not alter the

facts: whites are not committing suicide; we are the targets of genocide.

18. Blaming whites for our present plight is analogous to a doctor treating lung cancer with a stern lecture about the necessity of quitting smoking. Yes, smokers are responsible for their cancers. But assigning blame is not the same thing as a cure. Once one already has cancer, it is too late to change one's lifestyle to prevent it. One must first excise the tumor. Then, if one survives the operation, one can work on the necessary lifestyle changes to make sure the cancer does not return.

Yes, whites are in large part responsible for our plight. We are suffering from bad leadership, bad values, and an ethnocidal political and economic system that has made us vulnerable to race-replacement and a takeover by a hostile Jewish elite. We'll work on those problems. But first we need to cut out the cancer that's killing us. We need to regain control of our destiny and separate ourselves from other races. Then, if we survive, we can work on creating a new system that ensures that this will never happen again.

Counter-Currents/*North American New Right*,
April 12, 2012

THE BURDEN OF HITLER

Adolf Hitler was born on April 20, 1889. Every April 20th, White Nationalist websites inevitably see an increase in discussion and debate about Hitler and his legacy. Positions usually array themselves between two poles: Hitler is the problem and Hitler is the solution.

The claim that Hitler is the problem is basically a rejection of an intolerable burden of guilt by association. Hitler is the most hated man in our whole Judaized culture. Indeed, hating Hitler is the only moral judgment not stigmatized by modern moral relativists. The only absolute moral standard we are allowed is Hitler, the incarnation of evil, and all lesser evils are evil by being "like Hitler"—which ultimately means that all white people are evil due to our kinship with Hitler.

The "blame Hitler" argument boils down to this: If only Adolf Hitler had not started World War II, killed six million Jews, and tried to conquer the world, White Nationalism would get good press and perhaps make some progress in the political realm. Hitler is the reason why race realism, eugenics, immigration control, and nationalism have been discredited in the eyes of whites the world over. Thus if White Nationalism is to have any chance of changing the world, we need to ritually condemn and repudiate Hitler and everything he stood for, as well as all his present-day followers.

I find this argument to be morally contemptible and politically naïve.

It is contemptible, because it is essentially an attempt to curry favor with our enemies and pander to ignoramuses and fools by throwing a loyal white man under the bus. And make no mistake: Adolf Hitler, whatever his faults, was a loyal white man who fought and died not just for Germany, but for our race as a whole.

Blaming Hitler is also morally obscene because it absolves a whole host of villains who are the real architects of our race's doom: the slave traders and plantation owners who introduced blacks into the Americas, the railroad magnates and other plutocrats who brought Orientals to our shores, the traitorous capitalists who are destroying the white working and middle classes by importing non-white labor (legal or illegal) and shipping American jobs to the Third World, the egalitarians who have not hesitated to spill oceans of white blood to promote the moral and political equality of non-whites—and of course every politician who has done the bidding of all of the above.

Blame must also be placed on the organized Jewish community which has used its control over the entertainment and news media, academia, and the professions, as well as its vast wealth, to corrupt all aspects of American politics, business, and culture and to engineer and promote multiculturalism, mass non-white immigration, miscegenation, racial integration, and a poisonous culture of white self-hatred and non-white truculence.

Blaming Hitler is also politically naïve. Our race was not set on the path to destruction when Hitler was elected Chancellor of Germany in 1933. The problem started long before then, but a real turning point began in the 1880s with the immigration of millions of Jews from Eastern Europe to the United States, a country that was simply not culturally or politically capable of understanding and containing the threat they posed. By 1917, the organized Jewish community—operating through a cabal around Woodrow Wilson—had sufficient power to bring the United States into the First World War as a *quid pro quo* for the British Empire's Balfour Declaration, which paved the way for the foundation of the state of Israel.

When Jews arrived in America *en masse*, they found a largely innocent and trusting people and only the weakest barriers to their rise to wealth and power. And what gratitude did the Jewish community feel toward America and its people? As soon as they were able, they traded the lives of 116,000 of the sons of those trusting Americans, plus the suffering of 205,000 more young men who were wounded, some of them unspeakably, plus the mental anguished suffered by ten million soldiers and their loved ones, plus the years robbed from the lives of the ten million soldiers and all those who worked to support them, plus the untold millions of Europeans who suffered and died because America's entrance prolonged the war—all in order to gain a British promise to allow Jews to displace the Arabs of Palestine to found a Jewish state.

This was a pivotal moment in world history: In the United States, it became clear that whites had lost control of our destiny to Jews, and ever since then, Jews have been able to use their hegemony in the United States to take control of the destinies of white nations around the world and turn more and more of them onto the path to extinction.

No, their control was not absolute. In 1924, white Americans passed immigration restriction. But by 1941, Jews and their allies had delivered America into another world war; in the 1950s and '60s they spearheaded, funded, and controlled the civil rights movement; and by 1965, after more than 40 years of lobbying, Jews were pivotal in opening America's borders to non-white immigration.

If Hitler had never been elected Chancellor of Germany, if the Second World War had never happened, Jews would still have lobbied for open borders; they would still have promoted multiculturalism, feminism, and generalized cultural decadence; they would still have promoted pseudoscientific race denial, racial egalitarianism, and racial integration; they would still have corrupted our political system to pursue Jewish interests at the expense of American interests. How do I know this? Because they were *already* doing all these things long before Hitler came to power.

Jews are promoting conditions that are leading to the genocide of the white race. They are not doing this out of "self-defense" against Hitler's aggression, since they were doing it when Hitler was just a common soldier in the Great War. Indeed, the truth is that Hitler did whatever he did in self-defense against Jewish aggression—the same Jewish aggression that we are suffering today in a much intensified form.

The "blame Hitler" argument also commits what I like to call the "one little thing" fallacy. The way some people talk, Adolf Hitler is the one thing standing in the way of our victory. If only he had remained a painter, we would be living in a White Republic today. But history is not that simple. History is the net result of billions of causal factors interacting with one another. Therefore, chances are "one little thing" is never responsible for any large scale historical phenomenon, good or bad.

A choice example of the "one little thing" fallacy is a spurious quote attributed to Benjamin Franklin that floats around Right-wing circles. According to this legend, Franklin claimed that America needed to exclude Jews from the very beginning, else that one little thing will undo our otherwise perfect culture and political system. This kind of thinking is appealing because it simplifies matters considerably and a spares us from the necessity of reflecting on broader, deeper, systematic problems that might implicate us as well.

Blaming Hitler is just another form of blaming ourselves for our ongoing racial decline. It deflects attention from the real culprits — white traitors and aliens — and replaces righteous anger at our enemies with demoralizing self-reproach and self-doubt. Anger motivates action. Self-reproach promotes passivity. So our march to oblivion continues uninterrupted.

White Nationalists who feel like Hitler is a burden on our cause need to recognize that ritually condemning him on his birthday does no good. Hitler is dead and cannot be harmed. And they are still *goyim* slated for extinction. The only thing that has changed is their own moral status. They may have won the esteem of knaves and fools, but better men see them as ignorant and vile. What good is the friendship of the corrupt and cowardly if it costs you the friendship of the honorable and upright?

How, then, can one lessen the burden of "Hitler" — the Hitler of anti-white propaganda? If a person damages your car, cursing him might *feel* good, but the only way to *fix* things is to get some sort of compensation.

How can Hitler compensate us for the burden of "Hitler"? All he has to offer us today is knowledge. So if we can *learn* something from Hitler that actually helps our race, that would at least contribute to lessening or lifting the burden of "Hitler." If you really believe that "Hitler" is keeping the white race down, then pick Hitler up: read *Mein Kampf, Hitler's Table Talk*, etc., and see if you can glean some useful truths.

There is a lot of truth there: about race, history, the Jewish question, political philosophy, economics, culture, religion, and the dead ends of bourgeois liberalism and conservatism. *Mein Kampf* is filled with practical advice about radical political organizing and propaganda that remains valid to this day.

Hitler was right about another thing as well: The ideas behind National Socialism may be universally and eternally true, but the National Socialist movement—its political platforms, symbolism, and other external trappings—are the products of a particular time and place. Thus people who dress up like Storm Troopers in 21st-century America have only a superficial understanding of Hitler's teachings. Today, a real follower of the Leader would look as American as apple pie. White Nationalists should strive to be historical actors, not mere re-enactors.

The North American New Right does, however, part ways with Hitler on one fundamental matter: he wished to reduce fellow Europeans, specifically Slavs, to colonized peoples, which contradicts the basic principle of ethnonationalism. The North American New Right stands for ethnonationalism for all nations, and we reject the totalitarianism, imperialism, and genocide of the Old Right.

The Second World War was, of course, a human catastrophe. But Adolf Hitler was not solely or even primarily responsible for that war. It takes a world to make a world war. Hitler's attempts to bring oppressed German populations into the Reich were entirely legitimate applications of the ethnonationalist principle.

It was tragic that Poland was ruled by criminal adventurers who wished to hold on to the German city of Danzig. But Hitler started a war with Poland. It was the British and French who declared war on Germany, leading to a world conflagration. The fact that they did not also declare war on the USSR, which also invaded Poland, shows that their concern with Polish independence was nothing but a hollow pretense used to stoke Polish intransigence in order to decrease the possibility of a negotiated settlement and increase the likelihood of war.

One cannot justify every action taken in a war, particularly in hindsight, but the Germans committed no crimes that the Allies did not match or exceed.

As for Operation Barbarossa against the Soviet Union: aside from the fact that Stalin and his regime richly deserved destruction, there is credible evidence that the Soviets, seeking to gain advantage from the war in the West, were poised to launch a massive invasion to seize the whole of Western Europe some time in 1941. The Soviets had already invaded Finland, Romania, and the Baltic countries, as well as Poland, in 1939 and 1940. Such an attack on the West was, of course, a predictable consequence of the war that apparently never entered into the calculations of the British and French.

Hitler and his Axis partners pre-empted that invasion and almost destroyed the Soviet Union, which survived due in large part to American aid. Although the Axis was defeated, and Stalin conquered Eastern and Central Europe, it was due only to the titanic struggle and sacrifice of Hitler, the German people, and their Axis partners that all of Western Europe was not engulfed by Communism. Adolf Hitler was, in short, the savior of the West.

I recommend that you pick up a few books about Hitler and the Second World War, just so you do not fall into the trap of discussing them in terms of preposterous war propaganda like "Hitler started the Second World War" and "Hitler was out to conquer the world." Begin with R. H. S. Stolfi's magnificent *Hitler: Beyond Evil and Tyranny*.[1] Then look at Patrick Buchanan's *Churchill, Hitler, and "The Unnecessary War": How Britain Lost Its Empire and the West Lost the World*. I would also look at A. J. P. Taylor's *The Origins of the Second World War*. And be sure to read David Irving's enthralling and fact-packed books *The War Path* and *Hitler's War*, available in a single volume: *Hitler's War and the War Path*. Lesser researchers routinely plunder them, so you might as well go back to the source. (Also, to appreciate Hitler's works of peace, read Frederic Spotts' *Hitler and the Power of Aesthetics*, which is my favorite book on Hitler.)

I do not think that the progress of White Nationalism in the

---

[1] http://www.counter-currents.com/2013/05/r-h-s-stolfis-hitler-beyond-evil-and-tyranny-part-1/

21st century *requires* the rehabilitation of Hitler and the Third Reich, which in any case would be an infinite task for scholars and a distraction for political activists. But when historical clichés are regularly lobbed at us like grenades, every responsible adult needs the basic knowledge necessary to defuse them. We don't need to be learned doctors of revisionism, but we should be able to apply some battlefield first aid.

Perhaps the most subversive thing one can do regarding Adolf Hitler is simply to ignore those who hate or love him blindly and instead discuss him rationally and objectively, like any other historical figure. If you follow this advice, I guarantee that the burden of "Hitler" will begin slowly to fade.

But you may also discover that the burden of thinking "Hitler" was wrong is nothing compared to the burden of believing that Hitler was right.

Counter-Currents/*North American New Right*,
April 20, 2013

Dealing with the Holocaust

INTRODUCTION

White Nationalists need to deal with the holocaust just as we need to deal with the Jewish question in general.

It is futile to focus on white advocacy alone and ignore the Jews, simply because the Jews will not return the favor. You might not pick Jews as the enemy, but they will pick you. You might wish to see Jews as whites, but Jews see themselves as a distinct people. Thus they see any nationalism but their own as a threat.

It is futile for White Nationalists to ignore the holocaust, for the holocaust is one of the principal tools by which Jews seek to stigmatize white ethnic pride and self-assertion. As soon as a white person expresses the barest inkling of nationalism or racial consciousness, he will be asked "What about the holocaust? You're not defending *genocide*, are you?"

The holocaust is specifically a weapon of *moral* intimidation. It is routinely put forward as the worst thing that has ever happened, *the world's supreme evil*. Anybody who would defend it, or anything connected to it, is therefore evil by association. The holocaust is evoked to cast uppity whites into the world's deepest moral pit, from which they will have to extricate themselves before they can say another word. And that word had better be an apology. To borrow a turn of phrase from Jonathan Bowden, the holocaust is a moral "cloud" over the heads of whites.

So how can White Nationalists dispel that cloud? We need an answer to the holocaust question. As a New Rightist, the short answer is simply this: the New Right stands for ethnonationalism for *all* peoples. We believe that this idea can become hegemonic through the transformation of culture and consciousness. We believe that it can be achieved by peaceful territorial divisions and population transfers. Thus we retain the values, aims, and intellectual framework of the Old Right. Where we differ is that we reject Old Right party politics, totalitarianism, imperialism, and genocide.

The idea of ethnonationalism is true and good, regardless of the real and imagined crimes, mistakes, and misfortunes of the Old Right. Thus we feel no need to "deny," minimize, or revise the holocaust, just as the New Left felt no need to tie its projects to "Gulag revisionism."

WHAT IS THE HOLOCAUST?

I understand the holocaust to mean the claim that up to six million European Jews were put to death during the Second World War by the Third Reich and its allies as part of a policy of systematic and intentional genocide, i.e., the extermination of a whole people or group.

WHAT IS REVISIONISM?

History is what really happened. *Historiography* is the *record* and *interpretation* of history created by finite and fallible human beings. As we discover new historical facts and the lies, errors, and biases of past historians, we must accordingly *revise* historiography. Historical revisionism is simply the process of criticizing historical narratives to bring them in line with historical facts.

Historical revisionism is, in principle, an infinite task, for every historian interprets limited data within particular frameworks. But data can always change, and interpretations can always be questioned. Revisionism is, therefore, a necessary and permanent feature of the pursuit of historical truth.

WHAT IS HOLOCAUST REVISIONISM?

Holocaust revisionism primarily challenges the facts of the holocaust narrative, usually focusing on death totals and techniques of extermination. Holocaust revisionism is a completely legitimate field of historical inquiry, simply because *all* historical narratives are subject to revision.

Beyond that, revisionism about wartime atrocities is necessary because wars always generate propaganda, and much of war propaganda is untrue. In the case of the holocaust, for instance, the old stories about human soap and lampshades have now been recognized as false even by mainstream historians, including Jewish historians. And so many holocaust memoirs have been unmasked as false that they constitute a whole new literary genre.

Holocaust revisionism is not the same thing as revisionism about the Third Reich or the causes, conduct, and consequences of the Second World War. Nor does it constitute holocaust revisionism to compare the holocaust to other genocides or discuss its overall meaning.

For instance, Irmin Vinson's *Some Thoughts on Hitler and Other Essays*,[1] deals with the role of the holocaust in stigmatizing and suppressing white racial consciousness today. But it is not a revisionist account of the actual events of the holocaust.

HOLOCAUST REVISIONISM IS NOT NECESSARY FOR WHITE NATIONALISM

Just so we are clear: I believe that holocaust revisionism is a legitimate field of historical research, because *all* forms of historical revisionism are legitimate, due to the necessarily partial, finite, and therefore revisable nature of historiography. I believe that all laws that penalize holocaust revisionism should be scrapped as anti-intellectual, quasi-religious obscurantism. I believe that all revisionists should be released from jail. I have met many leading revisionists, and with only a couple of exceptions, I think they are honest and honorable people. I wish them well in their endeavors.

I am not arguing that we should avoid holocaust revisionism because it will garner bad press. I don't worry about such things, because we will always have bad press—until we control the press.

I simply wish to argue that holocaust revisionism is not a *necessary* component of our intellectual project. We don't *need* it. Which is not the same thing as saying that it is a hindrance,

---

[1] Irmin Vinson, *Some Thoughts on Hitler and Other Essays*, ed. Greg Johnson (San Francisco: Counter-Currents, 2011).

or that it cannot help under any circumstances, although I will argue that it is often a *distraction*.

Personally speaking, since becoming involved with the White Nationalist scene, I have never been all that interested in holocaust revisionism, simply because my main concern is with *the genocide being committed against our own people today*, not the real or imagined crimes committed by our people in the past. And the holocaust strikes me as having little to do with the *deep* causes of our racial plight and even less to do with the solutions.

There is a weak sense in which holocaust revisionism is not *necessarily connected* to White Nationalism, namely they have very different aims which makes them very different endeavors. The proper aim of holocaust revisionism is historical truth. The aim of White Nationalism is the creation of white homelands. Although the ranks of revisionists and White Nationalists overlap, there is no necessary connection between these two aims. Which is not to say that they necessarily conflict.

For instance, there are holocaust revisionists who are not White Nationalists, such as Bradley Smith, Robert Faurisson, and Roger Garaudy. And there are White Nationalists who are not holocaust revisionists. Indeed, there are some who hope that the revisionists are wrong.

Others, like me, simply hold that revisionism, whether true or false, is simply not *necessary* to the White Nationalist project. The standard account of the holocaust could be completely true, and it would still not imply that there is anything wrong with White Nationalism and the goal of breaking Jewish power over our destiny and physically separating whites and Jews.

Of course for German and Austrian nationalists, particularly those who want to rehabilitate old-style National Socialism, there seems to be an inextricable connection between holocaust revisionism and their practical political aims. But I wish to argue that even in this case, holocaust revisionism is not necessary for German and Austrian nationalism to re-emerge from the flames.

Nothing prevents German or Austrian nationalists from saying: "If the lessons of the holocaust are that genocide is evil and the best defense against genocide is to have one's own state, then we think this lesson applies to us too. We will cease to exist as a people if we do not have control over our own borders and destinies. It is time for a new nationalism. We simply refuse to tie our destiny to what happened in the Second World War. We're over it. We've moved on. Jews are no longer being subjected to active, ongoing genocide, but we are."

So if one's goal is historical truth about the holocaust, to rehabilitate National Socialism and the Third Reich, or to cleanse the German people of blood libels, then holocaust revisionism makes perfect sense. Nothing else will really do. But if one's aim is White Nationalism, holocaust revisionism is not necessary.

THE HOLOCAUST & JEWISH POWER

Those who argue that holocaust revisionism is a necessary component of White Nationalism usually claim that the holocaust is the foundation of the post-World War II regime of anti-white genocide.

The holocaust really is the principal source of white guilt, the principal tool to stigmatize white national and ethnic consciousness.

What are the "lessons" of the holocaust? The holocaust is used, simultaneously, to justify Jewish racism, Jewish nationalism, and Jewish self-assertion and to stigmatize white racism, nationalism, and self-assertion.

Thus, some White Nationalists reason, if the principal claims about the holocaust could be refuted—if the death toll could be lowered, if the homicidal gas chambers could be exposed as a myth, etc.—then the whole racket of anti-white guilt and extortion would crumble.

But is this true?

Revisionists have been chipping away at holocaust claims since 1945. The shrunken heads, human soap, and human lampshades have been quietly withdrawn. The homicidal gas chambers have migrated from Germany and Austria to Poland. Death tolls at individual sites have been revised downward. Scores of fake memoirs and testimonies have been unmasked.

And all of these findings have been accepted by mainstream historians.

Yet has this decreased the cultural power of the holocaust over whites? Maybe it has slowed the juggernaut down a bit, but from what I see, it is still rolling over us. Furthermore, I see no effect on broader Jewish cultural and political hegemony, which has never been stronger.

Of course if the revisionists could score a major hit—if, for instance, they are right about the gas chambers at Auschwitz—there is no question that the Jewish establishment would suffer considerable embarrassment and loss of credibility and prestige in the eyes of whites. That certainly *couldn't hurt* White Nationalism. But would it really constitute a decisive blow against Jewish power?

I think not, for the following reasons.

First, as Mark Weber has pointed out, the cultural and political power of the holocaust is not the *foundation* of Jewish power, it is an *expression* of pre-existing Jewish power.[2] Before the Second World War, Jews already had an enormous amount of power in the United States: enough power to deliver the United States into two world wars, for instance. Jewish power was based on over-representation in banking, business, law, politics, academia, and the news and entertainment media.

If the holocaust suddenly lost its potency as a tool of moral intimidation, Jews surely have the talent, money, power, and ill-will to foist a new one on us. Whites will never be free until we identify and defeat the real sources of Jewish power. And from that point of view, focusing too much on the holocaust is superficial and can function as a distraction. The holocaust is like the toreador's red cape. We bulls need to stop charging the cape and start focusing on the man who wields it.

Second, holocaust death totals are never going to be revised to zero. In a war in which countless innocent people of all nations died, countless innocent Jews surely died as well, and ultimately that's all the holocaust needs to survive. The gas chambers, the genocidal intent, and the rest of it could be

---

[2] http://www.ihr.org/weber_revisionism_jan09.html

dropped, but poor little Anne Frank and many others like her would still be dead.

Third, the pity for innocent Jewish victims that our people feel will not be altered even if they are convinced that many holocaust survivors and the Allied powers exploited their deaths for political and financial gain and embellished them with outrageous blood libels against the German people. The victims told no lies about the holocaust (soap, lampshades, etc.). The survivors did. The Allied governments did. The Jewish leadership did. But dead men tell no tales.

Fourth, if many key holocaust claims were proven false, holocaust survivors could still present themselves as victims, this time of the Allied powers that fabricated German atrocities to retroactively justify their own war crimes. Jews who were duped into thinking that their entire families had been exterminated might well have lost the opportunity to find their loved ones because they believed them to be dead.

This would actually be a political windfall for Jews, because Jews have worked very hard to make *all* whites feel a spurious guilt for the holocaust, even the citizens of the Allied powers that brought the holocaust to the end. If, however, the Allies fabricated key elements of the holocaust narrative, then they really would be guilty of a great crime against the Jews, opening up vast new prospects for reparations.

Fifth, the holocaust may be the anti-white guilt trip most useful to Jews—since it simultaneously supports their nationalism and undermines ours—but it is certainly not the only one. There are all too many whites who are happily abasing and immolating themselves for such historic crimes as Negro slavery, the conquest and dispossession of indigenous peoples around the globe, even the extermination of countless animal species. Some whites seem almost eager to believe that our ancestors exterminated the Neanderthals, so they can feel guilty about that as well. Of course it would be nice to set the historical record straight on all these issues, but the real problem here is moral.

THE MORAL ROOTS OF WHITE DECLINE

It is our own people's grandiose propensity toward collective guilt and self-abasement that is the ultimate source of the holocaust's power over us. No amount of Jewish propaganda could sell us the "lessons" of the holocaust if we were not willing to buy them. *The real problem of the holocaust is moral and psychological, and historical revisionism simply does not address it. It is a problem that can only be addressed by moral and psychological means.* Unless we deal with the real root of the problem, whites will be just as willing to abase and ruin themselves over 600,000 dead Jews as over six million.

The fact that the ultimate problem lies in ourselves does not, however, absolve the organized Jewish community of guilt for exploiting it to serve evil ends.

Just to be clear, I am not objecting to feeling sympathy with the victims of injustice. Nor am I objecting to feeling shame for one's own misbehavior or the misbehavior of others, especially those who act in one's name. These are signs of moral health.

What I object to is collective guilt and collective atonement: the idea that whites today are collectively guilty for what whites have done in the past and must collectively atone for those crimes. I believe there are collective goods and evils. I am all for collective pride and collective shame. But I do not believe in collective guilt. Individuals are only guilty of the things that they do, even when individuals act in groups. It is perfectly reasonable to feel pity and shame for the extinction of the dodo or great auk. But I am not guilty of actions taken by others long before I was born.

One of the most disgusting but least harmful manifestations of collective guilt and atonement is the issuing of collective apologies for past wrongs. The King of Spain, for instance, was asked to apologize for the *Reconquista,* i.e., the reversal of the Moorish conquest of Spain. A healthy people would have responded to such insolence with laughter (and tossed whoever suggested it down a well, for good measure). After all, where is the Moorish apology for the *Conquista*?

Then there is the group of white Christians who marched around wearing chains and yokes in the custody of blacks to apologize for the slave trade.³ Of course, Muslims, Jews, and African blacks felt no need to apologize for their people's roles in the slave trade.

It is this mentality that has allowed Jews to fashion the holocaust into a kind of moral fetish from which whites shrink like vampires from the cross.

The moral and psychological effect of collective guilt is *collective demoralization and self-hatred*, which leads to *a loss of a collective destiny*. We no longer think that the world is a better place because of our people, that we have something good to contribute to the universe.

A whole book could be written about the consequences of white demoralization. I believe it is a factor in everything from lower birth rates to miscegenation to our willingness to subject ourselves to annoying black music.

But the most important consequence of white demoralization is our unwillingness to take our own side in ethnic conflicts with every other group on the planet. And, as Michael Polignano has argued so cogently, refusing to take one's own side in an ethnic conflict is the path to collective dispossession and extinction.⁴ (This is why our enemies promote such attitudes in the first place.)

Our morality has made us sick, rotten, weak, and contemptible, and only a moral revolution, what Nietzsche called a transvaluation of values, will save us. This is not the place to fully explore that transvaluation. But I will touch on how it relates to the holocaust question.

REVISIONISM VS. TRANSVALUATION

Not only does holocaust revisionism fail to deal with the moral roots of the problem, it actually subtly strengthens them. Both holocaust promoters and revisionists share a common premise: If white racism, nationalism, self-assertion, etc. led to

---

³ http://www.assistnews.net/ansarticle.asp?URL=Stories/2007/s07030129.htm

⁴ http://www.counter-currents.com/2010/09/taking-our-own-side-2/

the holocaust, the slave trade, Jim Crow, etc., then they are evil. Revisionists do not challenge the moral part of this premise, they simply dispute the facts.

But the most fundamental response is to deny the *moral* premise: *There is nothing wrong with white racism, nationalism, and self-assertion. These do not necessarily conflict with the legitimate interests of other peoples, and in cases when our interests conflict with theirs, it is perfectly correct to take our own side.* Attacking the moral dimension of the problem is like hacking at the trunk of a tree, whereas revisionism is akin to merely trimming the branches.

How Much Should the Past Matter?

There is a sense in which *the past simply does not matter* to a people of sufficient vitality and destiny. Yes, we should honor our heritage. Yes, we should learn from history. But no healthy people should allow the past to turn into a dead weight impeding them from pursuing a better future.

From the point of view of a vital organism, memory should be as selective as the digestive process, which separates nutrients from poisons and dross, absorbing the nutrients and excreting, i.e., *forgetting*, the rest as swiftly as possible.

Individuals who have a long memory for negative things, like people with slow bowels, are sickened by retaining wastes that should be excreted. The same is true for whole peoples. Great men and great peoples need to have a capacity to forget the negative so they can get on with life.

The bigger the memory, the smaller the man, i.e., the longer the memory for slights, the pettier and sicklier the soul. The bigger the past, the smaller the future, i.e., the more tied to the past one is—especially past negatives—the less vitality one has, the less ability to project a future.

And, to extend the analogy one step further, people who constantly harp on past negatives are trying to make you eat the psychic equivalent of shit. They are trying to poison you. They do not have your best interests at heart.

Sure, it is good to set the historical record straight. But from the point of view of the existential, practical project of securing the existence of our people, it is not necessary. Because mere historical facts—no matter what they are—should never deter us.

The Holocaust from the White Point of View

Part of the power of the holocaust is the idea that it is history's greatest crime, the worst thing that ever happened. This is a factual claim, which can be easily refuted. Lenin, Stalin, and Mao each killed more than six million people. (As many as 15 million people died in the USSR under Lenin's leadership, during the revolution and civil war, *before* Stalin came to power.)

Tinkering with holocaust death totals is obviously relevant to where the holocaust fits into the hierarchy of human atrocities. Does it come before or after the millions of German civilians killed during and after the Second World War by the Allied powers? How does it relate to the 1.5 to 4 million people who died in the Bengal famine of 1943, caused by the British? How does it compare to the some two million Armenians, Assyrians, Kurds, and Greeks who were killed by the Turks between 1915 and 1920, or the 1.7 million Cambodians were killed by Pol Pot from 1975 to 1979?

But from a Jewish point of view, such tinkering is irrelevant, because whether the death toll is six million or 600,000, the holocaust is still the worst thing that ever happened *to Jews*.

The problem is that Jews have gotten the rest of us to accept the Jewish view of the holocaust as the only view, the view of "*humanity*," which for a Jew means only Jews, but for whites means everyone. Whites need to develop our own perspective on the holocaust.

From a general human point of view, holocaust numbers are irrelevant as well, because even if 16 million Jews perished in the Second World War, it is certainly not the worst thing that ever happened to the human race. That would be Communism.

From a white point of view, holocaust numbers are irrelevant too, because the worst thing that has ever happened to our race has also claimed far more than six million lives. That would be the rise of Jewish power over whites, whenever and wherever it has occurred, including Communism in the USSR and Eastern Europe, the delivery of the United States into the First World War, playing a major role in fomenting the Second World War, and playing a leading role in establishing the postwar system in which low white birth rates and the immigration of fast-breeding non-whites threaten white peoples the world over with political dispossession, cultural obliteration, and, if present trends continue, biological extinction.

But even if the holocaust were the worst thing that ever happened, 1) it is not our fault and (2) we have our own slow, ongoing genocide to worry about. So, in the end, do the numbers really matter to a people with the will to have a future?

Could "Another Holocaust" Really Happen?

The most urgently touted lesson of the holocaust is that whites had better not contemplate separating themselves from Jews ever again, lest it lead to "another holocaust." But this doesn't really follow.

First, if it really were a matter of "us or them," any healthy people would take its own side.

Second, Jews have been expelled many times from white lands, and not all of these expulsions resulted in massacres. Indeed, some of them probably prevented massacres.

Third, Jews now have some place to go: a homeland that will not refuse them refuge.

Fourth, Israel has hundreds of nuclear weapons which will effectively deter any future massacre of Jews.

The time has never been better for whites to separate ourselves from Jews.

Revisionism & Rhetoric

From a practical, political point of view, holocaust revisionism is a rather clumsy way of dealing with the holocaust question.

Imagine you are protesting some evil done by Jews and you are told that Jews have a right to do x because of the holocaust. Do you splutter that the holocaust is a "hoax" and then start disputing the numbers? Or do you simply say, "Two wrongs don't make a right"?

Imagine that you are passing out anti-immigration literature and somebody comes up to you and tells you "What you're doing is just like what led to the holocaust." Do you bring up the *Leuchter Report*? Or do you simply say, "Unless we don't stop immigration, white people have no future in this country, and that's genocide too. We're fighting against our own 'holocaust'"?

The first response is moral. The second can be characterized as political. As a general rule, moral and political arguments are more convincing than historical or scientific arguments, because the latter require specialized knowledge and lengthy explanations, whereas the former can be pithily formulated and draw upon common moral and political intuitions — and generally people's moral intuitions are healthier than the toxic moral swill ladled out by the churches, schools, and mass media.

THE TRUE LESSON OF THE HOLOCAUST

Generally the "lesson" of the holocaust boils down to: Jewish racism, nationalism, and self-assertion are good; white racism, nationalism, and self-assertion are evil. The flaw in this position has nothing to do with historical facts. It is simply the glaring moral double standard, which is the essence of Jewish tribal morality. The position is perfectly consistent with Jewish live-and-let-die morals, since both sides of the double standard benefit the Jews.

The white answer should be, for starters, to point out the double standard. But one cannot stop there, in a posture of naïve, aggrieved universalism. One should also point out that Jews are quite aware of such double standards and quite pleased with them: they are essential to the Jewish moral outlook. Jews are *morally different people*, and we need to recognize this.

But the answer is not to adopt our own version of Jewish ethics — preaching universalism for them while practicing ethnocentrism for us — for at least six reasons.

First, Jews aren't as stupid as whites, so they would never buy it.

Second, Jews can afford to maintain moral double standards

because they have the power to make them *work for them*. Whites do not have that kind of power, so there is nothing to gain by sacrificing our consistency.

Third, our fellow whites have a strong predisposition toward universalism, and flouting it makes our task that much harder.

Fourth, whites tend to be outraged at violations of universality and reciprocity. Why not channel all of that outrage toward our enemies rather than share in it ourselves?

Fifth, philosophically speaking, ethnocentrism, ethnonationalism, and ethnic self-assertion are *completely universalizable principles*. They can be accepted by all peoples. The New Right stands for ethnonationalism for everybody.

Finally, Jews have invested a great deal in genocide education and awareness. Why not make that work for us, for a change?

If the lesson of the holocaust is that peoples need their own states, ethnic pride, and ethnic separation in order to preserve themselves from genocide, then whites need to demand that this principle be applied to us as well, for although Jews have never been more secure—with their ethnostate sitting on a mountain of nuclear weapons—whites in all nations are faced with declining birth rates and teeming populations of non-white invaders, a trend incompatible with our long-term survival. That is genocide too, as defined by the United Nations. White Nationalism is all about resisting white genocide.

Followers of Bob Whitaker's mantra have made an important contribution to White Nationalism by injecting the white genocide meme far and wide into the culture. Clearly they understand that they will have a greater impact by building upon genocide awareness rather than trying to nibble away at its edges with holocaust revisionism. And one can do this in all earnestness, because, after all, *genocide really is evil*.

WHY IS REVISIONISM CRIMINALIZED?

Holocaust revisionism is illegal in 17 countries and counting. In France, Jean-Marie Le Pen, Roger Garaudy, Jean Plantin, and Robert Faurisson have been imprisoned and/or fined for holocaust revisionism. In Germany, Ernst Zündel, Germar Rudolf, Sylvia Stolz, Horst Mahler, Dirk Zimmerman, and Bishop Richard Williamson have been imprisoned and/or fined. In the cases of Zündel and Mahler, they were sentenced to five years. In Switzerland, Jürgen Graf, Gerhard Förster, and Gaston-Armand Amaudruz have been imprisoned and/or fined. In Austria, David Irving and Wolfgang Fröhlich have been imprisoned, the latter for six years. Others have been forced into exile.

One might argue that no one bans what he does not fear, thus if holocaust revisionism is banned, it must be feared by our rulers. One could make the same argument about the criminal assaults, bombs, arson, loss of employment, professional harassment, and social ostracism to which holocaust revisionists have also been subjected.

But the fact that holocaust revisionism is persecuted still does not imply that it is a *necessary* or *effective* component of White Nationalism. Furthermore, fear is not the only motive for persecution. Hatred probably plays a bigger role. The holocaust is a highly emotional topic among Jews, thus revisionism would probably be persecuted even if it bore no connection to any particular political agenda and threatened no political powers. Indeed, holocaust revisionists who have no ties to White Nationalism have also been persecuted. Finally, if White Nationalists who do not link themselves to holocaust revisionism become more effective (as I think they will), then they might have even worse persecutions in store.

Conclusion

To sum up, I have argued that White Nationalists need to deal with the problem of the holocaust. I have argued that the root of the problem is our people's willingness to accept unearned guilt and punish ourselves for it. The problem, in short, is psychological and moral, not historical. Thus holocaust revisionism is not the answer. It is not necessary for White Nationalism. At best, it can supplement an essentially moral argument for White Nationalism. At worst, it distracts us from dealing with the deeper roots of Jewish power and white weakness.

I wish to end with a few words from Jonathan Bowden, who has been a major inspiration for what I have written here. When an exponent of white revival is asked, "Well what's your view of the *Shoah* then?" Bowden recommends simply saying: "We've stepped over that."[5] Meaning that we have overcome it, that we are moving forward, that the future calls, and we are a people who wish to have a future again, and we recognize that the holocaust is being used to abort that future.

To the retort, "What do you mean you've 'stepped over' that? Are you *minimizing its importance to humanity*?" Bowden counsels the reply, "We are minimizing its importance to *our* form of humanity!"

I wish I could ask Bowden what he meant by "our form of humanity." Obviously he is referring to white people. But, whether he knew it or not, I think he is referring to only a subset of whites.

Today whites, as a whole, are a race without a future. White Nationalists wish to save our people, but the sad truth is that we can't save all of them. We are too few, the rot is too deep, and the hour is too late.

Thus, ultimately, we are not so much saving our people as becoming a *new* people. Hence "our form of humanity" consists specifically of whites who have, through a Nietzschean revolution in values, overcome Jewish power and white weakness *at their roots*, thus becoming whites who, once again, have a future.

The Occidental Observer, July 20, 2012

---

[5] http://www.counter-currents.com/2012/05/revisionism/

WHITE NATIONALISM &
JEWISH NATIONALISM

Guillaume Faye's speech at the 2006 *American Renaissance* conference was quite eventful. Most people have heard of the infamous Michael Hart incident.[1] But to my mind, something far more significant occurred during Faye's speech, something that later struck me as revelatory.

In Faye's view, the "Global South," organized under the banner of Islam, is the mortal enemy of Europe. The United States, which favors the Islamization of Europe, is not the primary enemy of Europe, but merely an adversary. Faye does not, however, classify the Jewish community as an enemy or adversary of Europe at all. Instead, Faye views the Jews as a potential ally in the fight against Islamization.

---

[1] After Faye's speech, a member of the audience stood up and asked Faye, in a roundabout way, if the organized Jewish community in France played the same role as it played in the United States in opening the gates to non-white immigration. It was a fair question, one that had also occurred to me. If I had any objection, it was to the fact that the questioner was unaware of the long line of people behind him and took too much time to get to his point.

But before Faye could answer, a Jew (author Michael Hart), angrily jumped up and denounced the questioner, David Duke, as a "fucking Nazi" and a "disgrace to the conference." This rude and foul-mouthed tirade, was, moreover, delivered in front of the children of one conference-goer. "Surely," I thought, "Jared Taylor needs to be more selective about who comes to his conferences. This Hart guy should be shunned."

Others felt similarly. Indeed, one group concluded that the incident proved it was high time for Jared Taylor to crack down on anti-Semites, the kind of people who goaded the poor victim Michael Hart until he couldn't take it anymore. This brazen little cabal, led by Lawrence Auster, even framed the whole affair as the "David Duke incident," and a lot of White Nationalists who should have known better went right along with it.

Thus, at a certain point in his speech, as Faye enumerated the possible negative consequences of the unchecked march of Islam, he said, "The state of Israel may cease to exist." But, to his obvious astonishment, this statement was met by enthusiastic applause.

Now, to be fair, I admit I joined in the applause too, in a spirit of pure mischief. But later I thought better of it. After all, as a friend pointed out, "If the Jews lose Israel, where do these people who were clapping think the Jews will go? They'll all be here or Europe. Do they really want that?" I knew that, of course, and I am sure a lot of the other people clapping knew it too.

But some people hate Jews more than they love their own people. They hate Jews so much that they want them to be harmed, even if it harms us too—even if it harms us more. Call it the white version of the "Samson Option." But if we are going to think rationally about the Jewish problem, we first have to identify and isolate this strand of suicidal spitefulness, which obviously conflicts with cool calculations of how to pursue our long term racial interests.

I would like to offer some notes on White Nationalism and Jewish nationalism in order to clarify my thoughts and provide material for discussion.

1. As ethnonationalists, we believe in the "Ein Volk, ein Reich" principle: "One people, one state" (*at least* one state per people, although there could be more than one). This means that we support, at least in principle, the nationalism of all nations, the ethnic self-determination of all peoples. We envision a kind of classical liberalism for all nations, in which each people has a place of its own, whose legitimate rights need not conflict with the legitimate rights of all other nations. If this vision came to pass, we would have a world of perpetual peace. It is an appealing ideal, even though there may be insuperable impediments to its realization.

2. Zionism is a species of ethnonationalism. It was conceived during the heyday of 19th-century European ethnonationalism as a solution to the so-called "Jewish question." The idea was to address the underlying causes of anti-Semitism by creating a

sovereign Jewish homeland and encouraging a Jewish ingathering, a reversal of the diaspora.

3. As an ethnonationalist, I do not object to Israel or Zionism *per se*. Yes, I object to our foreign policy toward Israel and its neighbors, which is dictated by Israeli interests rather than US interests. Yes, I object to foreign aid to Israel that does not serve US interests. But let us be perfectly clear here: These are not problems with Israel *per se*. *They are problems with the Jewish diaspora community in the United States.*

I do not oppose the existence of Israel. I oppose the Jewish diaspora in the United States and other white societies. I would like to see the white peoples of the world break the power of the Jewish diaspora and send the Jews to Israel, where they will have to learn how to be a normal nation.

4. But what about the Palestinians? First, let me state unequivocally that I sympathize with the Palestinians, because I too live under Zionist occupation. Second, I must also state that I admire the Palestinians, because unlike Americans and Europeans, they are fully aware that they are an occupied people. Third, and most importantly, the Palestinians are fighting against their oppressors, and I wish my people would do the same.

5. But, ultimately, white interests and Palestinian interests do not coincide. Palestinians, quite naturally, want their country back. They want to send the Jews back whence they came. As a White Nationalist, I want all our Jews to go to Israel, and that means that I want Israel to stay put.

What about Palestinian self-determination? I support a Palestinian homeland, right next to the Jewish homeland, because I want to send the Palestinian diaspora home as well.

In short, I favor a two-state solution. I do not favor the destruction of Israel, because I want the Jews to live there, not among my people. I favor a Palestinian state, because I want the Palestinians to live there, not among my people.

6. Unfortunately, when it comes to the Palestine question, the views of many White Nationalists are clouded by the fact that

they hate Jews more than they love their own people, thus they are willing to beat Jews with any stick handy, including the appeal to principles that are deadly to our people as well.

7. For instance, I think it is self-defeating to oppose Zionism on anti-colonialist grounds, for the simple reason anti-colonialism undermines the legitimacy of the founding of the United States and practically every other white nation if you go far back enough. Some guilt-besotted souls have actually contemplated resurrecting the Neanderthals, presumably so they can apologize to them for the genocide allegedly committed by our Cro-Magnon ancestors. But fretting over past wrongs distracts us from something far more important, namely preventing future ones. And the most pragmatic approach is to give both Palestinians and Jews their own homelands.

8. It is also self-defeating for White Nationalists to attack Israel on the grounds of multiculturalism. Yes, some of the very same people who complain of the Jewish double standard of promoting multiculturalism in the diaspora and an ethnostate in Israel, lament Jewish-promoted multiculturalism at home while demanding that Jews adopt it in Israel! Of course the Jewish double standard is logical, insofar as it actually advances the interests of the Jews as a diaspora community and the interests of the ethnostate of Israel.

But for White Nationalists, such a double standard serves no rational purpose at all, since we do not have political power anywhere in the world, and our only hope of gaining such power is first to build a coherent intellectual case for a white ethnostate and then to build a cultural and political movement that will actually be able to take power and create one. But one cannot build a coherent intellectual foundation by appealing to contradictory principles because one's only concern is venting hate on the internet.

9. The same argument applies to attacking Zionism because it is a form of nationalism. Since Jews have invested so much in demonizing Hitler, many think it terribly clever to liken Zionism to Nazism and Jews to Hitler. (Most White Nationalists don't go

quite that far, of course.) As a White Nationalist, however, my quarrel is with diaspora Jewry's promotion of multiculturalism and suppression of healthy nationalism in white nations. I do not oppose Zionism because it is a form of nationalism. If Jews agree with nationalism (or National Socialism, for that matter), that is to their credit.

The same argument applies to the charge that Zionism is a form of racism.

I sincerely believe that a lot of the support for Israel among American and European conservatives is merely a form of sublimated white racial nationalism. That was certainly true of me when I was a conservative. So let's leave the Jews to their racial nationalism and have our own instead.

10. It is also self-defeating to attack Israel on grounds of human rights, international law, and opposition to violence. Because everyone except complete pacifists recognizes that there are circumstances in which violence, revolution, and war are justified. Jews, moreover, have invested a great deal in promoting the idea that resisting genocide can justify pretty much any means necessary. That's convenient, since we wish to resist our own genocide, and our enemies are not likely to give up without a fight. Any measures that Jews justified against Nazis in the past and against Palestinians today can be justified against our enemies tomorrow.

11. Since people fight more fanatically if their backs are against the wall, Machiavelli argued that it is always prudent to leave an enemy a means of retreat, as it increases the likelihood of victory and reduces its costs. Diaspora Jewry regards Israel as a refuge, an insurance policy in case things go bad. The continued existence of Israel may, therefore, make it easier for whites to combat the power of diaspora Jewish communities in our various homelands.

Part of Jewish psychological intensity is their propensity to treat every issue as a matter of life and death, which produces the absurd spectacle of the leaders of the world's most powerful ethnic group comporting themselves with the hysteria of cornered rats. The actual destruction of Israel would really give them something to whine about. It would immensely heighten the Jewish siege mentality and toughen Jewish resistance to white interests.

12. I have argued that White Nationalists have an interest in the continued existence of the state of Israel. Does this mean that European nationalists like Guillaume Faye, Nick Griffin, Geert Wilders, and Anders Breivik are justified in allying themselves with Jews, whether in Israel or the diaspora?

Absolutely not, for a host of reasons.

13. The foundation of this proposed alliance is an alleged common interest of native Europeans and diaspora Jews in resisting Islam. But does that common cause even exist? After all, the state of Israel, which diaspora Jewry regards as their last line of defense, exists in a sea of Muslims. There are, moreover, millions of Muslims within Israel's borders. Thus one has to ask: Do Muslims really make Jews feel insecure? Or, if Jews are afraid of Muslims, is there something they fear even more?

Jews in Israel seem willing to exist at close quarters with Muslims to avoid a greater evil. What greater evil? European anti-Semitism, of course. The Zionist project was conceived as a refuge from European anti-Semitism. The state of Israel was founded after the Second World War. The holocaust is upheld as the justification for Israel's founding and for all of its subsequent wars, annexations, and acts of oppression against the indigenous population. Jews definitely fear and hate Muslims. But they fear and hate white Europeans even more.

Given Jewish fear of European anti-Semitism, it follows, that Jews would actually feel safer in Europe if its indigenous population were diluted with non-Europeans, including Muslims. This hypothesis is, moreover, completely consistent with the policies supported by the leading Jewish organizations, which oppose European nationalism while supporting multiculturalism and Muslim immigration into Europe.

14. But what about instances in which Jews have been attacked and killed by Muslims in Europe? Is this not a basis for a common interest in resisting Islam? I think not. Jews pursue pol-

icies in Israel that virtually guarantee Muslim terrorist reprisals. Yet Jews pursue these policies anyway, because they think they are worthwhile, even figuring in the inevitable Jewish casualties.

The same logic is at work within Jewish diaspora populations. Yes, supporting Muslim immigration into Europe does expose diaspora Jews to Muslim violence. But the Jewish community regards this violence as a small price to pay compared to the benefit of the dilution and ultimate destruction of the indigenous European population.

15. Jews feel safer around Muslims than around Europeans. Jews do not, therefore, believe it is in their interests to ally themselves with European nationalists to resist Muslim immigration into Europe. But even if it were in their interest, that still might not be enough to alter Jewish policy. *After all, it may be the case that Jews hate whites more than they love themselves.*

16. It may be a mistake to ascribe too much rationality to Jews. Jewish power may be less a product of rational calculation than of the irrational and compulsive repetition of a set of evolved strategies for achieving dominance over other groups. If these strategies are applied compulsively rather than rationally, one would expect Jews to continue to apply them even when they are becoming counterproductive. And indeed, this has been the Jewish pattern for centuries. Jews have continually risen to positions of wealth, power, and influence. But they have a tendency to push their host populations too far, leading to sudden backlashes and terrible reversals of fortune. You can't drive a car without brakes, and Jews have no brakes.

17. Even if Jews turned against Europe's Muslims, Muslims aren't the only problem. There are plenty of other fast-breeding non-white groups that could just as effectively dilute and then destroy European whites. By using "Muslims" as a politically correct proxy for non-whites, European nationalists have painted themselves into a rhetorical corner, in much the same way that American conservatives have by using "illegal" immigration as a proxy for non-white immigration. Muslims, however, can become Christians with a splash of holy water, and illegals

can be legalized simply by changing the law.

18. If Jews wanted to limit Muslim immigration into Europe, they would not need small European nationalist parties to accomplish it. Virtually overnight, they could have the conservative parties opposing Muslims on conservative grounds, the liberal parties opposing Muslims on liberal grounds, the Greens opposing them on Green grounds, the socialists on socialist grounds, etc. That is what intellectual and political hegemony means.

19. Political alliances are not based merely on common interests, real or perceived. Nobody seeks alliances with powerless parties. And the European nationalist parties have little or no power. Even those parties that have achieved parliamentary representation have been unable to effect real change. European nationalist parties have nothing to offer Jews, who have real wealth and real power.

20. Why, then, do some Jews seek to join European nationalist groups, as well as White Nationalist groups in America? A variety of motives are possible, including sincere conviction, insanity, hedging, spying, and sabotage. Unfortunately, there is no foolproof way of determining what a given person's real motives are. But I'm betting that most of them are up to no good.

Since we are fighting for nothing less than the biological survival of our race, and since the vast bulk of Jews oppose us, we need to err on the side of caution and have no association with Jews whatsoever. Any genuine Jewish well-wishers will understand, since they know what their people are like better than we ever can.

Saving our race is something that we will have to do ourselves alone.

Counter-Currents/North American New Right,
August 5, 2011

The Christian Question in White Nationalism

There is a strong anti-Christian tendency in contemporary White Nationalism.

The argument goes something like this: Christianity is one of the primary causes of the decline of the white race for two reasons. First, it gives the Jews a privileged place in the sacred history of mankind, a role that they have used to gain their enormous power over us today. Second, Christian moral teachings—inborn collective guilt, magical redemption, universalism, altruism, humility, meekness, turning the other cheek, etc.—are the primary cause of the white race's ongoing suicide and the main impediment to turning the tide. These values are no less Christian in origin just because secular liberals and socialists discard their supernatural trappings. The usual conclusion is that the white race will not be able to save itself unless it rejects Christianity.

I think that this argument is half-right. I do believe that Christianity is one of the main causes of white decline, for the reasons given above. But I do not believe that discarding Christianity is a necessary condition of white revival. I am not a Christian. But the fact that I am not a Christian might lend credibility to my argument that the White Nationalist movement need not and indeed should not be anti-Christian.

First, although intellectual debate is definitely part of White Nationalism (perhaps too large a part), we must never lose sight of the fact that White Nationalism is a *political* movement, not a purely intellectual one. Intellectual movements require agreement on first principles as well as ultimate goals. Political movements require agreement only on practical goals.

Our goal is a white homeland in North America. This political goal is, as a matter of fact, shared by Christians and non-Christians alike. To achieve a white homeland, we have to work with our allies, not against them. We might wish that they agree with us on other matters besides the goal of a white homeland. But this is not necessary, and emphasizing differences of opinion is not productive. When one is on the barricades, one does not turn to one's comrades and start finding fault.

Not emphasizing differences of opinion is not the same thing as hiding them, however. A mature and healthy White Nationalist movement should cultivate a culture of openness and frankness. We need to be as willing to express our differences in a civil manner as we are to put them aside to work for the common good.

Second, Christianity may be a necessary condition of white racial suicide, but it is not really the driving force. Christianity has long ceased to be the ruling power in Western societies or individual Christian lives. Instead, the churches preach white suicide and Christian Zionism because they wish to suck up to the real intellectual and political power structure, and today that power structure is overwhelmingly dominated and defined by Jews and Jewish interests.

This is not a new phenomenon, either. The church has long trimmed its sails to the winds of expediency. When there were absolute monarchs, the church preached the divine right of kings. When there was slavery, it bade slaves to obey their masters. When there was patriarchy, it taught wives to obey their husbands.

It is tempting to condemn this tendency as mere political opportunism, but that would be a mistake. The church has always been supple at bending to the reigning political and intellectual orthodoxies because, ultimately, its kingdom is not of this world. In spite of aberrations like the Social Gospel movement, the church has always been more concerned with saving individual souls than with social justice. Thus churchmen regard sucking up to the secular powers as a small price to pay to stay in the soul-saving business.

What this implies for White Nationalism is that the church will resist us less fervently than those whose aims are primarily secular, such as Jewish organizations, non-white ethnic organizations, and the secular Left. And when we gain power, ministers will begin hunting for Bible verses to justify the new regime. There is no reason why a White Nationalist regime cannot become a new Caesar, to whom Christians render their secular loyalty while reserving their religious loyalty for God.

Third, it is a basic principle of political struggle that one should always work to preserve the unity of one's ranks while sowing division among the enemy. Christian resistance to White Nationalism will be weaker if the churches are divided, and they can be divided if there are Christians in our ranks, especially Christians with personal ties to church leaders. Resistance will be stronger, however, if White Nationalism ceases being a merely political movement and takes on the aspect of an anti-Christian crusade.

Once a White Nationalist regime emerges, White Nationalist Christians can use their ties with the churches to better bring them into compliance with the new order.

Although the presence of Christians in the White Nationalist movement will help split the churches and weaken their resistance, their presence will not split or weaken White Nationalism as long as it remains a purely political movement unified solely by the pursuit of a white homeland.

Today White Nationalism is a movement of the political Right. Someday, however, it may become the common sense of white people up and down the political spectrum. To my mind, this would be a positive development, because when it comes to religion and politics, I am very much a liberal: I believe in the separation of religion and politics and in basing political decisions on secular reason.

To me, it seems fortunate that the separation of church and state in the white homeland may well be necessitated by political reality. The White Nationalist movement must unite whites of widely different religious convictions in the struggle for a homeland. That means we must build religious pluralism and tolerance into our movement today, which means they will be built into our homeland tomorrow.

The Occidental Observer, May 14, 2010

RACIAL CIVIL RELIGION

For my purposes, I will define a religion as the communal practice of honoring the holy. By the holy, I do not necessarily mean a God or gods or any supernatural beings, whether immanent or transcendent. What I mean is the *highest good* in any belief system, that to which all lower values must defer and, in a conflict, be sacrificed.

One can either duly honor the highest value, or one can ignore, denigrate, and profane it. Religion honors it. But it is not enough merely to honor the highest good in thought. One must do so in action. But even that is not yet religion. To actively honor the highest good individually is to lead a righteous life. To honor the highest good collectively, in community with others, *that* is religion. Such collective honors to the highest good are rituals.

Religion, on this view, is inherently communal and inherently ritualistic. But it is not inherently theistic or supernatural. A community could hold itself—its origins, its existence, and its destiny—to be the highest good and make itself the object of a civil religion, of communal rituals of self-remembrance and self-perpetuation: honoring heroes and ancestors, sanctifying marriage and family life, sacralizing education and coming-of-age, solemnly commemorating great historical events, demonizing enemies, damning traitors, and so forth.

I believe that there is one highest good for any community that persists over time. For religion—a common hierarchy of values combined with a means for collectively honoring and perpetuating them—is the primary preserver of unity. A community with multiple highest goods and religions may appear in a historical freeze-frame, but I would argue that if you let the film run, you will see that such a society is actually in the process of decomposition. There are many values and forces that pull societies apart. A society will perish, therefore, if its continued unity is not valued, and if that value is not made into an actual cohesive force by being given collective honor through a civil religion. Mere external, legal force is not enough if its goals are not seen as legitimate in the minds of the people.

What *makes* a community one need not have anything to do with religion. A community can emerge simply because of geographical isolation and shared blood, language, and customs. But what *sustains* a community as one over time has everything to do with religion. There are, of course, deep-seated, entirely natural inclinations to *love one's own* and to *distrust strangers*. But these alone are not enough to preserve distinct communities.

Communities can perish by splitting apart and by merging with others. Sometimes communities with common values split because they fall into quarreling due to scarcity. Sometimes radically different communities and races merge and blend with one other, due to greed and lust. For communities to stick together, they have to make unity a higher value than family and factional loyalties and individual greed, lust, and ambition. Making such priorities *stick* is a matter of religion.

Of course, the unity of a community may still be threatened if there are still higher values above it, for instance universal brotherhood, or capitalist wealth accumulation, or Communist wealth redistribution. Thus the best way to preserve a community is to make it the *highest* value, i.e., to erect a civil religion.

If a common religion preserves the unity of a society, whence the religious pluralism of modern Western societies? There are essentially two explanations. First, the pluralism could be illusory. Second, the unity could be illusory or transitory. Both are true of the West.

Western religious pluralism is in part illusory. It is a mistake to identify the plurality of Christian sects with genuine religious pluralism, for since the 17th century, Christianity has not been the dominant religion of the West. In 1648, the Peace of Westphalia ended the Thirty Years War between Protestants and Catholics. In 1660, the Restoration ended Puritan rule in England. Both events in fact replaced Christianity as the dominant religion of the West with a new civil religion of Liberal

Universalism. In effect, the values of religious tolerance, social peace, and secular progress were raised above Christianity, and ever since, Christianity has submitted — sometimes eagerly, sometimes grudgingly, but submitted — to this new civil religion.

Second, Western unity is in part illusory, because Liberal Universalism has opened Europe to subversion and colonization by peoples who pay lip service to Liberal Universalism even as they practice tribal forms of particularism (most prominently, Jews, but also East and South Asians and other Third World immigrants) or rival, illiberal forms of universalism (Islam, Marxism). Liberal Universalist society, because it does not insist on genuine reciprocity from others, is a self-subverting system that will be dismembered by the aliens it has allowed in its midst.

White Nationalism, as I conceive of it, is not just a political philosophy, competing with other political philosophies for power under Liberal Universalist hegemony. Rather, we must aim at displacing Liberal Universalism and establishing a White Nationalist hegemony, a new civil religion for the West which treats the preservation and flourishing of our race as the highest good, to which all lesser values must be subordinated. White Nationalism must make the highest good of our race the center of a public cult celebrating our identity, our heritage, our heroes, and our Faustian destiny.

From this point of view, the debates about Christianity vs. paganism in White Nationalist circles seem beside the point.

The critics of Christianity are right: Christian values are at best indifferent to racial preservation and at root hostile to it. Beyond that, Christianity is not really an alternative to Liberal Universalism, which has simply secularized Christian values and eschatological fantasies.

But the critics of Christianity are wrong to think that Christianity is, today, the primary enemy. For the real religion of our time is Liberal Universalism, to which even the Pope bends his knee.

Besides, most of the people who counsel a return to Christendom actually picture just an earlier, less overtly decadent period in the history of Western Liberal Universalism. If they actually knew anything about the real history of Christendom—if they read a history of the Albigensian Crusade, the Thirty Years War, or the English Civil War, for instance—most of them would reject a real Christian restoration in horror.

I have no doubt that the indigenous European folk religions can be revivified through studying the fragments that have come down to us, accessing traces of living traditions, and having direct experiences of the numinous. I have no doubt that European folk religions are more consistent with European identity politics than Christianity, Islam, Liberal Universalism, etc.

But I see no sign that neo-pagans seriously wish to establish a pagan civil religion. Most neo-pagans seem entirely content with being socially marginal, "tolerated" outsiders in what they imagine is a Christian society.

Moreover, when politics comes up, neo-pagans basically divide themselves into two camps: Liberal Universalists and White Nationalists. And let us be frank: the vast majority are Liberal Universalists and White Nationalists *first*, and neo-pagans second.

For White Nationalists, the real religious struggle of our time should not be between Christians and neo-pagans. Christianity does not rule, and neo-pagans don't even know what that would entail. The real struggle is between Liberal Universalism and White Nationalism.

So what would the religious landscape look like under White Nationalist hegemony?

First of all, under Liberal Universalist hegemony there is complete unity on Liberal Universalist values. Likewise, under White Nationalism, there would be complete unity on the supreme importance of white racial preservation and progress. The denigration or destruction of our race would lie outside the parameters of acceptable opinion, just as White Nationalism is currently outside the boundaries of polite society. All rival civil religions and hegemonies would be suppressed: Liberalism, Marxism, Islam, Judaism, etc.

Second, just as under Liberal Universalist hegemony, there

would be complete pluralism and tolerance in all *unimportant* matters. As long as Christian denominations do not challenge the racial civil religion, they will enjoy the same status as they do today under Liberal Universalism. The same goes for all forms of neo-paganism, imports from the Far East, and any other religion you care to make up.

Since Christianity's kingdom is not of this world, and since the church has a long history of supple accommodation to whatever Caesar is in power, Christianity will quickly reconcile itself with racial civil religion.

Many of the values of Liberal Universalism—private enterprise, private life, freedom of thought, speech, and creativity, etc.—can also be preserved under a White Nationalist hegemony insofar as they are consistent with racial survival and health.

Under a White Nationalist hegemony, it would be understood that the racial civil religion would not fully satisfy the spiritual needs of everyone. But, as in antiquity, everyone would be free to explore mystery cults and foreign faiths as long as they do not undermine our race. But for me, my race is not just my nation, it is my religion as well.

Counter-Currents/*North American New Right*,
August 2, 2013

THAT OLD-TIME LIBERALISM

When White Nationalists point out the undeniable fact that throughout the white world, the Christian churches are actively aiding white race-replacement through non-white immigration and colonization—or, *at best*, not opposing it—the standard response of Christian apologists is that we should not criticize the churches today because, centuries ago, the church fought against the Muslim invasion of Europe and launched the Crusades to take back the Holy Land.

I call it the "Old-Time Religion" argument, and it strikes me as lame for a number of reasons.

1. That was then; this is now.

2. Warriors defended Europe, not priests. It was swords, axes, and maces wielded by brawny men that hewed down the invaders, not the crosses, incense, and spells of pedophiles in skirts. Islam attacked many different peoples with many different religions. But regardless of whether their priests were Hindu or Zoroastrian or Christian, it was warriors who fought to defend their homelands. Pre-Christian European warriors fought to defend their homelands at Thermopylae and Salamis, and post-Christian Europeans can do so as well.

3. If Christians want to own the Battle of Tours, do they also want to own everything that came before that, namely the loss of Christian North Africa and Spain to Islam?

4. If Christians want to own the Crusades, do they also want to own the initial loss of the Holy Land by the Byzantines? Do they want to own the Fourth Crusade and the sack of Constantinople? Do they want to own the Children's Crusade? Do they want to own the ultimate loss of the Holy Land to the Muslims? Because—remember—the Crusades were a giant failure in the end.

5. If Christians want to own the Battle of Lepanto, do they also wish to own the fall of Constantinople and every other de-

feat leading up to and following from it? Do they want to own the bargains and alliances struck with the Turks by Christian princes angling to gain advantages over one another?

The best way to appreciate the folly of putting our hopes in a revival of a fighting form of Christianity—a religion that was displaced from hegemony in white lands in the 17th century and has been withering ever since—is to compare Christianity to a much more vital religion, the religion that displaced it, the dominant religion of the West: Liberalism.

Like Christianity, Liberalism is a universal creed. Just as all men can be brothers in Christ, all men can be citizens of a Liberal society. But that did not stop liberals less than 100 years ago from being race realists and from taking their own side in ethnic conflicts. Liberals and progressives were also advocates of immigration restrictionism and eugenics. One of the ongoing projects of Counter-Currents is to document the existence of a racially conscious Left, which has included such figures as Jack London and Denis Kearney in California and Rex Fairburn in New Zealand. It strikes me as far more reasonable for White Nationalists to hope for a revival of a race-conscious and militant form of our living, dominant religion than of a medieval form of a displaced and dying faith.

Not only is that Old-Time Liberalism of relatively recent date, it is possible to reform Liberalism in ways not open to Christianity and other revealed religions of the book. There is no "bible" of Liberalism—except vestigial traces of the Bible itself, which is the source of many of its problems. Thus Liberalism is relatively more open to interpretation and change. A Christianity stripped of egalitarianism, universalism, and eschatological hope for the future is unthinkable. But a Liberalism stripped of these vestiges of Christianity is entirely conceivable. It is possible to believe that Liberalism is the best form of society, but *only for white people*, because the races are not equal, and there is no hope of them ever becoming that way in some future utopia.

1. White liberals are actually deeply racist. Every single white liberal I know believes that blacks and mestizos are, on average, mentally inferior to and less attractive than whites.

They also believe that Asians are mentally equal to whites but less attractive and interesting to be around. You can infer this from their behavior, but many will actually say it as well, if they feel safe to do so.

But white liberals will not openly state or act on such beliefs for the same reasons that most White Nationalists won't: guilt because of the internalization of false values, plus the desire to preserve money and status in a system that rewards conformity and punishes dissent. They fear that they are all alone in their beliefs. Or they fear that even if they are not alone, nobody would come to their defense while others would seek advantage from their disgrace. When those mechanisms of control break down, many new things will be possible.

2. White liberals are actually "white supremacists," indeed, to such a degree that I find it frankly embarrassing and offensive. Liberals believe that whites are the only agents in history. This view gives rise to two related thought patterns: white grandiosity and white guilt. White grandiosity is the view that whites are responsible for all good things. White liberals believe that they set the standards of civilized life to which all other peoples aspire, or should aspire, if they knew what's good for them. The flip side of white grandiosity is white guilt, the belief that whites are actually responsible for all the bad things in the world. If white liberals could be weaned away from this unrealistic sense of omnipotence, if they could accept that other races are agents, for good or ill, but retain a more sober sense of white pride and white guilt, that would open a whole new world of possibilities.

3. White liberals and progressives generally embrace Darwinism over creationism, except when it comes to the human brain. Egalitarianism is just liberal creationism. The idea that race is a social construct is just a metaphysical postulate of egalitarian social uplift schemes. When it comes to science, white liberals are 99% of the way to White Nationalism. Christian creationists, however, are 0% of the way. Thus they are capable of embracing racial egalitarianism without reservation. Indeed, eventually they will be the only people in our society who actually believe in it.

4. A distinct advantage of reviving a racially realistic and militant form of liberalism is that, unlike conservatives, Liberals are winners: they understand power. They know how to gain it and how to keep it. White Nationalists have much to learn from them.

Ultimately, of course, if Liberalism were to undergo a racial reformation, that would mark its loss of intellectual hegemony to White Nationalism, which would then replace it as the civil religion of the West.

Counter-Currents/*North American New Right*,
August 14, 2013

THE WOMAN QUESTION IN WHITE NATIONALISM

It is a perennial question: Why are there so few women in the White Nationalist movement?

Before venturing an analysis of this question, I need to say a few words about what White Nationalism is. White Nationalism is about preserving the *biological integrity* of the white race by making our race's survival and flourishing the number one political priority. White Nationalists represent the genetic interests of all whites, men and women, adults and children.

But preserving our race's biological integrity requires more than defeating multiculturalism and multiracialism. It also requires the defeat of feminism and emasculation (male infantilization) and the restoration of sexual roles that are not just traditional but also biological: men as protectors and providers, women as nurturers.

These sex roles are *norms*, meaning *ideals*. Realistically, not every man or woman will be able to function according to them. (That's what makes them ideals!) But a White Nationalist society needs to maintain these ideals as norms nevertheless, for even in a racially homogeneous society like Japan, feminism and male infantilization are causes of personal and social misery and below-replacement birth rates, particularly among the educated and intelligent who should be reproducing more rather than less.

Many men who genuinely wish to become husbands and fathers shy away from marriage because every man knows another man who has been emotionally and financially savaged by the punitive feminist biases now codified in laws governing marriage, divorce, and child custody. White Nationalists will change that.

Many women who genuinely wish to become wives and mothers nevertheless feel forced to pursue a career first because of a lack of men who wish to assume the protector and provider role. They want a Prince Charming, but all they see are Peter Pans. White Nationalists will change that as well.

The restoration of traditional and biological sexual norms will affect men as well as women. Indeed, it will be harder for men than for women. In a White Nationalist society, men will no longer be allowed to prolong their adolescence into their 30s and 40s. They will be expected, encouraged, and enabled to take on adult responsibilities as soon as they are able. They will become husbands and fathers, providers and protectors for their families. White Nationalism will demand that men "man up" so women do not have to.

White Nationalism promises women a society in which they are free from the fear of the black and brown predators who commit the overwhelming majority of rapes. Nobody will stop women who wish to remain single and childless to pursue their careers. But the overwhelming majority of women who wish to marry and raise families will be able to find husbands who can support them and their children in stable, monogamous marriages. No matter what their income, they will be able to live in safe, homogeneously white neighborhoods. No matter what their income, they will be able to send their children to safe, homogeneously white schools. In a White Nationalist society, no mother will need to fear that her children's livelihoods will be lost because of affirmative action, non-white immigration, or shipping jobs overseas. In a White Nationalist society, no mother need fear that her children will die on battlefields to serve the interests of other races. In short, White Nationalism has a great deal to offer to women.

So again, why are there so few women in the White Nationalist movement?

My answer is simple: Most women see politics as a largely masculine enterprise. They are correct in this. Thus women are waiting for men to build a White Nationalist movement that credibly advances the interests of our race. When we accomplish that, the women will come, and they have an important role to play as natural networkers, nurturers, and multitaskers.

So White Nationalist men need to focus first and foremost on advancing our cause: building community and raising consciousness, honing our message and developing new ways of communicating it, organizing to pursue aims in the social and political realms. If we take care of those things, the woman question will take care of itself.

As for the few women who are already in our cause: that is to their credit. They are in the vanguard of their sex as well as the vanguard of our race.

The last thing the movement should do is soften our message or compromise the pursuit of our ultimate aims simply in order to court women.

First of all, we have to ask: Is the lack of women in the movement even a problem? Yes, of course, we need all the people and resources we can get. But is the existence of overwhelmingly or exclusively male groups *by its very nature* a problem? Yes, by all means, let's bring women into the movement. But does that mean that all groups need to be open to women or have "gender parity"? Is our struggle against racial diversity strengthened by sexual diversity? Are we feminists, then? Are we building a rainbow? Are we nuts?

Michael Walker's otherwise excellent speech at the 2008 *American Renaissance* conference was marred by his claim that he would like to see every other seat filled with a woman. That would, of course, be excellent advice if we were a ballroom dancing society. But it was not so long ago that politics was an exclusively male thing. Armies and police and fire departments were also exclusively male. Were these organizations less able to look out for the interests of women when they were exclusively male?

The truth is that sexual diversity in an organizational context, like racial diversity in all contexts, is often a source of division, conflict, and weakness — particularly if the organization is involved in something quintessentially male like fighting and self-sacrifice for the common good. Thus all-male police and fire departments were probably more effective at protecting the interests of women than today's integrated forces.

We have to ask ourselves if this might not also be true of some White Nationalist organizations. And might some White Nationalist groups be more effective if they were all female? See, for example, Amanda Bradley's excellent review of Glen Jeansonne's *Women of the Far Right*, which deals largely with women-only organizations.[1] We need a lot more of such groups.

If sexual diversity is a source of weakness for all other political movements, shouldn't White Nationalists—who can't afford to pass up any tiny advantage—be eager to experiment with sexually homogeneous organizations? If our enemies are slowing themselves down by tying themselves to women in three-legged races, why should we be eager to adopt their handicaps instead of sprinting unencumbered for the finish line?

I am all for pluralism. White Nationalists need to recruit the full diversity of whites in order to reach the full diversity of whites. We need to have people from all different groups and walks of life adapting and delivering our message. We need a whole range of different organizations and strategies. Some of those organizations might be exclusively male. Others might be exclusively female. Still others will be mixed. But there is no *a priori* reason to think that something is wrong if a White Nationalist group or the movement as a whole does not have a 50/50 male to female ratio.

The main reason why men want more women at White Nationalist meetings is they wish to find ideologically compatible mates. But as our community grows we will be able to separate political gatherings from purely social ones, and some of those political organizations might function better by being sexually segregated. (Every normal society tends organically toward having at least some sexually segregated organizations.)

The White Nationalist community is often characterized as "misogynist." Many White Nationalists are so afraid of that label that they will actually censor, shun, and betray other White Nationalists who are accused of misogyny. Just how cowardly and contemptible this is should be obvious.

"Hate" is the stock accusation of the enemy. Even if you offer up the most sober, scientific accounts of racial differences, you will be labeled a race hater. Oppose multiculturalism and

---

[1] http://www.counter-currents.com/tag/glen-jeansonne/

you are a race hater. Offer up the same sort of accounts of sexual differences and you will be called a woman hater. Oppose feminism and emasculation and you are a woman hater.

The enemy controls the media and status system in this society. *Of course* they are going to use harsh words to stigmatize us. And that is just for starters. But if someone is able to stand up to the first accusation, he should be able to stand up to the second. The inability to do so strikes me as the sign of scandalous intellectual confusion and moral weakness. Jewish power will not be overthrown by men who are terrified of their own wives.

That said, just as there are White Nationalists who are race haters by any reasonable definition of the term, there are genuine woman haters. They are not found everywhere, but they have their bastions. They are not the majority, but they are a sizable and vocal enough minority that the movement as a whole has been characterized as misogynist. (There are also passionate man haters, but like women in general, they are few in number.)

But why the intense mutual hatred between the sexes? Such hatred is not natural and healthy. It is the product of a sick social order.

White Nationalists hold that racial hatred is an inevitable result of breaking down racial boundaries and introducing racial competition within the same realms. Diversity and integration are not cures for racial hatred, they are causes of it.

Hatred between the sexes is also a product of the breakdown of natural and traditional sexual roles and the introduction of competition within the same realms. Feminism has brought women into formerly male bastions, creating enormous resentment from men. Feminism and its corollary, male infantilization, have caused untold conflict and suffering for both sexes. Feminism in the legal system has made life hell for countless divorced husbands and fathers. Feminism is not a cure for misogyny, it is a cause of it. This means that a White Nationalist society will be the cure for misogyny as well as race hatred.

So what do we do about misogynists in our ranks? I vote we

do nothing. In the appropriate venues, we need to let their voices be heard, in spite of frequent crudity and excesses. Also, remember: much of what is stigmatized as misogyny is simply salutary "sex realism" and the absolutely necessary project of restoring traditional/biological sex roles.

White men are the victims of a pincer movement. We are victimized as whites and as men. How can our movement claim any moral credibility and leadership if we demand that our racial brothers who are often in extreme pain be censored, whether the motives be feminism or misplaced conservative chivalry?

I understand that this sort of atmosphere makes female vanguardists uncomfortable, but I will simply ask you, as a personal sacrifice to the greater good, to be tolerant and understanding. Honest communication even about unpleasant matters is one of the things that sets our movement apart. And cultivating this kind of openness is absolutely necessary if we are to establish an intellectually sound vision of a white society and a strategically and tactically sound path to achieving it.

One false explanation for why there are so few women in the movement is the presence of weird men: curmudgeons, cranks, nerds, people who have been locked in mental institutions, and so forth. This would, of course, explain the relative absence of *normal* women. But there are plenty of weird women out there. And the reason they are not White Nationalists is that they are waiting for their weird male counterparts to make some progress before they will hop on board. In that, at least, they are perfectly normal.

Savitri Devi once said that she could never love a man who loved her more than he loved his ideals. What makes a man worthy of respect is his ability to look above himself and his personal interests to serve the common good. This is what Julius Evola called Uranian masculinity. The best women respect that. They are right to despise a man who compromises his principles in order to court their favor.

The same principle applies to our movement. Women will become White Nationalism's most fanatical and devoted supporters once we demonstrate that we are truly able to secure the existence of our people and a future for white children. If we neglect that end, soften our message, and split our camp with needless witch-hunts and finger-pointing, all in the name of catering to the ignorant and foolish, the best women will hold us in well-deserved contempt as we listen to the sirens singing our race to its doom.

Counter-Currents/*North American New Right*,
May 25, 2011

NOTES ON POPULISM, ELITISM, & DEMOCRACY

Is democracy a good system from the perspective of racially conscious whites?

1. When both the United States and North Korea describe themselves as democracies, it is safe to conclude that "democracy" means close to everything and next to nothing. For my purpose, I will define democracy as the idea that *the power to make political decisions should reside with the "many."*

By the "many," I mean more than a minority, but less than everybody. A society can be ruled by one man, a few men, or many men. But it cannot be ruled by *all* men, since in every society there will be at least some people who cannot be allowed to exercise political power, e.g., minors, the insane, criminals, etc.

2. Most White Nationalists are strongly inclined towards elitism, even though the opinions of the majority on such questions as economic nationalism and non-white immigration are far more sensible than those of the ruling elites who are imposing globalization and race-replacement on the people. If white societies were truly democratic on these issues, we would be a lot better off. But, although today's so-called democracies could be improved by being more democratic, that is hardly an argument for democracy as such.

3. I would like to argue that democracy, defined as placing political sovereignty in the hands of the many, is not a good system for racially conscious whites, or anybody else for that matter. To make my case, however, I must distinguish democracy, plain and simple, from two good ideas that are so similar to democracy that they are often confused with it.

4. The first good idea mistaken for democracy is what I shall call "populism," or the principle of popular sovereignty, or the

principle of the common good. I define this principle as the idea that government is legitimate only if it serves the common good of a people.

In his *Politics*, Aristotle makes this principle the highest law and the criterion for distinguishing between good and bad forms of government.[1] When a single man rules for the common good, we have monarchy. When he rules for his own private good, we have tyranny. When the few rule for the common good, we have aristocracy. When the few rule for their private and factional interests, we have oligarchy. When the many rule for the common good, we have what Aristotle calls "polity." When the many rule for their private and factional interests, we have democracy.

Yes, for Aristotle democracy is *by definition* a bad form of government. But he believes that "polity" — popular government for the common good — is at least conceivable.

The idea that the common good is the proper aim of politics is often mistaken for democracy, but they are not the same thing. The common good can be served by one man, the few, or the many. Furthermore, it is an open question as to which group — the one, the few, or the many — is most capable of securing the good of all.

White Nationalists are, of course, racial populists. We believe that the only legitimate regime is one that secures the existence of our people and a future for white children.

5. The second good idea that is often mistaken for democracy is a so-called "mixed" regime that has a democratic element. For instance, the United States has a mixed constitution with elements of monarchy (the President), aristocracy (the Supreme Court and the Senate before it was popularly elected), and democracy (the House of Representatives). Representative democracy itself is a hybrid system, since the many appoint one man or a few to represent their interests. Virtually every European society today has a mixed constitution with monarchical,

---

[1] Greg Johnson, "An Introduction to Aristotle's *Politics*," online at http://www.counter-currents.com/2012/06/introduction-to-aristotles-politics-part-1/

aristocratic, and democratic elements, as did ancient Rome and Sparta (which was technically not monarchical, since it had two kings at the same time).

In his *Politics*, Aristotle argues that a mixed regime is more likely to secure the common good than an unmixed one. In an unmixed regime, the one, the few, or the many are liable to pursue their factional interests at the expense of the commonweal, simply because the other elements of society are not empowered to resist them. In a mixed regime, all three groups are sufficiently empowered to resist the attempts of the others to serve their interests at the expense of the common good. Yes, Aristotle was the first theorist of "checks and balances."

In an unmixed regime, we have to depend on the virtue of the rulers, since their selfishness can lead society to ruin. In a mixed regime, we do not have to depend entirely on the virtue of the rulers, since the one, the few, and the many all take part in rule, and even when their virtue fails them, they will still oppose the selfishness of the other factions out of selfish motives of their own.

Thus Aristotle long anticipated Machiavelli's critique of ancient political theory, namely that it was too dependent on human virtue. Aristotle would, however, reject the idea of modern political theorists that a good society can arise out of base motives. A good society can only be the product of virtuous statesmen, although he would grant that base motives can be harnessed to preserve the products of virtue, even when virtue occasionally nods.

6. Why is democracy, pure and simple, a bad system? Simply because men are unequal.

To understand and pursue the common good, statesmen need certain moral and intellectual virtues: wisdom, intelligence, courage, justice, self-control, etc. But these virtues are not evenly distributed in the population. Thus it is very unlikely that the majority, by deliberating together, will ever hit on policies that are conducive to the common good (or even their own factional interests, for that matter).

Nor would majorities working together be able to enact and

sustain such policies over the long run.

Moreover, the many cannot even be trusted to elect superior individuals to represent their interests, since they tend to fall for the bribes and flattery of slick and unscrupulous demagogues.

7. If the majority do not have the necessary virtues to serve the common good, then the only question is whether rule by one man (monarchy) or a few men (aristocracy) is best suited to serve the common good.

If virtue is the sole criterion for rulership, then monarchy is the best system only under extraordinary and highly unlikely circumstances. For a monarch would have to be superlative in a whole range of virtues that are seldom combined in a single individual, and even more seldom combined to a superlative degree.

Aristocracies can draw upon a whole range of men of consummate virtue: the wisest sages, the most stirring orators, the most cunning strategists, the bravest warriors. Only a god could possess all of these virtues at the same time. If one could find such a god-king, that would be the best of all systems of government. For he would combine all the virtues necessary for wise decisions with *the power to actually decide*.

But it is folly to repose all one's hope in a miracle. Thus aristocracy is a better system than monarchy, because only real regimes can serve the common good.

Furthermore, all existing monarchies are actually aristocracies in practice, for if a king is to rule well, he must of necessity select advisors, delegate powers, and thus create "peers."

8. However, aristocracy also has its limits. The main problem of aristocracy is that whenever power is exercised by groups, they must deliberate, and their deliberations must be able to produce decisions. Ideally, these decisions should be the wisest possible. But sometimes any decision, even a reckless one, is preferable to no decision at all.

There are many procedures to terminate deliberation and force a decision. One can put a time limit on discussion. One can put matters to a vote. One can even leave it up to the toss of a coin. But in such cases, human beings are essentially abdicating their responsibility to an impersonal system.

But if one needs more than just a decision, if one needs *accountability* for decisions, and if one needs an *executor* of decisions, then one needs a *person* who can decide. This is particularly the case during an emergency such as a war or a time of constitutional crisis when the existing laws and institutions prove themselves inadequate.

In the end, one cannot be governed merely by laws and institutions. Legislators cannot envision and provide for every future possibility. Thus there will always be circumstances where individuals have to make decisions in the face of novel circumstances.

And even if legislators could foresee every possible circumstance, one still needs individuals to *apply* the laws. And the application of laws cannot simply be governed by a higher set of laws, for how would one apply *them*? One cannot appeal to a third set of laws, for those laws also need to be applied. In short, the idea of general rules to govern the application of general rules leads to an infinite regress.

The only way out of that regress is to recognize another kind of intelligence, which can judge the applicability of general rules to particular circumstances. This is the faculty of *judgment*. But if judgment cannot be reduced to abstract general rules and incarnated in law books, it must be incarnated in a particular individual, the judge, who has the intellect to understand the general rules, the vision to apprehend and the tact to appreciate concrete circumstances, and the insight to apply the former to the latter.

Judgment is required on all levels of a system, from traffic courts to matters of life and death for the entire nation. Thus even the most exalted and refined aristocracy has need of a monarch: someone who has the responsibility and the power to exercise judgment in exceptional situations regarding the destiny of the nation as a whole.

Aristocracy by necessity is driven to embrace monarchy just as monarchy is driven by necessity to embrace aristocracy. Aristocracy is the best principle in normal circumstances, monarchy in emergency situations. In normal circumstances, the monarch should take his throne and preside over deliberations but give maximum latitude to aristocratic rule to ensure the most intelligent possible decisions. In emergencies, the aristocracy should give maximum support to the monarch to help him, and them, and the body politic, to weather the storm.

9. But although the few are far more likely to be able to discern and execute policies conducive to the commonweal, once they have power, how can we be sure they will actually do so?

To answer this, we must face a difficult fact: a White Nationalist society will never happen unless we can assemble an elite of extraordinary individuals who create it and endow it with sound institutions. Since such a society can only be created by an elite, it must, of necessity, be led by it. So, again, how can we ensure that such an elite, once installed, actually pursues the common good?

The answer is twofold. First, one must structure the elite so that it can perpetuate and improve itself. Second, one must structure the system as a whole so that the many have the power to keep the elite serving the common good rather than its own factional interests.

10. Although White Nationalists have a strong tendency to hereditarianism, hereditary aristocracy and monarchy are not the best systems, because there is a strong random factor in heredity that makes it possible for superior parents to have inferior children and inferior parents to have superior children.

Thus if we are to be ruled by the best, we need ways to (a) recruit and promote the best children of the masses to elite positions, and (b) identify and demote the inferior children of elites to stations that better suit them.

Elite parents will quite naturally love their children more than the common good. They will give their children every advantage of their station. Thus a well-governed society needs to take active measures to negate these advantages and to cultivate and promote geniuses from humbler circumstances.

One of the best ways to do this is a rigorous and entirely *public* education system, as opposed to the present mixed public-private system which is designed to perpetuate the current corrupt elites while smothering or co-opting their potential rivals from humbler circumstances.

The best institutional model for a White Nationalist society is the Catholic Church, which is ruled by a non-hereditary aristocracy which it recruits and promotes from its own ranks, and which elects a monarch from among the aristocracy.

Another useful model is the Venetian system. Although Venice was ruled by a commercial elite, it maintained an aristocratic rather than a merely oligarchical form of government by promoting to, and demoting from, the ruling stratum based on merit. Venice also had an elective form of monarchy, like the Papacy and other Italian city-states, such as Genoa.

Of course a White Nationalist society will be founded neither by a priestly nor a commercial aristocracy.

For the Old Right, a White Nationalist society would be founded by a martial/political aristocracy, which would more closely resemble the knightly orders of the Middle Ages or another militant order, the Jesuits, both of which were models for Himmler's SS.

The New Right seeks to create a White Nationalist society by dethroning the current hegemony of anti-white ideas and instituting a counter-hegemony of pro-white ideas, propagating this hegemony through the educational system and culture and colonizing the entire political spectrum with a range of pro-white options.

The vehicle for creating and perpetuating white hegemony is an intellectual and spiritual aristocracy, organized as a non-hierarchical network that can penetrate, subvert, and control all existing institutions that shape consciousness and culture.

Such an intellectual and spiritual aristocracy need not worry about exercising power, so long as it sufficiently shapes the consciousness of those who do, which is merely to say that the New Right is a metapolitical rather than political movement. Politics is guided from afar by metapolitics.

But a society sufficiently penetrated by New Right metapolitics would take on the form of a mixed regime with an aristocratic/monarchical leadership. Of course, most white societies already have that essential system, albeit in more or less degenerated forms. Thus New Right metapolitics aims at pouring a new, racially conscious spirit into the existing institutional bottles.

11. Recall that the two good ideas that are often called democracy are (a) the populist principle that a system is just only if it serves the common good, and (b) the mixed regime with monarchical, aristocratic, and popular elements.

With that in mind, we can raise the question: Do monarchy and aristocracy have need of a popular element? The answer is: Yes. If monarchy and aristocracy are to serve the common good, the people need to be empowered to constrain them.

But what form can this popular element take, given the obvious failure of representative democracy?

First, representative democracy can be improved by increasing the quality and decreasing the quantity of the electorate. One could limit votes to heads of households, property owners, or the gainfully employed. One could raise the minimum voting age. One could institute educational and public service requirements. One could give extra votes to the highly intelligent. In short, a democracy is more likely to elect an aristocracy if the aristocratic principle is used to determine the electorate.

Second, since democracy works best in small, homogeneous communities, one should adopt the principle of "subsidiarity," meaning that any issue should be handled by the authority that is smallest, least-centralized, and closest to the "grass roots," as long as it is capable of dealing with the problem effectively. Subsidiarity would allow deliberative, "direct" democracy and also improve representative democracy, since the smaller the community, the more accountable the elected representatives.

Third, although the many are less qualified to frame and execute national policies than the few, the people are acutely aware of damaging policies, such as free trade and race-replacement immigration.

Thus the people or their representatives should have the power to veto legislation that is inimical to the common good. The people should also have the power to depose public officials, including judges, who are inimical to the public good.

To prevent the people and demagogues from abusing these processes, they should, of course, be confined to extraordinary circumstances. They could, for instance, be carried out by calling special elections, referenda, or plebiscites.

Fourth, the people should also be able to propose and impose legislation of their own through ballot initiatives and special elections. Again, to prevent abuse, these would have to be confined to extraordinary circumstances.

Fifth, to keep the elites honest, the ancient Greeks gave the people the power to audit public accounts.

A little imagination could expand this list further. None of these measures would impede honest servants of the common good. But they would provide powerful deterrents to corruption.

12. The powers that be have invested a great deal in promoting the value of diversity, even while pursuing policies that systematically destroy it. This has played into the hands of the New Right, since we are the true defenders of human biological and cultural diversity.

In a similar manner, the establishment has invested a great deal into making an idol of democracy, even as they ignore the will of the people and trample the common good.

This can redound to the New Right's benefit as well, for although we are frank and unapologetic elitists, we can argue in all honesty that we represent "true democracy," or what is true *in* democracy, namely the principle of the common good and the idea that, in the name of the common good, the people must be empowered to resist the corruption of elites.

Counter-Currents/*North American New Right*,
September 4, 2012

The Perils of Positive Thinking

> "Time to stop talking falsely now.
> The hour is getting late."
> — Bob Dylan, "All Along the Watchtower"

The best way to get people to take bitter pills is to coat them with something sweet. The principle applies to poisons as well as medicines, and it applies in the intellectual as well as the material realm. The most insidious and destructive ideas are often served in the syrup of high-minded sentiments. A case in the point is the perennial cliché that white advocates need to "keep it positive": focus on the things we love rather than the things we hate.

This is a false alternative. The best approach is to do both: we must love what is good and hate what is evil — i.e., that which opposes and threatens the good. We must promote the good and combat evil. And you can't really be serious about promoting the good if you are unwilling to name and fight the evils that oppose you.

The root of White Nationalism is, of course, the love of our own people. The aim of White Nationalism is, of course, to perpetuate our race and ensure its well-being. These are positive goals. But if that's all we have to say, then white advocacy remains merely sentimental, abstract, and high-minded, merely a matter of feeling and thinking, as opposed to saying and doing.

As soon as we act upon our love, as soon as we step outside the online echo chamber and enter the realm of public debate, as soon as we try to promote the well-being of our people in the real world, we will discover that there are people who actually *oppose* us, people who have conflicting interests, including people who simply hate us, and whom we should heartily hate in return.

The peril of positive thinking is that it is ultimately ineffectual. It cannot save our people, because it is *abstract* rather than *concrete, high-minded* rather than *realistic*. I am all for abstractions and ideals, but they are not ends in themselves. They have to illuminate reality and lead to realistic, effective action. High-minded happy-talk divorced from ugly facts will not save our race, whose existence in the real world is being threatened by concrete forces including real, flesh-and-blood enemies.

Keeping it positive basically boils down to a resolution to be *superficial* rather than *radical*. No matter how positive one's spin is, one can't avoid dealing with the surface reality of white dispossession. So to "keep it positive," one has to refuse to examine the underlying causes of our plight, specifically the people who are to blame, lest we discover reasons to hate.

But the best way to treat an illness is to understand the cause. The best way to kill a weed is to pull up the roots. The best way to stop white dispossession is to discover who is behind it, and why, and stop them.

There really are people who become so fixated on harming their enemies that they end up harming their own interests. This is the psychology of spite, and it is self-defeating. For instance, some White Nationalists are so fixated on scoring points against the Jews that they attack Israel for being racist and nationalistic, even though White Nationalists should be defending the principles of racial nationalism, rather than attacking them on liberal, egalitarian, universalist grounds.

But the solution to suicidal spitefulness is not a priggish refusal to confront the reality of enmity. Instead, one must simply keep one's priorities straight. Our overriding goal is to serve the positive interests of our own people. Becoming too fixated on our enemies can conflict with that goal. Ultimately, however, ignoring or downplaying the reality of enmity is a far bigger threat to our people than self-destructive spitefulness. The cure offered by the "keep it positive" crowd is worse than the disease.

The "keep it positive" meme is repeated for many reasons, including sincere, naïve, high-mindedness. But as with the "white suicide" meme—with which it is often conjoined—I suspect that the motives behind its propagation are usually morally squalid: cowardice or outright enemy subversion.

The picture becomes clearer when we ask what, exactly, are the positive thinkers trying to conceal? Are they trying, for instance, to avert our gaze from black depravity? Are they demanding that we not ask them "the Negro question"? Are they telling us that we need to focus simply on spreading the "white genocide" meme rather than dwelling on black crime, corruption, and chaos? Consistency demands that they would, but I am not seeing it.

Instead, the "keep it positive" meme, like the suicide meme, is almost always employed to avert our gaze from the Jewish problem, i.e., the fact that Jews are massively over-represented among the forces both promoting white dispossession and preventing whites from organizing to stop it.

It is easy to understand why Jewish infiltrators wish to spread this meme. But what motivates whites? Ultimately, I think it is a combination of cowardice and naïveté: cowardice in the face of Jewish oppression and white social disapproval and the naïve notion that one might still be able to win a struggle without naming and confronting one's most committed enemies. Indeed, some are so naïve as to think that we can win while allowing one's organizations to be infiltrated and influenced by Jewish "sympathizers." (These Jews may even be sincere, but enemy agents always seem sincere too, and the hour is too late for such foolishness.)

Advocates of keeping it positive often claim that their opponents talk "only" about the Jewish problem, whereas they prefer to speak entirely about positive actions they can take for our cause.

Now, I will grant there are White Nationalists who are obsessed with Jews almost as much as Jews are. I grant that there are White Nationalists who act *as if* Jews are the sole cause of our problems. In the past, when I published articles that did not deal with the Jewish problem, certain commentators would show up to accuse me or the author of conspiring to cover up Jewish perfidy. But even these people probably do not believe that Jews are the *sole cause* of our problems or the *sole impediment* to solving them, although they often act like it.

The idea that one can talk only about positive things rather than negative things, or only about negative things rather than positive things, is not really true. One can, of course, speak of certain topics by abstracting and isolating them from the bigger picture. But abstraction entails a kind of falsification, because one is dealing with parts, not the whole—and, in the real world, everything is interconnected. Thus if one really thinks through one's abstractions, if one tries to understand how they are related to the rest of the world, how they are meshed in networks of meaning and causality, then one inevitably deals with other matters. And one has to, if one is going to affect real changes in the real world. Thus, dealing with matters in isolation is not really dealing with them at all.

If, for example, one actually thinks through how one is going to take positive steps toward saving our people, one is going to have to confront certain negatives, including the vast and essential role of the organized Jewish community in promoting white dispossession and preventing whites from resisting it. Or, if one starts with the Jewish problem and deals with it thoroughly, certain positive steps toward rectification will suggest themselves.

In a world in which everything is interconnected, truly radical thinking—thinking that can lead to action that can change the world—is concrete and holistic. But attempting to focus entirely on positives or negatives condemns one to being abstract and superficial—and thus, from a practical standpoint, ineffectual as well.

What about people who have a broad and concrete understanding of the white predicament but who choose to abstract out certain elements and focus on them in particular? It is a big world after all. People can't know everything about everything. Specialization is inevitable and indeed necessary for progress. What about people who wish to focus on race, or immigration, or the Jewish problem in isolation from the rest of the picture?

There's a right way to specialize and a wrong way. One can specialize but still keep a sense of the larger whole, and when people ask about the bigger picture, one simply needs to refer them to other specialists and then get back on message. One should not, however, engage in evasions and obfuscations of the larger picture.

Of course, these evasions only flow one way. Kevin MacDonald does not, for instance, treat biological race differences or non-white immigration as a hot potato. Not so with the Jewish question, which is consistently dodged by people who wish to position themselves closer to the political mainstream.

Of course, when writers refrain from dealing with the Jewish question, they come under suspicion of working for the other side. But there is an easy way to dispel such doubts (at least the reasonable ones). When the Jewish question is raised, they must simply state that they do not focus on that issue, acknowledge that there is genuine debate on the topic, refer the questioner to Kevin MacDonald, and then get back on topic.

Under no circumstances, however, should they resort to obfuscations and disinformation. The entire media and educational establishment are working 24/7, 365, cradle-to-grave to mislead our people about race and the Jewish question. Thus it is frankly disgusting when White Nationalists join in the lies because they are working some clever and self-regarding angle of their own.

Counter-Currents/*North American New Right*,
September 3, 2013

THE POLITICS OF RESENTMENT

White Nationalists believe that the existing multiracial, multicultural system has set our race on the path to extinction.

White birth rates worldwide are below replacement, while our homelands are being flooded with fast-breeding non-whites who undermine white wages and take far more from our welfare states than they contribute to them, meaning that indigenous whites pay the bills.

Whites are disproportionately the victims of non-white criminals, from black and brown murderers, rapists, and petty thieves in the streets to Jewish mega-swindlers and warmongers in the citadels of power. Whites are disproportionately dying in Iraq and Afghanistan, and of course we are disproportionately paying the bills for those wars as well.

While non-whites enjoy a baby boom at white expense, we are being sold miscegenation, homosexuality, abortion, perpetual adolescence, interracial adoption, selfish careerism, environmental altruism—anything, really, as long as cradles are not filled with white babies.

Our standards have been debased, our morals debauched, our culture liquidated in order to feign equality with primitives. Every healthy form of white ethnic consciousness is stigmatized, while white guilt and non-white assertiveness are promoted. We are told that we are not entitled to our nations, our wealth, our standards, our way of life. We have no pride, no backbone, no birthright, no sense of destiny or purpose, no conviction that we make the world a better place.

We behave like a conquered people. A conquered people exists at the sufferance of others. A conquered people cannot say no. When a non-white demands something, we must give in. If this keeps up, we will become minorities in our homelands within a few decades. We will cede the power to determine our destiny to people who hate us, people who will plunder and persecute our ever-dwindling descendants until our race simply ceases to exist—and then they'll keep blaming us for their failures long after we are gone.

Whites are being victimized *simply because we are white*. And while Channon Christian and Christopher Newsom, who were tortured and murdered by blacks, obviously suffered more than heiress Casey Johnson or poetess Sylvia Plath, who were killed softly by a poisonous cultural atmosphere of anti-white hatred, *all whites are targeted for destruction*, simply because we are white.

White Nationalism, therefore, has the potential to become a *mass* movement, encompassing all whites, since we represent and fight for the genuine and legitimate racial interests of all our people. Furthermore, White Nationalism can appeal to the most powerful passions that drive mass political movements: *resentment, victimhood, anger, hatred* of a system designed not merely to swindle and degrade us, but ultimately to destroy us.

Moreover, White Nationalism will never amount to anything unless it *aspires* to be a mass movement, harnessing resentment, victimhood, and hatred to smash the existing system and set our people free.

But this kind of politics does not sit well with many White Nationalists.

A lot of White Nationalists are just warmed-over bourgeois conservatives who tremble for their bank accounts when they hear populist rumblings or catch wind of the politics of resentment. I have known shady capitalists who have enriched themselves in ways no decent society should permit. But to a man they are convinced that any objection to their way of life is motivated solely by envy and resentment, much as Jews always attribute anti-Semitism to the defects of their enemies.

Other White Nationalists tend to be elitists with a fondness for traditional hierarchical societies: monarchies, aristocracies, classical republics. We are contemptuous of the rise of mass man and mass society: democracy, socialism, Communism.

But if we are going to found a classical aristocracy, we need to learn martial arts, invent a time machine, go back 1,000 years, conquer a country, and then mellow for 900 years. Then politics can be based on the nobler sentiments, not the crude tastes and resentment of the rabble.

To my mind, no system of government was more perfect than the English monarchy at the middle of the 19th century — except, of course, for the fact that a hundred years later England was Airstrip One, liquidating its empire to rain fire and death on Europe, to the profit of Jews, Bolsheviks, and Americans, none of them conspicuously noble and cultured.

Once you follow your ideal aristocracy to its end and rejoin us in the present, we can set about the task of saving our race in the real world. To do that, however, we need to face the fact that *we are the rabble*, the uppity, ungrateful peasants slated by our Judeo-plutocratic overlords for replacement by dumber, darker, more docile *fellaheen*.

We need to rouse our rabble by making our racial brothers and sisters aware of their victimization. We need to free them from the white guilt that makes them easy marks. One does not really feel victimized unless one believes that one's plight is *wrong*. We need to stoke their resentment and outrage until they are fighting mad.

"Now, Greg," you might be wondering, "how does this agenda of crude rabble-rousing fit in with your professed elitism and your focus on 'metapolitics' and your endless stream of articles mentioning Nietzsche, Spengler, Evola, and Heidegger?" That's a fair question. My answer is that metapolitics is *necessary* but not *sufficient* to save us.

Metapolitics as I understand it embraces two things: (1) intellectual activity, namely constructing our worldview and deconstructing the enemy's, and (2) community organizing, namely building a White Nationalist community, a counter-culture and counter-community that will be the seed of a new White Nationalist order to come. Those things are absolutely necessary, but alone they are not enough to save us. To save us, White Nationalism must ultimately become a political movement.

I do think it is *too early* for a political movement, and that we should spend our time and money on metapolitics. At best, political activism today should be regarded as a kind of metapolitical education, since we need to have a tradition of people with concrete political experience if we are to someday get involved with politics and play for keeps. (Looking at it that way will also prevent the kind of burnout fostered by false hopes of actually making political headway in the present climate. Managing expectations is always crucial.)

But when the time for politics comes, it will necessarily be a form of *modern mass politics fueled by resentment* — in our case *righteous* resentment. My metapolitical role, and the aim of this little essay, is to make sure that we are clear about that fact right now and adjust our attitudes and plans accordingly.

It needs saying, because two writers whom I regularly read — Richard Spencer and Brett Stevens — have recently been critical of attempts to stoke white resentment at our ongoing dispossession, and their attitudes are not idiosyncratic but widely shared.

In "Poor Little Oppressed White People,"[1] Spencer discusses Colby Bohannan of the Former Majority Association for Equality and Lou Calabro of the European/American Issues Forum, both of whom seek to promote white ethnic consciousness in a multicultural society, the first by sponsoring a scholarship for whites, the second by lobbying for California schools to recognize European Americans as an ethnic group.

Spencer likens both men to "entitlement-mongers like Al Sharpton — poor, little oppressed White people will apparently now plead for handouts from the welfare state." Spencer recognizes the potential of these projects to awaken white resistance to racial dispossession, but apparently it does not seem sufficiently high-minded or revolutionary for his tastes.

Stevens also identifies mass resentment politics with low-minded "liberalism," which he contrasts to high-minded, elitist conservatism.[2] He also claims that thinking of oneself as a victim is unhealthy.[3] In my view, however, it is *being* a victim that is unhealthy. *Feeling* victimized, by contrast, is not necessarily bad if it motivates one to get mad and get even. Besides, this is poli-

---

[1] http://www.theoccidentalobserver.net/2011/03/poor-little-oppressed-white-people/

[2] http://www.amerika.org/politics/forward/

[3] http://www.amerika.org/politics/naming-the-jew-and-why-you-wont-see-it-here/

tics, not therapy. Frankly, I am willing to sacrifice some peace of mind if that is what it takes to win.

White Nationalism incorporates both populist and elitist elements. We are populists because we believe that a just society aims at the common good of our people—all of them. Yet the knowledge and ability to pursue the common good are the property of the few, not the many. So a genuinely populist society needs an elite to guide it. (By the same token, the masses need a say in politics to keep the elites from pursuing their factional good at the expense of the common good.) The only real choice is whether we are ruled by our own elite whose selfish tendencies are mitigated by kinship or an alien and hostile one with no such barriers to exploitation. Our model is a hierarchically differentiated, organically unified society, a body politic.

If we are to create this kind of society tomorrow, our movement needs to embody that same blend of populism and elitism today. We are not going to win without engaging in mass politics, and the masses are moved by resentment. There is nothing dirty about that, because our grievances are just. And even if it were dirty, a race that is fighting for its survival can no longer afford to be led by high-minded gentlemen who take swords to gunfights because they would rather lose than violate their sense of honor and sportsmanship. Instead, we need leaders who are willing to make the same sacrifice as Frodo in *The Lord of the Rings*, who saved the Shire, but not for himself, for in the battle he lost something of his own soul.

Counter-Currents/*North American New Right*,
March 23, 2011

"Worse is Better"

It sounds like Newspeak. White Nationalists and other radicals often pepper their political discussions with the sentence "Worse is better." But what do they mean?

The phrase is deceptively short and categorical, which tempts one to think it is offered as a universal law. But if one treats it that way, it is child's play to "refute" it with a counter-example or two. After all, worse almost always is . . . worse.

"Worse is better" is not a universal or categorical claim. Its meaning entirely depends on context, and removing it from that context turns it into nonsense, thus doing so is a form of sophistry, a way of winning an easy victory in argument.

If a Republican says "Worse is better," he usually means, "Worse for the Democrats is better for the Republicans." If a Democrat says it, he usually means, "Worse for the Republicans is better for the Democrats." A hallmark of primitive thinking — to which "modern" people feel so superior, by virtue of their birth (the most democratic form of snobbery!) — is that the king is responsible for the crops. If the crops are blighted, the king must die. The same thinking reigns today. The president is responsible for the economy. If the economy is bad, the president must be replaced — with a president of the opposite party.

Within a two-party system, "Worse is better" functions to create a blank check on power for whatever party holds it. If a party were installed in power based on its platform and promises, they might actually feel pressured to act on them. But if a party is elected simply because they are *not* the other party, then they enjoy power not on their own merits, but on the demerits of their opponents, which means they can pretty much do anything as long as they seem sufficiently *unlike* the other party.

And of course, we White Nationalists know that none of the system parties are really that different. They are just heads of the same hydra, sock puppets of the same octopus, masks of the same alien oligarchy. (And I don't mean Kang and Kodos.) So the two-party system feeds on its own failures, rotating the front men while continually accumulating power.

When a White Nationalist takes a step back from the system and says "Worse is better," what does he mean? He usually means one of three things.

1. "The worse for the system as a whole, the better for white people in the long run." Why? Because White Nationalists believe that we will never have a White Republic by working within the current system. But since we do not have the power to destroy the system outright, we need it to destroy itself. Thus, whatever drives the system toward a breakdown—economic depression, corruption, apathy, cynicism, mass chimp outs, fiat currency, etc.—is better for the long-term interests of whites than maintaining the present system.

2. "The worse white dispossession is today, the better for white people in the long run." Why? Because whites are being done to death slowly—with demographic trends that unfold over decades—so that most of us will not even notice what is happening until it is too late. How does one boil a frog without him jumping out of the pot? Increase the heat slowly, so that when he realizes he is being boiled, it is too late. Thus, "worse is better" in this context means: The acceleration of white dispossession will raise white racial consciousness.

This, of course, is risky. If the process accelerates too quickly—to *The Camp of the Saints* levels—we might be swamped anyway, even if we do regain our racial consciousness. My great fear is that the system will collapse too soon, and White Nationalists will not be in a position to have a say about what comes next. But even this is less risky than allowing our dispossession to unfold slowly.

The most advantageous form of white dispossession to accelerate is on the symbolic plane, which shapes consciousness while leaving us materially able to fight when we are so inclined. As I have argued elsewhere, the election of Barack Obama was symbolically very good for white racial consciousness, because now our president no longer looks like us.

Obama's election has also made blacks far more uppity, greedy, and reckless. Black flash mobs are a reflection of this, and they are highly educational on the symbolic plane without incurring debilitating real world costs.

3. "The worse the American economy today, the better for white people in the long run." Americans are narcotized with prosperity and individualism. These drugs allow us to make our separate peaces with the system that is destroying us. In spite of a lot of patriotic bluster about fighting for freedom, Americans don't fight for our freedom. We run away for our freedom. We move one more exit down the interstate to another subdivision for our freedom.

As long as Americans have the money, we will insulate ourselves and our loved ones from social decay and racial dispossession—letting the dark masses cull the weaker and poorer among us. But the predators will work their way up the economic ladder eventually, and when they come for the upper middle class, there won't be enough white people left to band together to resist them.

Economic hardship also increases racial conflict and thus increases racial consciousness. Thus the worse the economy gets for white Americans today, the faster we will gain racial consciousness and the sooner we will stand up for ourselves. This is why I believe that Ron Paul-like figures, who promise to put the economy on firmer footing while maintaining race-replacement, are far greater enemies of whites than Barack Obama, who looks like he might destroy the dollar in only one term.

Many people find the "worse is better" notion morally objectionable because it is all mean and vanguardy. And in truth cyberspace is full of creeps who revel in visions of hated liberals and "SWPLs" being murdered by black mobs so they can cackle and say "I told you so." Their *Schadenfreude* and wounded vanity are palpable. Our movement is plagued with people who are kooks and haters *first*. They come to White Nationalism because they believe the enemy propaganda about us and think they have found a home.

But true White Nationalists do not rejoice in the idea that "worse is better." We wish that it were not so. We wish we lived in a world in which worse is always worse. We wish that our people had heeded the warnings about the follies of racial egalitarianism and non-white immigration from farsighted whites of generations past like Lothrop Stoddard. But, sadly, few ever heard the warnings, and most of those ignored them.

The ultimate premise of "worse is better" is the old "*pathema, mathema*" (suffer and learn) principle: Most people do not learn from intellectual warnings, which are abstract and universal, but through experience, which is concrete and individual. Good parents of course want to spare their children unnecessary suffering. So they warn them about hazards. But still, many children learn only through painful experiences.

White Nationalists, like good parents, have tried to spare our people from the tribulations to come. But our race is a sleepwalker approaching a precipice. Now we have only a choice of horrors: catastrophe's rude awakening or extinction's eternal sleep.

Counter-Currents/*North American New Right*,
July 19, 2011

LEARNING FROM THE LEFT:
DOUGLAS HYDE'S
Dedication & Leadership

White Nationalism is at present confined largely to the political Right, i.e., the people who have been on a losing streak since Stalingrad. European Rightists do, of course, have much practical wisdom to impart, even if they failed in the end.

But American Rightists have not even managed to learn what they can from the losers, much less take an interest in learning from the winners: the Left, which has now established ideological hegemony up and down the political spectrum, defining the Limbaughs and libertarians of the "respectable" (viz., ineffectual) opposition as surely as the liberals they huff and puff about.

For those Rightists who want to learn from the winners, Douglas Hyde's *Dedication and Leadership* is a good place to begin.[1] Hyde was a 20-year veteran of Communist activism, serving as news editor of the Communist London *Daily Worker*, until 1948, when he resigned, renounced Communism, and announced his conversion to Catholicism.

Although Hyde rejected the ideals and aims of Communism, he thought that the party's highly effective organizational techniques should be emulated by those who wish to change the world for the better. *Dedication and Leadership* is a 150-page distillation of his experiences and insights.

Communism has killed more than 100 million people worldwide and is still racking up victims. Thus it is hard to think of Communism as anything but evil. But even evil is an accomplishment, and prodigious evil is a prodigious accomplishment.

How did tiny minorities of Communists accomplish so much? Because they worked harder and smarter than their opponents. They were particularly effective in mobilizing im-

---

[1] Douglas Hyde, *Dedication and Leadership* (South Bend, Ind.: University of Notre Dame Press, 1966).

portant moral qualities: idealism, dedication, and self-sacrifice. (One tends to feel licensed to kill for causes that one is willing to die for oneself.)

The fact that these moral qualities were bent toward evil ends does not make them any less praiseworthy.

How does one find and mobilize idealism, dedication, and sacrifice? Hyde advises the following.

First, recruit people who are *already* idealistic.

Young people tend to be idealistic, so special efforts should be focused on recruiting them.

Second, if you want to *get* a lot from people, *demand* a lot from them.

Communists inspired tremendous efforts simply because they asked for them. Communists were taught not to ask what they party can do for them, but what they can do for the party. The US Marine Corps has no shortage of recruits for the same reason: their recruitment propaganda emphasizes sacrifice and discipline, not the perks of membership.

I was particularly impressed by one example of the dedication and self-sacrifice that was routine in Communist circles. Hyde and his fellow party employees took eight-fourteenths of their income—more than 50%—and *tithed it back to the party*. They did this *every payday*, not just on special occasions.

How many White Nationalists are willing to tithe *any* percentage of their income to the cause they claim is sacred to them?

There are legions of professional Jews and blacks. But there are fewer than ten full-time White Nationalists in the entire United States, and most of them make so little from the cause that it would be inconceivable that they could tithe anything back to it. Poverty is their sacrifice.

It is not that money is lacking. There are individual White Nationalists whose wealth runs not just into tens, but hundreds of millions of dollars. Something else is lacking: the qualities of character that give rise to *real, effective* idealism, dedication, and sacrifice.

The truth is on our side. But truth is not enough to win if it remains locked in our hearts and heads, without consequences in the real world. When the first White Nationalist pledges eight-fourteenths of his income to securing the existence of our people and a future for White children, I'll believe that we will win.

But beyond asking for eight-fourteenths of an employee's income, Communism asked for 100% of each member, body and soul. And they got it.

Yes, demanding heroic dedication did make some hesitate before joining the party, but when they did, they were prepared to give their all. It also kept out lukewarm sympathizers and fellow travelers. But the party still had ways of utilizing the talents and resources of those who were unready or unable to take the plunge.

Third, aim high.

If one is going to ask for everything, one has to have a good reason. The Communists asked everything of their activists because they had a world to win. Grandiose aims are only a problem if there is nothing concrete one can do in the here and now to realize them. But if one can forge that link, then even the humblest drudgery suddenly takes on a deeper and higher meaning.

I once asked an audience at a meeting on White community organizing why they were there. There were many answers: meeting new people, networking, seeing old friends, even learning about White community organizing. All of these were good enough reasons to get people there.

But then I offered a better reason: to save the world. Make no mistake, White Nationalists are not just struggling to save the white race, since the welfare of the whole world depends upon our triumph. If we perish, the other races will breed recklessly and despoil the planet unchecked, and the one place in the universe where we know there is life will end up nothing but a burnt-out cinder in the vastness of space.

So the next time you attend a White Nationalist gathering, remind yourself that you are saving the world. It will make the commute a little easier, parking less of a hassle.

The Communists realized that demanding heroic dedication to a higher cause does not drain people but energizes them. It does not hollow out their personalities but deepens them. Those who live for themselves alone have less meaningful lives than those who dedicate themselves to a higher cause.

Fourth, be the best.

The Communists taught that there is no contradiction between being a good Communist and being good in every other area of one's life. The same should be true of White Nationalists. If you are going to be a good White Nationalist, you also have to be a good student, worker, employer, artist, spouse, parent, and neighbor.

One is a more credible and effective advocate for White Nationalism if one is well-regarded in other areas of one's life. The Communists found that personal relationships with exemplary individuals were more important than ideology in recruiting new people to the cause.

Also, if one finds that one's political commitments are interfering with excellence in other areas of one's life, then one needs to scale back and regain balance. This prevents activists from burning out and keeps them in the fight.

Fifth, activism is essential.

Most individuals who joined the Communist Party were *immediately* required to engage in some form of public activism. (A few with important social connections were trained as Communist secret agents.)

Public activism came *before* ideological instruction. By acting publicly as a Communist, one makes one's commitment open and irreversible. By acting before one receives ideological instruction, one learns in a very personal and sometimes painful fashion the necessity of such instruction. Such activism also helps weed out people who lack moral and physical courage before anything is invested in indoctrinating them.

Activism has a twofold purpose: to change the world and to change the activists. Since the party must act until the world changes, it must be organized for perpetual activism. Campaigns should be designed to (1) demonstrate that the party cares about its constituency, (2) to heighten the conflicts between the system and the party's constituency, and (3) by building character, skills, and camaraderie among activists.

Hyde illustrates these and many other points with vivid anecdotes. His discussion of Communist cadre indoctrination techniques deserves an article of its own. I have not read many books that pack as much food for thought into so few pages.

Some White Nationalists might find *Dedication and Leadership* a depressing read, since it highlights the truly primitive, pathetic, unserious nature of the movement today. But that is the wrong way to look at it.

One does not need to read Douglas Hyde to see that White Nationalism in America today is full of kooks, losers, and dilettantes. One needs Hyde and authors like him if one is serious about creating a movement that can win.

The Occidental Observer, June 8, 2010

EXPLICIT WHITE NATIONALISM

White Nationalism is the monstrous and immoral idea that the white race, a unique biological subspecies that is in long-term danger of extinction (due to loss of habitat and competition from hardier invasive subspecies) deserves the same protections as snail darters, spotted owls, and California condors.

White Americans will become a minority in this country by 2050. I know for a fact that a vast number of white Americans — liberals, centrists, and conservatives — are profoundly uncomfortable with this transformation. They know that it threatens the things they value. Rightists realize that individualism, capitalism, and constitutional government will not survive in a black and brown America. Liberals know that women's rights, gay rights, environmentalism, animal welfare, and support for "the arts" have little place in a nation dominated by Mexicans, Muslims, and blacks. (Sadly, nobody in the white political mainstream thinks of the perpetuation of their extended racial family as a political good in itself. But we are working on that.)

I also know that white Americans will become even more uncomfortable as the tipping point approaches, perhaps restless enough to actually *do something* to slow down or reverse the process.

I know this, because I am already living in that future. Yes, I have access to a time machine. Just buy a plane ticket to California, where it is 2050 today.

White Americans know that our country is being taken from us, and we are afraid. But white Americans also know that it is dangerous to express these fears for the future, out of fears for much more immediate consequences. We fear that expressing ourselves will make us many enemies and few friends.

But what if the majority of white Americans comes to feel this way? What if a majority decides that there are already too few white European states in the Western hemisphere, and far too many backward, Spanish-speaking non-white states? This country is still democratic enough to change policy, if the people stand up and demand it.

But it is not enough that the majority merely *believes* something. Majority members have to *know* that they are the majority, and the politicians have to know it too. But that means that people have to declare their beliefs publicly, so a self-conscious majority can coalesce. A silent majority is powerless.

But for a silent majority to become self-conscious, at least some people have to speak out. A courageous minority have to declare themselves and hold their ground long enough for the less courageous to gin up the courage to join them. Gradually the crowd grows by adding layer upon layer of ever more timid and tepid people, until finally it attracts the necessary ballast of every mass movement: the people who join simply because they want to be on the winning side. At that point, the most contemptible people of all—the politicians—will throw in, and the new majority will carry the day. It is a process that can only begin, however, with a few men of courage who will risk raising a standard to which their less courageous fellows may or may not repair.

In short, we need *explicit* White Nationalists. We need a lot of them. And we need them to appear sooner rather than later.

Ideally, explicit White Nationalists should be come from all walks of life, social classes, regions, religions, cultures, subcultures, and ethnic groups, so that people from all those groups can identify with concrete examples of explicit White Nationalists.

Furthermore, it would also be ideal if explicit White Nationalists were on average smarter, better looking, and more successful than the other members of their particular groups, since we want people not merely to identify with them but also to look up to them.

Obviously, we have a long way to go.

But there are good reasons for this.

In the United States, it is not illegal to be a White Nationalist. Not yet anyway. White Nationalists are not arrested, imprisoned, tortured, or murdered by the state. Although we know that our government is doing these very things to non-US citizens around the globe.

Being an explicit White Nationalist does, however, open one to all kinds of private harassment, both legal and illegal. Explicit White Nationalists are subjected to verbal abuse, including moral shaming. Explicit White Nationalists can lose business opportunities and employment. Sometimes one loses friends. One can even be shunned by one's family or lose one's marriage. In very rare instances, explicit White Nationalists are subjected to criminal violence because of their beliefs, or are framed as criminals by the government.

But usually the penalties are pretty mild. One might have a few heated exchanges that can get one's heart rate elevated. One might have to endure an uncomfortable work environment. One might lose the company of tepid and cowardly friends. (Since one is dealing with cowardice, one often never really knows why certain friends and acquaintances drift away.) But one is well rid of such people and will eventually come to find new friends who are capable of deeper and more significant relationships—friends who also understand the greatest problem facing the world today.

Because of these difficulties, many people who come to White Nationalism prefer to remain silent about it. They reason that there is nothing to be gained by going public, since so few people think the way we do, and very few of them would come to the defense of someone who is publicly attacked for advocating the continued existence of our race.

This is particularly true of White Nationalists who have a lot to lose—money and status; business, social, and political connections—and who want themselves and their families to stay on an upward social trajectory.

These are exactly the kind of people White Nationalists need on our side.

The only people who have nothing to fear from social opprobrium are those who have nothing to lose. But people who have nothing to lose also have little to offer. And we have enough people like that already.

One of the most popular ways of engaging in white advocacy

while protecting oneself is to use a pen name. It provides most of the protections of silence yet allows one to speak out. A good percentage of the best white advocates fall into this category.

So how do we build a winning team from mainstream types who are mostly silent and explicit types who are mostly marginal?

A natural division of labor suggests itself. Explicit White Nationalists need to go public, stand their ground, and buckle down for the long, hard, grinding task of winning more people to our side. Silent White Nationalists need to write checks. Or, if they are afraid of writing checks, they need to stuff cash in envelopes.

According to one of his friends, Wilmot Robertson recounted that over the years, he would hear from wealthy and powerful people who expressed their agreement with him but told him that they dare not speak out themselves. When he asked them to support him, so he could speak for them, they said that they didn't dare do that either. Were they afraid that their checks would be traced? Maybe so, but in all his years of publishing *Instauration*, Robertson never received an anonymous envelope of cash either.

How can we forge cordial and productive relationships between explicit White Nationalists, including those who use pen names, and those who choose to remain silent? A couple of points of etiquette are a good start:

1. Everyone who comes to White Nationalism needs to determine his own level of involvement and explicitness.

2. Everybody else needs to respect those decisions. White Nationalists have the right to be silent. White Nationalists have the right to use pen names.

This implies that:

1. It is wrong for explicit White Nationalists to denigrate people who choose to remain silent or use pen names.

2. It is wrong for explicit White Nationalists to "out" people who choose to remain silent or use pen names.

Human motives and decisions are complex. From the outside, we cannot presume to know why people choose to remain silent or adopt pen names. These decisions cannot, therefore, be taken *ipso facto* as evidence of cowardice, venality, stupidity, or dishonesty. And even if such motives do play a role, people can grow in courage, idealism, and understanding.

People of *good character* can have *good reasons* for remaining silent or concealing their names. Explicit White Nationalists who cannot or will not understand that are a danger to the movement. They drive people away who could otherwise contribute. And they create a climate of fear and suspicion that makes it difficult for the people who do stay to work together.

When explicit White Nationalists hector and browbeat silent White Nationalists to get off the bench, or when they excoriate people who use pen names, the natural conclusion of sensible and cautious people is: "Somewhere down the road, this guy is going to start 'outing' people." They are right to be worried, and explicit White Nationalists need to step up and say something about it. The scolds and outers need to be reprimanded, and if they persist, they need to be shunned. It is the only way that the explicit movement can gain credibility and begin to grow.

Silent or anonymous White Nationalists need to reciprocate these courtesies as follows:

1. Don't complain about the marginal nature of explicit White Nationalists.

The main reason that explicit White Nationalists are less mainstream than the rest is because the more mainstream ones prefer silence or anonymity. The quickest way to change that is not by complaining, but by going explicit. If you are not ready for that, then cut us some slack. We get enough flak from the system. We don't need our own people chiming in too. Just as there are good reasons why you are silent or anonymous, there are good reasons why many explicit White Nationalists are eccentric. Eccentric ideas attract eccentric people. Once our ideas become more mainstream, mainstream people will be attracted to them. Eccentric White Nationalists, however, are not to be blamed for the bad press White Nationalists get. The bad press comes from offering a fundamental critique of the system.

2. Don't come to our gatherings and start rehearsing all the reasons why it is best to remain silent and anonymous.

We are all well aware of the world we live in. Flogging that dead horse only makes it more difficult for us to recruit and activate good people, which reinforces the marginality of the movement, which makes it smart to stay silent, and so the cycle continues. Break the cycle by remaining silent. Or, better yet, offer words of encouragement and constructive advice for insulating oneself from the negative consequences of explicit white advocacy.

Counter-Currents/*North American New Right*,
October 4, 2010

SECRET AGENTS

One of the great pleasures of being an explicit White Nationalist is that I get to meet other White Nationalists. If you state your views openly and honestly, you will hear from people who actually agree with you, people who will respect you for your views and for your forthrightness. If you spend your life hiding your beliefs—aside from an occasional wink, nudge, or hint—you will surround yourself with dupes or squishy people who would flee from and denounce the real you. I just don't see the value in that.

I have always prized intellectual probity over social approval and true friends over false ones, so I have a low tolerance for political dissimulation. I believe that ultimately we are not going to get what we want unless we level with people about what, exactly, we *do* want (a society of and for white people) and *who and what*, exactly, we are fighting against (the Christian values that have programmed us for collective suicide and the Jews who are organizing and egging the process along).

I tend toward tolerance, but in this area I have a moralistic streak, and I am quite a bastard when I sense cowardice and dishonesty in people. Really, what I despise is dishonesty *out of cowardice*. As we will see, there is another kind of dishonesty, a dishonesty of strength and self-overcoming, that I do admire. It is a dishonesty I am too weak to practice. It makes my frankness seem like mere self-indulgence.

One of the great pleasures of editing Counter-Currents and *North American New Right*—and before them *The Occidental Quarterly* and *TOQ Online*—is that "highbrow" publications attract intelligent readers, so I have gotten to know the brightest and the bravest people in our cause. Our enemies—and, sadly, all too many of our advocates—constantly reinforce the image that racially conscious white people are dumb and/or unhinged. I enjoy receiving daily empirical proof that this is untrue.

I am not claiming that I have been especially virtuous here. Indeed, for me there really is no alternative. There are many people in the racialist movement who publish dumb and crude material, either because they are dumb or because they think acting dumb is the only way to reach "the masses." The trouble with this strategy is that it repulses smart people and attracts dumb ones. Since our movement is small and is likely to remain so for the foreseeable future, I would rather it be smart than dumb. History, after all, is not shaped by small elites of dumb people.

Simply by publishing and selling intelligent material, I have found myself at the center of a nascent network of highly intelligent racialists. Who are they? Of course I can't say. People who have something to lose take risks every time they contact people in our movement. The only way they will contact me is if they can be assured that I will keep their information confidential. And I will. My mission depends upon it, and nothing is more important to me than the cause.

But I can tell you what types of people they are. First of all, they are far above average in intelligence, intellectual curiosity, idealism, and creativity. They include college professors, writers, artists, designers, publishers, creative people working in the film industry, businessmen, and professionals, some of them quite prominent in their fields.

They include a disproportionate number of people in their late teens, 20s, and 30s—far younger than the average audience at an *American Renaissance* conference or a Council of Conservative Citizens gathering—many of them from upper and upper middle class backgrounds who are headed to or who have graduated from leading universities. With a little luck and a little guidance, they are destined to have a disproportionate influence on society.

In short, I believe that I have the makings of a new intellectual and creative elite, an elite that might be able to play a leading role in our people's victory.

But it is not an elite yet.

First, I am often the only racial nationalist these people know, and for the most part, our relationships are merely commercial (they buy books from me) or virtual (email pen pals). We do not have a network yet, just a lot of isolated individuals connected to me by the slimmest of strands. To have a network, we have to create lateral ties between the different strands, linking individuals to the network at multiple points. I am working on that, putting like-minded individuals in touch with one another.

Second, we are few in number and widely scattered around the world. There need to be more of us, and we need to have concrete, face-to-face interactions from time to time. I'm working on that. I am working on bringing in more people and creating safe spaces for face-to-face interactions.

Third, we need people who are plugged into the system and have a lot to lose. But because of these very traits, they cannot afford to be explicit White Nationalists. Not yet, anyway. Nothing would be gained by these people losing their positions in the system by openly avowing White Nationalism in today's climate.

So what is to be done? We need to keep building our network until we become strong enough, and the system becomes weak enough, for open struggle to have a chance of success. Until then, most of us will have to remain publicly silent, sharing our views with only small circles of trusted friends.

But psychologically, that is very difficult to do. The truth matters to us, or we would not be White Nationalists. Courage matters to us, or we would not be White Nationalists. So it is very difficult for us to withhold the truth, or even pay lip service to lies, without feeling in our hearts like cowards.

For instance, recently a comrade who is in the position to hire people for his firm told me that he was dreading a conversation with his superior about diversity. He told me that he was planning to flatly declare that he would base his decisions solely on merit. He said that he couldn't live with himself otherwise.

I told him that this was an immoral self-indulgence. His protests would not change his institution's commitment to diversity. It would only harm his position in the institution and very likely lead to somebody else being given the power to hire people.

I persuaded him that it would be much better to pay lip service to diversity, keep his power to hire people, and then use that power to hire fellow comrades. To hell with "merit" if the best candidate is a racial or ideological enemy. In such a process, "diversity" could actually help us, since he could use considerations of diversity to exclude Jews on the grounds that they are white people.

Being a White Nationalist has many risks and no rewards. One of my goals is to change this by building mutual aid into our network.

To help square this with his conscience, I suggested that he see himself as a secret agent, as a disciplined political soldier. When James Bond is undercover, he doesn't reproach himself as a coward for not revealing his true identity. He just thinks of his mission, of his duty. A secret agent does not lie out of cowardice, but out of strength and self-overcoming. He suppresses any self-indulgent frankness for the greater good.

Yes, we need more explicit White Nationalists. But if you cannot be one, don't reproach yourself as a coward, don't create an inner conflict that exhausts your energies and may lead you to self-destructively blurt out the truth in a moment of mere weakness and self-indulgence.

Instead, you need to fully adopt the role of a secret agent, burrow deep, rise high, bring your comrades along with you, and be proud.

We know that the present system is unsustainable, but we do not know when it will collapse or how. It could be sudden and unanticipated, like the collapse of Communism. Or it could be long and slow. However it happens, though, the people who will pick up the pieces and build a new order are likely to be an organized, networked elite already plugged into the existing power structure.

Let's just make sure that next elite is *ours*. The best way to do that is to adopt the role and the discipline of secret agents.

Counter-Currents/*North American New Right*,
November 21, 2010

THE PSYCHOLOGY OF APOSTASY

In July of 2013, it was announced that Derek Black, son of Stormfront founder Don Black, had renounced White Nationalism. This raises questions of wider significance about how people form and reject beliefs. There are two basic kinds of beliefs: those you think are true based on *reality and reason* vs. those you think are true based on *other people's opinions*.

If you base your beliefs on reality and reason, then you will change them as new facts come to light or as better arguments are presented. For example, I used to be a classical liberal, but classical liberalism grants no importance to racial and cultural differences, and when I realized that these were more important than individual freedom and capitalist economics, I rejected classical liberalism as subversive of higher values.

WHY I AM A WHITE NATIONALIST

I am a White Nationalist because I believe that the survival of my race is threatened by the present political and economic system, which prizes individualist, capitalist, liberal, multicultural, and multiracial values. I see that these "race blind" and "race neutral" values are incompatible with the preservation and flourishing of my race. Race is real. Racial conflict is real. The other races are not going to trade racial competition for race-blind universalism. And any race that will not take its own side in racial conflict has no future.

I am concerned to preserve my race *simply because it is mine*, because it is my extended family. I also wish to preserve my race because I believe that it most closely approximates to the aesthetic and moral ideals I hold dear, ideals which may be race-specific but which seem to be universal because they are cherished by other races as well, so far as they are able. Finally, I want to preserve my race because I believe that biology has a huge impact on culture, thus many of my most cherished cultural, political, and scientific values could not have arisen without white people and will not be appreciated or preserved without white people.

Because the survival of my race is threatened by the current political and economic system, I believe that we need a new system that puts race at the center of political priorities — not individual freedom, capitalism, or tolerance and pluralism, which are genuine values, but lesser values than the preservation of the race that creates and sustains them. I believe that each race and each distinct people should have a nation or nations of its own, in which it can live according to its own identity and values and pursue its own destiny, free from the interference of other races and peoples. Finally, I believe that the main enemy of the idea of nationalism for every nation is the organized Jewish community, which promotes race-destroying values for other societies as a tool of ethnic warfare.

THE DEREK BLACK CASE

It is my understanding that Derek Black more or less believed the same things I do. Because I strive to base my views on reality and reason, I was naturally curious to hear why Derek Black had rejected White Nationalism. Did he have new arguments that I could not answer? Had he discovered hitherto unknown facts about race, the Jewish question, and the present-day political system? With these questions in mind, I eagerly scanned the news reports, only to be disappointed.

Derek Black has apparently rejected White Nationalism not for new truths but for old lies: pure Leftist boilerplate that rejects biology and biological inequality and explains unequal group performance in terms of social injustice, which in America means white injustice, for which whites can atone though affirmative action, non-white immigration, and all other forms of white dispossession and self-abasement.

Many people have speculated about Derek Black's motives for abandoning White Nationalism for this kind of mush. Is it peer pressure? Rebellion against his parents? Love? Perversion? Blackmail? Insanity? Did he grow tired of alienation and want to be plugged into the Matrix?

I am less interested in Derek Black's particular motives, or in the Derek Black case in general, than in what would make it possible *for anyone* to abandon truth *for any reason*. Two factors strike me as relevant, the first having to do with the basis of belief, the second having to do with strength of character.

OBJECTIVE TRUTH VS. COMMON OPINION

People who base their beliefs on reason and reality generally will change them only if given better facts and better arguments. People who base their beliefs on the opinions of others generally hold the beliefs of the people around them, particularly the most important people around them. When one grows up, one's beliefs are shaped primarily by one's parents and other authority figures. As one grows older, one's beliefs are shaped primarily by one's peers. Derek Black may simply have adopted White Nationalism because it was the worldview of his father, whom he wished to please. When he went off to college, he found a new, politically correct peer group and authority figures, and he may have changed his opinions to suit them.

If this is the case, then we can say that it is possible to reject White Nationalism for Political Correctness—truth for falsehood—if one *never really thought that White Nationalism was true in the first place*—if one never really understood that *truth means correspondence with reality*, not mere *agreement with other people*. I don't believe that it is possible to reject truth for lies if one really believes that truths are based on objective reality and lies are not. But if one merely adopts beliefs to please other people, then truth and falsehood have no objective meaning. They are just different ways that people express approval and disapproval. Then it becomes possible to adopt and discard radically different beliefs at will, based on the audience and aims of the moment.

Of course, there are two kinds of apostasy: one in which one actually changes one's beliefs, the other in which one merely verbally renounces them under duress without changing one's inner convictions. The first kind can be explained entirely in terms of a deep-dyed conventionalism, but the latter can't. Moral factors come into play.

Furthermore, nobody is entirely unconcerned with objective

truth. It matters when you balance your checkbook, or if you are falsely accused of a crime. But when it comes to the moral and political opinions that one has to profess to be considered cool or enlightened or just mainstream, their connection to the real world is nebulous to begin with. For one thing, the worst consequences of multiculturalism lie far into the future. And since at present most liberals occupy reality-free bubbles of prosperity and security—college campuses, college towns, resort communities, wealthy urban and suburban enclaves—they are insulated from the costs of diversity and even positioned to profit from it, financially and in terms of status, by abasing themselves before the black idols of white guilt. Thus for most people, politically correct opinions are entirely divorced from objective reality in terms of their grounds and consequences. Instead, they function as cheap tokens of status, easy ways of seeking social approval.

The closer you are to reality, and the more accountable you are for the objective consequences of your actions, the greater the importance of objective truth in determining your belief system. The further you are from reality and the less accountable you are for the objective consequences of your actions and beliefs, the greater the importance of social approval in selecting one's opinions.

THE ISSUE OF CHARACTER

Strength of character comes in as follows. All human beings value truth *and* the good opinions of their fellows to some extent. But these values often conflict. Strength of character is required to cleave to the greater good. The truth of White Nationalism is, of course, more important than the approval of a decadent society based on lies and hell-bent on destruction. This does not mean that you are a coward if you choose not discuss White Nationalism where it is not socially appropriate (over Thanksgiving dinner) or where it is not likely to produce a positive effect (with your boss, or your congressman, or your Jewish dentist). But if *forced to choose* publicly between White Nationalism and Political Correctness, the man of character will choose truth over lies.

Of course, many people have good reasons to want to avoid having to make that choice. They require the approval of their families, friends, colleagues, employers, and customers to lead good lives. Some of them wish to burrow into the system, gain as much wealth and influence as possible, and use it to advance our cause. They are secret agents. So they keep their views secret. And the rest of us have to respect that. If the system were able to socially and economically destroy every White Nationalist, it would be stronger and our movement would be weaker.

I have argued that if White Nationalism is to grow as a force, we have to follow two basic rules:

> 1. Everyone gets to choose his own level of involvement with White Nationalism and explicitness in advocating it.
>
> 2. Everybody else has to respect those decisions, while, of course, maintaining that the most admirable position is that of the fully explicit and proud White Nationalist.

In particular, everyone has to respect the anonymity of fellow White Nationalists. Anyone who "outs" fellow White Nationalists to expose them to harm from the system should suffer the social death of shunning. Similarly, any White Nationalist who through lax security measures allows personal information about White Nationalists to fall into the hands of "anti-fa" hackers, or movement kooks with track records of "outing" people, should suffer social death as well.

In exchange for these courtesies from explicit White Nationalists, I have asked implicit White Nationalists to reciprocate as follows.

> 1. Stop complaining about the eccentric and marginal people who are willing to be explicit White Nationalists. It is easier to be brave when you have less to lose. Courage and principle are also often paired with prickly or eccentric personalities.
>
> 2. Stop rehearsing horror stories and gloom and doom scenarios that make it harder for White Nationalists to become or remain explicit.

WHAT IF YOU ARE OUTED?

Another bit of advice for White Nationalists who wish to remain anonymous or silent: If you are outed—whether by yourself, a group like the Southern Poverty Law Center, or a turncoat in our own ranks—*do not apologize or surrender or go groveling for absolution from our enemies.* It doesn't help you or the cause.

Don't focus on how being exposed as a White Nationalist will ruin your credibility. Instead, try to control the damage. Try to maintain your credibility and moral stature by not apologizing and not backing down. Then, think of how you can *lend some of your dignity and credibility* to our ideas.

Don't count the "friends" you are losing. They're gone anyway. Surrender and groveling will not win them back. That will merely disgust and dishearten movement people who would otherwise be sympathetic to your plight. So instead count the friends that you will be gaining by not backing down.

Don't let the online kooks fool you. The White Nationalist community is filled with highly intelligent, accomplished, morally upright, and neurologically normal people. Many of the finest people I have met are White Nationalists. You should be proud to count them as friends and ashamed to dishonor them with your apostasy. Furthermore, outside the movement, there are still people who admire moral character, even in people with whom they disagree.

It is easy to understand and even forgive a Galileo, who paid lip service to the church's dogmas when threatened with torture and death. But White Nationalists today are being threatened with nothing worse than social disapproval and employment discrimination. Furthermore, the church had the power to force Galileo into apostasy in part because of a long litany of Christian martyrs who chose differently: they preferred death before apostasy, or even mere lip service to ideas they considered false. All things being equal, the side that is willing to fight the hardest and give up the most—even life itself—will win.

Ultimately, White Nationalism will not win until we can inspire people to prefer death to dishonor—until we can inspire people to martyr themselves for our racial survival. People who will suffer dishonor to preserve their economic status and the good opinion of complete strangers are natural slaves. The system can easily control them. But it cannot control people who would rather die than submit. It fears them, because a man who has conquered the fear of death has conquered all lesser fears, and he may inspire others to do so as well.

Thus White Nationalists must give the highest honors to explicit White Nationalists who demonstrate that they are willing to give everything to the cause by living a warrior's life and dying a martyr's death.

High honors are also due explicit White Nationalists who fight for our cause but never face the ultimate defining choice of martyrdom.

White Nationalists like Charles Krafft, who stand their ground when the system outs them and targets them for economic and social destruction, also deserve high honors.

Explicit White Nationalists need, in turn, to respect those who choose to remain secret agents within the system, particularly those who give active support to explicit White Nationalists.

TEACH YOUR CHILDREN WELL

With the apostasy of Derek Black—and the somewhat similar case of Lynx and Lamb Gaede of Prussian Blue—there is a significant mitigating factor. They were brought into public roles in White Nationalism as children. They were not allowed to determine their own level of explicitness and involvement. Their parents played a large role as well. Thus it was perfectly natural, when they grew up, to decide for themselves how involved they wanted to be, and to revise matters accordingly. One may quarrel with how they went about it, particularly in the case of Derek Black. But, in principle, I think they have the right to decide to leave the movement and lead private lives, as far as that is possible.

I think it is unethical for parents to involve their children *publicly* in White Nationalism, just as it is unethical to involve them in acting, modeling, and beauty pageants. These scenes are psychologically stressful for even the strongest adults. For children, whose characters and tastes are still developing, they can be psychologically crushing. The whole thing smacks of another scarring decision foisted upon children by parents: infant circumcision. In both cases, part of a child—be it only his innocence, his privacy, his *childhood*—is snipped off and discarded by his parents to consecrate him to their idols.

I do not, however, subscribe to the common view that it is a waste of time to try to pass one's values on to one's children because they will only "rebel." Empirical studies confirm that the single most powerful influence on a child's values and worldview are those of his parents. Why, then, is the lie that it is futile to teach one's children values so widely circulated? The answer is simple: so that children are delivered to the schools and popular culture as blank slates for politically correct brainwashing, which has never been deterred by the argument that it is futile and will only lead to rebellion.

The model White Nationalist is a person whose convictions are founded on reason and reality and who has the strength of character to stand up for the truth and work for the salvation of our race despite social and economic pressures, threats of torture and imprisonment, and even a martyr's or a warrior's death. This is a heroic ideal, by which we can measure ourselves and which we can strive to emulate. The great problem of our movement is to find or form men who put truth before opinion and death before dishonor—men who are hard enough to shatter this system, not weaklings who will crawl through the mud before its idols to protect their credit ratings.

Counter-Currents/*North American New Right*,
July 23, 2013

First, Do No Harm

A friend recently asked me what happened to the Counter-Currents program that I planned to do for the Voice of Reason Network. The short answer is that I was not particularly suited for it, so I changed my mind. Yes, there are a lot of interesting people out there to interview. Yes, there were a lot of interesting questions I wanted to ask them. But when I sat down to actually do it, I realized that it was not my forte. Since *the cause is better served by doing something well than by doing something badly*, I decided to stick to writing and editing.

It should go without saying that any cause is better served by doing something well than by doing it badly. But it needs saying, because in my ten years of observing and participating in the White Nationalist scene, I have seen more than enough poorly planned and executed events, botched demonstrations, inept videos, ugly websites, and bad writing, all of which do the cause more harm than good. They set us back rather than move us forward.

In fact, it is better to do nothing for the cause at all than to do something that reflects badly on it.

If asked to explain these travesties, most of the well-meaning perps will surely say that they felt they had to "do something." They were mad as hell, and they weren't going to take it anymore. Well bless them. Obviously nothing would ever happen if people didn't "do something." But "something" can be "anything." And we don't want to do just anything. We want to advance our cause. We want a white homeland. So the first principle of responsible activism should not be "Do something." Instead, one should take a page from medical ethics and "First, do no harm." (Harm to the cause, that is.)

Why, then, do activists "do harm"?

There are many ways that things can go wrong through no fault of one's own. Websites can be hacked, software can have flaws, printers can botch a job, a demonstration can be rained out, etc. Whether you are responsible or not, the cause has been set back. In cases like that, the best thing to do is not to brood over it and keep picking the scab, but to learn what can be learned and get back in the game.

Others "do harm" simply from lack of forethought, knowledge, experience, or taste. There is nothing wrong with these traits as such. They are universal features of youth, and youth usually brings with it many compensating virtues. They become problems only if individuals are unaware of their inadequacies, or if they are unwilling to correct them, or if they lack proper guidance from more mature and experienced mentors.

There are very few mentors in the movement today. (I am not counting the people who set examples of what *not* to do.) This puts a heavy burden on those who are willing and able to provide guidance.

But the "first, do no harm" principle applies to mentors as well. At the very least, a would-be mentor has to level with those who come to him for advice. All-purpose words of encouragement do no good if someone is about to embark upon a project that puts him and the cause in a bad light.

It is particularly imprudent if one uses one's name to endorse harmful products and actions, since it depletes one's credibility, which is a precious commodity. Given that the system works overtime to "discredit" leading White Nationalists, it seems crazy to help them out.

I have not been particularly good as a mentor, but I am striving to improve. It is easy to mentor someone who is mature, self-confident, and emotionally healthy. But such people need very little mentoring. The hard cases are people who are immature, insecure, and neurotic. Unfortunately, our cause is filled with talented people of that description. And in those cases, I have not done all I could.

Ultimately, the root is fear: It is dangerous to level with a person who might be more than a little neurotic, and if he has serious mental problems, then the principle of "no harm" (to the cause and to oneself) means that one should not encourage him — or discourage him, for that matter — but just be silent and slowly back out of the room. From bitter experience with kooks, I am afraid that I err on the side of caution.

This brings us to one of the chief reasons White Nationalists "do harm": Personality disorders like narcissism and mental illnesses like depression and bipolar disorder are over-represented in our ranks. Learn the signs.

I want to deal with these problems at greater length in the future. But for now, I just wish to observe that even though White Nationalism is anti-egalitarian and elitist in theory, in practice White Nationalists tend to coddle and even promote people who are mentally and physically botched and unhealthy.

Part of this tendency is based on Christian "virtues," such as pity for the lame, the halt, and the blind, or the soul-body dualism that allows us to believe that noble souls might be hiding behind Halloween masks of rage, brooding, and insanity. But non-Christians fall for the same traps too.

As a rule, White Nationalists are so alienated and so desperate to find people with talent that we are blind to glaring faults, or turn a blind eye to them.

But in doing so, we tacitly confess that *we really don't take this all that seriously.* We aren't really looking for people who can become political soldiers in a world-historical struggle. We are looking for audiences, sounding boards, echo chambers, drinking buddies, dinner companions, pen pals, phone friends, racialist sewing circles and sorority sisters, and the like.

When we surround ourselves with crazies—or even mere ineffectual, well-meaning milquetoasts—we are confessing that we don't really think we can win, that none of us will "Die Fighting," but we are bound and determined to "Die Complaining"—complaining about the same stuff we have been complaining about for 40 or 50 years.

Serious activists don't associate with kooks, even kooks who are all about "doing something."

There are plenty of character flaws that keep White Nationalists silent and sidelined, but refusing to follow obvious kooks is not among them. These are good reasons for not getting involved, among many others.

I should note that I am not claiming that certain strains of White Nationalism "do harm" by their very nature. I am not, for example, one of those race-wise bourgeois conservatives who blame the failure of White Nationalism to gain traction in their circles on the mere existence of the Ku Klux Klan and neo-Nazis, as if more mainstream groups would magically begin to get good press if the "costume clowns" would just go away—as if fellow White Nationalists were a greater enemy than the establishment and its media mouthpieces.

Any costume can be a clown costume if worn by a fool, even a jacket and tie. And every kind of group can make a positive contribution to our cause—from the most radical vanguardists to the most accommodating mainstreamers—provided they choose realistic goals and rational means, then do something positive.

Of course the ultimate principle of activism is not "avoid harm" but "do good." Yet a distant good is often harder to determine than an immediate harm, and the White Nationalist movement is still making baby steps. So for us today, the most reliable way of pursuing that ultimate good is to first do no harm.

Counter-Currents/*North American New Right*,
September 18, 2010

White Nationalists & the Political "Mainstream"

White Nationalists want political power. We want to gain it, and keep it, and use it to turn our race from the path to extinction back to the path to the stars. We have truth and right on our side, and we're going to win.

But let's not lose sight of where we are today. White Nationalists are a tiny, powerless, despised minority. We are poorly organized, poorly funded, and poorly led. Aside from the internet, we have no way of getting our message to the masses. The political system is rigged against us. The reigning moral consensus holds racism to be the ultimate evil.

We are, moreover, a magnet for dysfunctional types: drunks, cranks, hobbyists, depressives, pathological liars, histrionic narcissists, grandiose maniacs, and outright psychotics. Until we learn to identify and avoid such people, the best we can hope for is two steps forward, one step back. All too often, it is two or three steps back.

A movement that combines lofty idealism with such real-world impotence and squalor is bound to breed a tendency toward wishful thinking and grandiose fantasies. Who could blame us for wanting an alternative to *this* reality?

What is the difference between healthy idealism and mere fantasy? The healthy idealist does not merely have a sense of where he is going, he also bears in mind where he is now, and how he is going to get there from here. The fantasist, by contrast, is so hell-bent on fleeing the squalor of the present that he launches himself into an idealistic fantasy world with no thought to how this fantasy can be achieved.

I want to discuss two kinds of fantasists: radicals and mainstreamers.

Radical Fantasists

The first kind is the easiest to spot. They are ideological purists who believe in articulating and sticking to the truth, no matter how radical and unpalatable it might seem to the mainstream. Purists believe that the social and political changes they desire will be achieved only after the present civilization collapses due to internal weakness and corruption. Until then, they are content to read Julius Evola and Savitri Devi, post comments on the internet, and maybe stockpile weapons, ammunition, and dried banana chips.

I think the purists are 95% correct. I agree that we need to speak the truth, stand our ground, and try to move the rest of the world in our direction. I believe that we will never be saved within the present social and political system. I believe that we will only get what we want when this system is destroyed. I agree with their implicit assumption that we will never be strong enough to destroy the system ourselves. I especially agree with the reading list.

But I don't believe in just waiting for history to do our work for us. We can also *do something* in the meantime. We can create real world communities. We can create networks and organizations. We can publish books and edit journals. We can mentor young people. We can convert people to our way of thinking.

We can do more than prepare to survive a collapse. We can already have a new community — the seeds of a new order — in place when the collapse comes. And who knows, we may even be able to lend our shoulders to the wheel of time, to speed up the process of dissolution and renewal. That which is falling should not just be cheered on. It should also be pushed.

Mainstream Fantasists

The second type of fantasist is harder to spot, because he pretends to be a hardbitten political realist, a shrewd wheeler-dealer, a pragmatic activist who scorns the radical fantasists as do-nothings.

But the mainstream fantasists are often more detached from reality than the radicals. Consider the following mainstream fantasist behaviors.

1. Election Enthusiasm

Mainstream fantasists followed the recent [2010] US elections with extreme interest, even though of the hundreds of candidates running for office, only one of them—Jim Russell of New York's 18th district—was concerned with representing the interests of white Americans (and even he might want to sue me for saying so).

Yes, of course, American politics affects us all. But that does not explain why *bona fide* White Nationalists are actually rooting for Republicans as if Republicans give a damn about white interests.

What explains that?

It is complex. In some cases I am sure it is just a matter of old habits dying hard. In other cases, it is less a love of Republicans than a hatred of the Left.

But the greater part of it is the power of make-believe. I have seen obese couch potatoes pantomiming slam dunks and then strutting and preening like star athletes. I have seen sports enthusiasts who take as much pride in calling a game as the athletes who actually win it. Rooting for the Republicans is the same thing. It is no fun to feel alienated and impotent, so many White Nationalists like to imagine that the Republicans are our team, because when one's team wins, one experiences a vicarious feeling of efficacy, even though one actually does nothing to contribute to the victory.

Mistaking political commentary for political power is the equivalent of feeling like a rock star by playing air guitar.

But it gets worse.

2. Supporting System Candidates

Some White Nationalists go much further than giving mere passive support to mainstream politicians. They actually give *money* and *work* to politicians who don't represent us. Indeed, if these politicians knew who we are, they would run away from us.

First it was Patrick Buchanan. Then it was Ron Paul. Now it is Rand Paul and the Tea Party. I personally know White Nationalists who have given thousands of dollars and countless hours of hard work to these candidates, even though there is no way we could influence them.

Again, the question is why?

Sure, the Left predictably accused them of racism. But that did not make it so. None of these people represent white interests. They would be furious if you accused them of that.

Some White Nationalists claimed they were prospecting for potential converts. But that did not require donating money and actually *working* for the candidates.

Others claimed that they simply wanted to make trouble for the establishment. But, again, there were enough *genuine* paleocons, libertarians, and Tea Partiers out there to do that. White Nationalists did not need to give a dime or lift a finger.

So why did they? Again, I think it offers them the illusion of efficacy in the real world.

But it is a very expensive illusion.

Indeed, I would argue that it is an immoral self-indulgence.

Wide awake White Nationalists are very rare. If you are wide awake, then you need to put all of your money and efforts into awakening others. Libertarians and paleocons can take care of their own. White Nationalists need to take care of our own.

To the White Nationalists who are wasting their time and money supporting system politicians, I ask: "If not you, who?" If you don't support our cause, then who will? White Nationalism is all about taking our own side. So why are White Nationalists working for the system instead?

The next time anyone reading this is thinking of spending $2,000 to eat rubber chicken in a ballroom with a system political candidate, get in touch with me first. For $2,000, I'll actually sit down to dinner with you and *listen* to what you have to say. I'll make sure your money will go directly to promoting White Nationalism. I'll keep you informed about the effects it is having. Hell, I'll even pick up the tab.

3. Self-Censorship

The system wants nothing more than to shut us up. But some White Nationalists actually fantasize that shutting up is the path to victory. They tell us that we have to censor ourselves of every idea that "won't play in Peoria." We have to distance ourselves from the radicals and extremists, the people with strange sounding, easily parodied ideas.

Instead, we have to "meet people where they are right now." We have to appeal to their existing attitudes and interests. Politics, after all, is the art of the possible. We have to work within the existing parameters and incrementally move people in the right direction.

It sounds so reasonable, so concrete and well-grounded. But it is actually abstract fantasy talk. The truth is, there is no *political* path that leads from Peoria to the White Republic. Between them stands a vast moral chasm that mere politics cannot bridge.

The problem is that the people in Peoria *want* the system that is poisoning their children's minds with self-hate and minority worship, flooding our nation with the detritus of the Third World, and setting our race on the road to extinction. They want that world—or they want the approval of their friends and neighbors and Baptist Sunday school teachers and Oprah *more* than they want to oppose the forces promoting our extinction.

The Tea Partiers *want* that world too, they just want to make sure that the brown hordes inherit a country with low taxes, limited government, and sound money—as if they'd have any use for them. The Tea Partiers will do nothing *explicitly* pro-white because they don't care enough about racial preservation to take the risk. They aren't racists just because the Rachel Maddows of the world say they are.

Politics always appeals to the existing value system. No White Nationalist politics is possible today, because the dominant value system is anti-racist. Anti-racism really is the only thing sacred in this country today. Unless we change that value system, any political progress we make will be at enormous cost and will probably be easily erased. Yes, one can swim against the current, but it is tiring, and one need only relax a second to see all one's gains swept away.

The conclusion: We need a metapolitical movement to create the context in which political change is possible, and creating that context requires: (1) changing people's values and (2) expanding their conceptions of what is really possible.

It can be done. But we have to say things that people will think are immoral or impractical, and then persuade them to change their minds. If we are going to save our race, we have to risk offending people.

Politics as usual is the path to perdition: to shutting up, blending in, not making waves, and going with the flow that is leading our people down to the sunless sea of extinction.

4. Self-Co-option

The system tries to co-opt and neutralize all political dissent. But some White Nationalists fantasize that co-opting ourselves is the path to victory.

I am all for creating front groups and publications controlled by *bona fide* White Nationalists that intersect with the outer edge of the mainstream. These fronts allow us to recruit and radicalize people, moving them in the right direction. We need a whole spectrum of organizations and messages spanning the gap between the mainstream and the advocates of a white ethnostate.

But no purpose is served by persuading White Nationalists to move toward the mainstream: to shut up, blend in, and devote our scarce money and time to promoting the success of marginally better system politicians. How, exactly, does this get us closer to the White Republic? Co-opting ourselves is not the path to power but to oblivion.

Again, the libertarians, paleocons, and Republicans can take care of themselves. We are a tiny, powerless, impoverished minority. If we do not devote all our resources to promoting our message, then who will?

Counter-Currents/*North American New Right*,
November 5, 2010

WHY CONSERVATIVES STILL CAN'T WIN

Recently I re-read William Pierce's classic 1971 essay "Why Conservatives Can't Win."[1] Like Pierce, if forced to choose between liberals and conservatives, I would side with conservatives. Conservatives have the indispensable political realism necessary for the preservation of any civilization. Liberalism, I will grant, does attract the best brains, blood, and spirit of our race. But though liberal idealism and imagination may adorn the heights of our civilization, they are undermining its foundations.

If, in the next national election, everybody who voted Republican dropped dead in the voting booth, the country would be finished. You can't have a functioning society consisting of bureaucrats, academics, welfare parasites, Jews, coloreds, feminists, fruit juice drinkers, and assorted busybodies. But if every Democratic voter dropped dead, my own family would be more than decimated, but society would go on. It would definitely be more orderly and more prosperous, although it would also be drab and hideously uptight.

Aside from politics, in which I completely reject egalitarianism and multiculturalism, I am pretty much a liberal. But one cannot deny that White Nationalism today is a phenomenon of the Right. If White Nationalism is to triumph, it will have to become the common sense of the whole political spectrum. But for the time being, we are Rightists, and we have to make the best of it.

But although we are Rightists, we are not conservatives. Conservatives share some of our values, but they don't share all of them, and they certainly don't share our goals. In fact, it is hard to speak of conservatives as goal-oriented at all. Conservatives are backward-looking or fixated on legalism, procedure, and

---

[1] http://www.counter-currents.com/2010/12/why-conservatives-cant-win/

rights, but they do not have an image of a perfected society that is the proper goal of political activity. White Nationalists, like Leftists, do have such a vision.

Conservative goals, such as they are, are confined to piecemeal resistance to the implementation of the grand designs of the Left. As often as not, conservatives are just trying to hold on to the Leftist programs of the past.

William F. Buckley's description of conservatism as "Standing athwart the tracks of history yelling stop" pretty much captures this mentality, as unseemly as it is for a serious-minded individual. We White Nationalists, however, want to be in the engine of history, steering it toward our goal, and cheerfully pouring on the steam when the Buckleys of the world try to get in our way.

The core of Pierce's argument is that conservatives can't win because they aren't really trying. The Left plays for keeps. They have an overriding goal. They have a world to win. Conservatives are just trying to hold on to the 1950s or the 1980s. Conservatives may fight ferociously from time to time, but they are always playing defense. They think the election of a Nixon or a Reagan is a great victory, then lapse into complacency, only to awaken a few years later to find that the Left has been on the march the whole time.

Other things being equal, the side that fights to win will defeat the side that fights for a draw. Fortune favors the bold, those who launch offenses, not those who merely play defense.

Conservatives also make a virtual cult out of being good sports, graceful losers, and ready compromisers.

Well, conservatives STILL can't win. But neither can they learn, so they continue to promote their folly to new generations. Recently, two White Nationalist publications that once showed real promise have been lost to conservatism: *Occidental Dissent* and *The Occidental Quarterly*, which I edited for two and a half years, along with its sister publication, *TOQ Online*, which I created and edited for a year. I have already dealt with *Occidental Dissent* in "White Nationalism and the Political 'Mainstream.'" Here I wish to deal with *TOQ*.

On November 6, 2010, John Gardner ("Yggdrasil"), the new publisher of *TOQ*, published "Why *The Occidental Quarterly* Exists"[2] in which he explains the aims of *TOQ* under his watch. This article contains sound advice to whites to become as independent as possible from the consumerist system and its values and to create mutual aid networks.

But when it comes to the political system, Gardner is still very much a conservative, a Republican even. He thinks that White Nationalists—a tiny, voiceless, despised, poorly funded, and poorly led movement—should aim at lobbying and "conditioning" Republicans to represent white interests. Gardner actually thinks that whites can vote and lobby and game ourselves out of this mess, as if our people have not been slated for slow and systematic genocide but are merely having a run of bad luck at the polls.

I think it is too early for White Nationalists to get involved in electoral politics and lobbying. We need to become a much bigger, richer, and more politically threatening group before we can make a difference in that realm. (And if we become powerful enough, we can dispense with electoral politics altogether.) But for any of that to happen, we need to invest our time, money, brains, and talent in community building and outreach. We need to win people over to our way of thinking, by packaging and delivering our message to every white group through every medium available. We need to build up our community so it has something more to offer prospective converts than ignominy and the company of the insane.

The John Gardner I knew was a race-wise, Jew-wise White Nationalist who believed in the goal of a white ethnostate. *The Occidental Quarterly* I knew was founded to be *explicitly* white and to deal *explicitly* with the Jewish question. But you would never know that from Gardner's *TOQ* 2.0 agenda. The most he says about race is that white Americans are being demonized and discriminated against because of our "skin color." (Which is the language of biological race deniers and minimizers.) And as for the Jewish question, all we get is this:

---

[2] http://www.toqonline.com/blog/featured/why-toq-exists/

Effective political motivation demands an identifiable "them."

Our competing racial groups have an identifiable "them" in their stereotype of the evil and undeserving White man.

We need our own identifiable "them" which is, of course, those who benefit from the current repression of Whites under the regime of "multiculturalism."

Then the trick is to make the "them" apparent to our own people without inflaming and motivating our opponents.

We should not name "them" explicitly. Rather, we advance policies that directly thwart the extractions and benefits "they" get from "us," thus generating the kind of policy-oriented anger that will motivate and unify "us."

If this is taken seriously as *TOQ* policy, then every back issue of the journal will have to be pulped and reprinted, with references to Jews replaced by euphemisms like "liberals" and "cultural Marxists." Furthermore, Kevin MacDonald now seems like an odd choice for Editor. And in the end, it will never work, because the SPLC will always be around to remind people of the truth about White Nationalists who scuttle crabwise toward the mainstream, begin speaking in riddles and euphemisms, and try to reinvent themselves as conservatives.

We few who know the most important truth in the world — that organized Jewry (not "liberals," not "cultural Marxists") have set the white race (not "conservatives," not "Christians," not "Western civilization") on the path to extinction — have an absolute duty to get this message out and wake our people up. Because if we don't do it, nobody else will. Those who know the truth but can't shout it from the rooftops have the duty to support those who can spread the word.

Gardner's claim that "the trick is to make the 'them' apparent to our own people without inflaming and motivating our opponents" is just a version of the old idea that we can "sneak up on the Jews" and catch them napping. But the enemy has millions of lidless, unsleeping eyes. And the idea that the enemy is not already inflamed and motivated and working against us at 99% capacity is laughable.

Gardner's "trick" is not to name "them" but to support policies that negatively impact the interests of the enemy, so they rise from their slumbers and attack us, which will then motivate us to fight back.

Where to start?

1. Aren't the Jews attacking us enough already? And if decades of Jewish attacks have not motivated whites to unite and fight back, then why does Gardner think that ratcheting up the Jewish pressure will produce a different result this time?

Our people have suffered enough. The role of White Nationalists should be to explain who has been attacking us, and why, and how to fight back. *That* is the leadership our race needs.

2. When and how are White Nationalists going to gain enough power to credibly threaten Jewish interests? How, exactly, is White Nationalism going to grow without first talking about race or Jewish power? If we don't say anything to set us apart from conservatives, if we don't act any more honest than system politicians, then why would we expect any growth? Gardner's strategy for gaining political power begins: First, gain sufficient power to threaten the interests of the enemy. It doesn't work that way.

3. It is a tried and true method of political agitation to present a moderate petition to an arrogant power and hope that it is denied. There is nothing wrong with using this technique from time to time, when it is appropriate. But to depend on this technique alone—because one has adopted a policy of never speaking the enemy's name—is an abdication of leadership. White Nationalists should be the primary educators and agitators of our people. Again, if we don't argue our case, nobody else will.

4. What exactly is the advantage to our people of being kept in the dark about our real enemies? The mainstream Right has been doing that for decades, and what has that gotten us? Richard Nixon knew the score, but he spoke the truth only in private. In public, he made a foreign-born Jew Secretary of State and created affirmative action. The enemy operates under no such self-imposed handicaps.

5. Gardner's strategy is obviously based on the experience of the Tea Party, a piously color-blind, universalistic movement promoting fiscal conservatism and constitutional government which was nevertheless viciously attacked as "racist" by the Left. These attacks have prompted ever-angrier denials of "racism" but not much more. Perhaps White Nationalists can reap some benefits from this polarization, but it is not a phenomenon that we need to imitate or encourage. It is doing quite well without us. Furthermore, Leftist attacks on the Tea Party might move some people in our direction, but we will not move them any further unless we stay true to our own message rather than blending in with conservatives.

Pierce was right. Conservatism can't win. It doesn't really conserve anything. It is so politically inept and hapless that it seems almost designed to lose. If doing the same thing again and again and expecting a different result is a definition of insanity, it is also a good definition of conservatism.

Counter-Currents/*North American New Right*,
December 28, 2010

Status Competition, Jews, & Racialist Mainstreaming

This following article was written in December of 2009 in response to an attack against Patrick Buchanan by Alex Linder of the Vanguard News Network. I am reprinting it here, essentially unaltered, because there are a few points here worth considering.

Linder believes that writers who occupy positions somewhere between paleoconservatism and outright White Nationalism, or who define White Nationalism in a manner that does not explicitly exclude Jews, need to be singled out for especially "vicious" attacks. The aim of these attacks is to "polarize" the political field, forcing people to choose between conservatism and explicit, anti-Semitic White Nationalism.

Linder's targets include writers like Patrick Buchanan, Samuel Francis, Jared Taylor, Peter Brimelow, Richard Spencer, and now Matt Parrot. Linder has even attacked Kevin MacDonald as an "implicit" conservative, which did nothing for Linder's credibility.

A staple of Linder's "vicious" attacks is to claim — based merely on speculation, of course — that Buchanan *et al.* are cowards, opportunists, traitors, and the like. Linder, of course, only pretends to know these people's true motives. I don't know these people's hearts any better than Linder does, but in the following response, I offer an account of the strategic thinking that might explain their behavior.

Matt Parrott has offered the best critique of Linder's polarizing strategy. Polarization is only advisable if one is positioned to actually *benefit* from forcing a choice. One has to actually have an *alternative* to offer: an alternative political vehicle, not merely an online version of Arkham Asylum. Forced to choose between mainstream conservatism and VNN Forum, a lot of White Nationalists would prefer to drop out altogether.

My own critique of "polarization" is very simple. If we are going to create channels of influence and pull the whole political spectrum and the cultural mainstream in our direction, we need white advocates to fill every shade of the political spectrum and address every white group and subgroup, and we need to find ways of productively networking between them.

I make clear my reasons for thinking that any alliance with Jews is folly in my article "White Nationalism and Jewish Nationalism" (chapter 13, above) and the associated online comment thread.[1]

I posted this as a reply to Alex's VNN article on Buchanan, but it never appeared, so I am posting it here.

I always love it when Alex writes an essay. I don't have time to sift through the discussion forum looking for his little gems. That said, I strongly disagree with his attitude here.

Pat Buchanan will not save us. Nor will Ron Paul. Nor will any politician. Nor will we be saved by race realist policy wonkery. I see no salvation for our race short of creating a new political system, either by replacing the US system as a whole or by seceding from it.

But Buchanan the writer and commentator has his virtues and his uses.

Linder constructs his argument about strategy in terms of crafting a message that gets to dim ordinary people. I am not sure that is the right audience. Historically speaking, dim masses don't count for much, because they are easily controlled by elites with access to political power and the power to shape attitudes through education, religion, and the press. How would Linder's strategy change if White Nationalists focused on changing white

---

[1] http://www.counter-currents.com/2011/08/white-nationalism-jewish-nationalism/#comment-9507

elite opinion?

The white elites in the US are not dim. If dim is the average, the elites are above dim. Some of them are fiendishly intelligent. The white elites in the US can, however, be characterized by high degrees of individualism, conformism (the two actually go hand in hand), materialism, and insecurity about their status. The richer they are, the more insecure they are, because the more they have to lose.

They can lose status, of course, because in the US, status depends more on achievement than birth. In more traditional societies, one has status through birth, whether one is a street sweeper or an aristocrat. Here, one's status is "earned."

Now, in both kinds of society, it is other people who "grant" one's status. If nobody will treat an aristocrat like an aristocrat, then he has no status. But for whatever reason, in a country like England, an aristocrat like Sir Oswald Mosley might take very radical political positions, and even go to jail for them, but enough people still recognized him as an aristocrat that his social standing was never destroyed. In the US, we are much more individualistic. We grant or withhold status based on what each person does or says, not who his parents were.

At first glance, that seems like a great system. There are certainly fewer barriers to upward mobility. In the United States, money buys anything.

Unfortunately, money also guarantees nothing. Thus the people who fight hard for upward social mobility are also haunted by downward mobility. They know that the very individualism that allowed them to rise also allows them to fall back down. For if their business partners, social contacts, and others turn their backs on them, they can easily be ruined, and whether this happens is merely a matter of individual choice, based upon nothing more stable than calculations of self-interest.

Tocqueville long ago observed that American individualism goes hand in hand with a high degree of social conformity. Why is this? Here is my theory: human beings are social animals, with a need for social approval and recognition. In individualist societies, however, the extension of social approval and recognition is highly conditional and constantly re-evaluated. Therefore, one has to be more attentive to gauging and conforming to public opinion in individualistic societies. Thus a high degree of individualism and social mobility promotes a high degree of social conformism, because people also value social approval and social stability. (The ambitious love upward mobility, but once they get theirs, they want to hold onto it.)

This is why social mobility in individualist societies is most available to people who combine intelligence and ambition with a shallow, extraverted, conformist personality type. Frat boys with MBAs.

Furthermore, the more ambitious one is, the more one needs social approval and recognition, because one needs to secure the cooperation of more people to do bigger things. Thus as one approaches the pinnacles of the white money and power elites, one finds individuals who have higher and higher levels of ambition, aggressiveness, narrow cunning intelligence, extroversion, social conformism, and a pathetic, childlike insecurity.

No sane society should be ruled by people like this. But we were far better off when we controlled our own "symbolic realm"—the realm of ideas, ideals, honors, and opinion that governs the granting and withholding of social status.

Unfortunately, that realm has now been captured by an alien, hostile elite, the Jews, who have rigged a new status system to reward whites who betray their own kind and promote and engage in race-destructive behavior. The segment of society most controlled by this hostile elite is the entertainment industry, which is thus on the cutting edge of race-destructive white behavior. Whites in Hollywood attain status through anti-natalism, feminism, homosexuality, miscegenation, adopting non-white babies, and the like. Where Hollywood goes, there goes America, if the Jews who are scripting our dispossession and extinction have their way.

The strategic question of White Nationalism, therefore, is: How do White Nationalists change elite opinion when our plutocrats tend to be shallow, extroverted, and insecure about their status, which happens to be determined by our polar opposites, the Jews?

The problem is compounded when White Nationalists themselves aspire to attain or hold onto elite status. Aside from the personal benefits of such status to White Nationalists, such status is also beneficial to the movement, since elite members have greater access to the elite.

I believe that this is the context in which one has to understand the strategies of such people as Samuel Francis, Patrick Buchanan, and Jared Taylor. If I wanted to (1) promote White Nationalism to status-conscious, insecure elites, and (2) maintain my own status and thus access to these elites, I would give a wide berth to the Jewish question, since the Jews now control the status system in our society, and if they felt sufficiently threatened by people like Francis, Buchanan, *et al.*, they would shut them down and destroy any access they might have to their preferred audience.

If I were Francis, Buchanan, *et al.*, I imagine I would play the following dangerous game with the Jews. Because they would work to shut down and marginalize anyone who was openly impervious to the Jews, one would have to signal a certain porousness to them, specifically by cooperating with whatever marginal Jews will associate with White Nationalism, e.g., Michael Hart, Michael Levin, Marcus Epstein, Paul Gottfried, etc. These Jews obviously think they are getting something by cooperating with White Nationalists, if only the chance to spy on our gatherings.

But we have to give White Nationalists some credit too, for they might think they are using these Jews to advance White Nationalism. Maybe they are foolish or naïve to think this, but that is probably what they think.

If Buchanan *et al.* were merely working as fronts for the Jews, in order to mislead and sabotage White Nationalism, then why would they have any public affiliation with Jews? Wouldn't that blow their cover? Wouldn't that make their task more difficult?

The mere fact that at people like Buchanan, Francis, and Taylor interact in a collegial fashion with certain marginal Jews does not constitute evidence that they are working for "the Jews" — meaning the organized Jewish community. It does not follow simply as a matter of logic. In fact, it would make more sense for them not to associate with Jews at all.

It is certainly reasonable and prudent to be suspicious of the judgment of White Nationalists who think they can manipulate Jewish opinion to advance our cause. It is certainly reasonable to be cautious in dealing with such people. But suspicion is not proof, and using such people cautiously does not mean that they cannot be used at all.

As an introvert, I have little patience for extroverts, and highly extroverted, status-insecure elite members like George W. Bush strike me as especially soulless and contemptible. Frankly, I wish we could save our race without dealing with such people. In my darker moods, I wonder if a race that allows itself to be led by people who put trivial issues of personal status ahead of collective survival can be saved, or even if it deserves to be saved. There is something disgusting about people who have all the money in the world and permit themselves less freedom to speak their minds than a truck driver or short order cook. As N. B. Forrest once asked on VNN about Mel Gibson: How much money does one need to give the Jews the finger? I wish I could shame these people, but I cannot, for their sense of shame is held captive by our enemies. Thus I have little patience for efforts to soft-sell these people on their own race's survival. What kind of people need to be soft-sold their own survival?

That said, Pat Buchanan has his uses. I recommend his books to skittish, insecure, status-conscious mainstream conservatives to nudge them in the right direction. If they like Buchanan and become comfortable advocating his take on the world, then perhaps they can be brought further still, by reading Sam Francis' *Essential Writings on Race*, then *American Renaissance*, then maybe Kevin MacDonald.

Even if Alex's worst suspicions about Buchanan are true, that would in no way lessen the value of his books. Even if the Jews are using him to mislead, we can still use him to wean people away from mainstream Republicanism in the direction of White Nationalism. To think that such attempts would be doomed to failure is to underestimate our own power and to ascribe to the Jews some sort of occult force of invincibility that they simply do not have. That is how losers think.

I do not think Pat Buchanan is our competitor. I do not think he is our enemy. And even if he were, we are strong and clever enough to use him for our own ends.

An afterthought: The depressing truth I am struggling to come to grips with is that our race must be saved *in spite of itself*, and *against its will*. No healthy organism needs to be provided with a moral justification for its survival. But white people do. From a biological point of view, this is morbid and decadent. But since we are not in a position to simply remove this weakness, we have to deal with it. That is the most important strategic question.

Counter-Currents/ *North American New Right*,
August 26, 2011

THE LAUGH TEST:
MULTICULTURALISTS GIVE ADVICE TO ETHNONATIONALISTS

On February 26th, 2011, *The Guardian* announced the results of a poll conducted by the Searchlight Institute in the UK:

> Huge numbers of Britons would support an anti-immigration English nationalist party if it was not associated with violence and fascist imagery, according to the largest survey into identity and extremism conducted in the UK.
>
> A Populus poll found that 48% of the population would consider supporting a new anti-immigration party committed to challenging Islamist extremism, and would support policies to make it statutory for all public buildings to fly the flag of St. George or the union flag.
>
> Anti-racism campaigners said the findings suggested Britain's mainstream parties were losing touch with public opinion on issues of identity and race.
>
> The poll suggests that the level of backing for a far-right party could equal or even outstrip that in countries such as France, the Netherlands and Austria. France's National Front party hopes to secure 20% in the first round of the presidential vote next year. The Dutch anti-Islam party led by Geert Wilders attracted 15.5% of the vote in last year's parliamentary elections.
>
> Anti-fascist groups said the poll's findings challenged the belief that Britons were more tolerant than other Europeans. "This is not because British people are more moderate, but simply because their views have not found a political articulation," said a report by the Searchlight Educational Trust, the anti-fascist charity that commissioned the poll.
>
> ... 63% of white Britons... agreed with the statement

that "immigration into Britain has been a bad thing for the country." Just over half of respondents—52%—agreed with the proposition that "Muslims create problems in the UK."

Jon Cruddas, the Labour MP who fought a successful campaign against the British National party in his Dagenham and Rainham constituency in east London, said that the findings pointed to a "very real threat of a new potent political constituency built around an assertive English nationalism." The report identified a resurgence of English identity, with 39% preferring to call themselves English rather than British. Just 5% labelled themselves European.[1]

On its surface this is good news. It indicates that 48% of Britons are just waiting for an excuse to vote for the British National Party, which has "mainstreamed" itself, distancing itself from its associations with neo-Nazis, fascists, and skinheads and diversifying itself with Sikhs and Jews. Of course, it also implies that the enemies of the BNP and their willing allies in the mainstream media will never cease reminding voters of these connections.

This brings to mind Kevin MacDonald's recent talk, "Nationalist Strategies,"[2] which focuses on Geert Wilders in the Netherlands. Wilders has gone about as far as possible to construct a European nationalist party that stays within the boundaries of what MacDonald calls "the post-World War II consensus" about race, nationalism, and Jews.

As MacDonald points out, Wilders is perhaps the most philo-Semitic politician in Europe today (and sincerely so, judging from his marriage to a Jewess). But still, Wilders has made barely a dent in Jewish opposition to Dutch nationalism. Indeed, fewer than 2% of Dutch Jews voted for Wilders' Freedom Party in the last election.

---

[1] http://www.guardian.co.uk/uk/2011/feb/27/support-poll-support-far-right

[2] http://www.counter-currents.com/2011/02/nationalist-strategies/

But, as MacDonald points out, by staying within politically correct boundaries regarding race and the Jews, Wilders has gained the votes of Dutchmen who have awakened to the dangers of multiculturalism and immigration but who remain brainwashed about race and the Jewish question.

All over Europe, there are strong winds of discontent over multiculturalism and immigration, and nationalist mainstreamers like Wilders are trimming their sails to catch them. It would be a good thing if these parties made some headway in ending multiculturalism and non-white immigration, just as it would be a good thing if the Tea Party made similar headway in the United States.

I'm a "let a thousand flowers bloom" kind of guy, and if this sort of stuff gets people who don't know any better excited and involved and even leads to actual political change, I am certainly not one to dampen their enthusiasm. (I want them to keep their enthusiasm, but discover who their true friends and their true enemies really are.)

But White Nationalists should not lose sight of the fact that the goals of people like Wilders and the Tea Party fall far short of a white ethnostate. Furthermore, they would rebuff any overt association with us as a threat to their already shaky mainstream legitimacy.

The common denominator of nationalists like Wilders in Europe, the Tea Party in the United States, and White Nationalist mainstreamers worldwide is that they wish to craft a message that stays within the boundaries of that post-World War II "consensus": racial preservation and betterment (eugenics) are evil; the only legitimate goal is cultural preservation; since we are only concerned about culture, we hold open the possibility of cultural assimilation to people of all races; anything that smacks of fascism or National Socialism is anathema; and, of course, the ultimate evil is anti-Semitism, thus any form of European ethnic self-assertion must embrace the right of Jews to come and go and live where they please.

But that consensus is merely an artifact, a product of Jewish power. Thus my question to the mainstreamers is this: How do you propose to achieve white power without dislodging Jewish power? Because without Jewish power, white nations around the world would not have embraced multiculturalism and non-white immigration in the first place. And Jews don't seem to be persuaded of the necessity of changing these policies. Thus I just don't see any way of winning without identifying the organized Jewish community as the principal enemy and removing them from power.

The Searchlight poll also should be greeted with some skepticism. The Searchlight Institute is the UK equivalent of the Southern Poverty Law Center. Now if the *New York Times* announced that the SPLC, based on extensive public opinion polls, advised American White Nationalists that they could win the allegiance of 48% of the voters simply by renouncing violence and fascist symbols, how many White Nationalists would be dumb enough to take the bait without wondering if it conceals poison or a hook? (I'd wager that the number is depressingly large.)

What is the Searchlight's agenda here? These people, of course, only tell the truth by accident, meaning that they only utter a truth if they see an ulterior angle in it. So none of their alleged facts should be taken at face value. Instead, they should be examined in light of how they advance the multiracialist agenda.

First of all, the Searchlight people are clearly worried about a real phenomenon: rising nationalist sentiment in the UK. Second, they wish to rally anti-racist forces to resist it. Third, they probably wish to scare up some funds from their donors. Fourth, they wish to do as much damage to their nationalist enemies as possible.

If I were the Searchlight Institute, I would craft my poll questions and massage my data to lead nationalists to conclude that doing something maximally dumb and self-destructive is the road to power. If the SPLC and the ADL were stupid enough to follow my advice, I would definitely advise them to do the most self-defeating thing that they could be persuaded to do.

What is the takeaway lesson of the Searchlight poll? Renounce violence and fascist symbolism and 48% of the vote will be yours. And in the UK, with its multiple parties, 48% of the vote means power.

The British National Party does, of course, have roots in National Socialism and the violent skinhead subculture. That is because National Socialists and skinheads saw the problems of multiculturalism and non-white immigration and were willing to fight them *decades before* the moderate, middle-class suburbanites who are now turning to the mainstreamed BNP.

Many of the most committed BNP vanguardists were driven out or left in disgust when Nick Griffin embarked on mainstreaming the party. But some disinterested old fighters still remain. (When Griffin began his reforms, they just chose to close their eyes and think of England.)

Now the Searchlight is suggesting to Griffin and the muggles that the only thing standing between them and power are the 16 remaining Nazis and skinheads in their ranks. If they take the bait, the result will be more internal strife in the BNP and White Nationalist circles worldwide. Mission accomplished.

I dream of the day when our movement is mature enough that such suggestions by our enemies do not pass the laugh test. Until then, I guess we can hope that our enemies will simply die laughing at us.

Counter-Currents/*North American New Right*,
March 6, 2011

Premature Populism

William Pierce's article "Skinheads and the Law"[1] is a useful point of departure for discussing an important problem with the White Nationalist movement, a problem that I call premature populism.

White Nationalism, as I define it, is a form of populism in the following sense: no system of government is legitimate unless it promotes the common good of a people. A system is illegitimate if it promotes the interests of one class or faction, or even aliens, at the expense of other parts of the body politic. But, as a populist, I believe that the interests of the whole are best served by an elitist political system, as long as the elite remains accountable to the rest of society. The problem of politics always boils down to how one can find leaders who are better than the common man. Furthermore, I believe that any movement that aims at creating a populist White Nationalist system needs to be as elitist as possible. Finally, I believe that to create such a movement, we need to focus first on creating the leadership caste before we reach out to the masses.

I also believe that White Nationalism needs to be populist in the more common sense of the word, for in terms of present-day society, the white social elites are disproportionately responsible for our decline and the white masses are disproportionately victims. Thus to gain power, White Nationalists should not merely represent the interests of all whites, but we should also be willing address the genuine and just resentments of the masses against the existing elites, who will not be allowed to keep the wealth and power they have accumulated by dismantling white America. Although my tastes in music and art are generally elitist, and my SWPL quotient is a matter of public record,[2] all of

---

[1] http://www.counter-currents.com/2013/04/skinheads-and-the-law/

[2] Greg Johnson, "Smells Like ... White Guilt: Christian Lander's

my political sympathies lie with the middle and working classes, who have suffered the most from white dispossession. But you won't catch me dead at a Taco Bell.

By "elites" in the strict sense of the word, I mean people of above average intelligence, taste, and virtue. I am not talking about the upper social classes—or the upper income brackets in the case of the United States and other Anglo-Saxon colonial societies which do not have real social classes. By "masses" in the strict sense of the word, I mean people of average or below average intelligence, taste, and virtue. I do not mean the lower classes or people in middle- and low-income brackets.

There is, of course, a correlation between income and IQ as well as certain virtues and tastes. But given the perilous state of white societies worldwide, we can say with confidence that these are not the kinds of intelligence and traits of character that White Nationalists should particularly prize.

The excellences of bourgeois man have brought our race to the edge of oblivion. Our salvation will come only by recovering the virtues of the sages, warriors, and bards of our premodern ancestors. And those traits can be found in all segments of existing society.

Thus premature populism does not mean recruiting a new elite from the best of our people, regardless of contemporary social distinctions.

Premature populism means recruiting people who are merely average or below average in intelligence, virtue, and taste *before* we have constituted ourselves as an elite with the authority and ability to lead them. Mobilizing the masses can also be premature if the historical situation makes it impossible to make real political headway.

By focusing on Pierce's essay on skinheads, I do not wish to give the impression that my criticisms are confined to Pierce or to skinheads, since the problem I am describing is much wider. Furthermore, I am not criticizing either Pierce or skinheads across the board. I have discussed my views of Pierce, both

---

Whiter Shades of Pale," in *Confessions of a Reluctant Hater* (San Francisco: Counter-Currents, 2010).

positive and negative, elsewhere,[3] and have I reprinted many of his articles. I also hasten to add that some of the finest people I have known have come out of the skinhead movement, in confirmation of my conviction that people of quality can be found in all segments of the existing society.

William Pierce was by conviction an elitist. But he was an elitist in a hurry. Thus he was tempted again and again by what he called, in his less hurried moments of reflection, the "buffoonery"[4] of populism. In his 1995 essay on skinheads, Pierce shows a realistic understanding of the problems of the skinhead subculture. But when he weighs the question of whether it would be better to direct scarce time and money to influencing college students or skinheads, Pierce, a Ph.D. in physics and a former college professor, shows a marked preference for skinheads. Pierce allows that college students are more likely to have greater power and influence within the current system. But Pierce was more impressed by the fact that skinheads are more racially aware, macho, and aggressive than your average college boy. (It is hard to say how many skinheads there are in the world, but it may well be that there are more tough, athletic college boys than there are skinheads, even though genuinely tough men might be a minority among college boys.)

Following this logic, in 1999, Pierce purchased Resistance Records, a skinhead music label. Pierce found the music unlistenable, but it gave him access to the skinhead scene worldwide and brought in quite a lot of money. Although the National Alliance continued to publish materials aimed at high- and middle-brow audiences, the skinhead outreach alienated some National Alliance members,[5] and after Pierce's death, the skinhead element (and other associated tough guys) took over the National Alliance and have pretty much run it into the ground. Pierce, of course, tried to raise up the best people in the skinhead move-

---

[3] http://www.counter-currents.com/2012/07/remembering-william-pierce/

[4] http://www.counter-currents.com/2011/01/our-cause/

[5] http://www.counter-currents.com/2012/07/some-reminiscences-of-dr-william-pierce/

ment, but the National Alliance was dragged down in the end.

The decline of the National Alliance is a textbook example of premature populism. Pierce's basic error was trying to imagine a viable White Nationalist political movement *in the present society*. If one asks who *today* is likely to go out and actually *fight* for a white society, the answer is obviously not people from upper and middle income brackets. The people who have the racial awareness, toughness, and meanness to fight for a white society are predominantly from the working and sub-working classes. These are the people who have been hardest hit by white dispossession. These are the people who have the least to lose and the most to gain from attempting a white revolution. But the problem is that, in the present circumstances, White Nationalists are not in the position to credibly organize and lead these people, and even if we were, we are in no position to destroy the current system.

Premature populism is bad because:

1. It undermines our ability to create and sustain viable elite vanguard White Nationalist organizations.

2. It encourages good, sound, salt-of-the-earth people to waste their time, money, and efforts in premature political activism when they could and should be pursuing families and careers.

3. It encourages tolerance of sleazy, skanky, crazy people, who destroy everything they touch and prevent us from attracting superior people (including the better sort of high-functioning eccentrics). If we really believe in our message, then we have to believe that it will appeal to sane and normal people. Thus we have to stop coddling every stray dog of humanity who shows up at our door because we are just so *desperate* to hear from new people who seem to understand. We have to stop counting the crazies in front of us and think instead of the legions of superior people they are keeping away.

4. It encourages what I call jock-sniffing: the fetishization of guns, muscles, and machismo—including one of the greatest self-inflicted plagues on our race, alcoholism—at a stage of history when our movement needs to focus more on building up brain power, technological competence, communication skills (especially writing and speaking skills), media savvy, organizational competence, and good taste, particularly in matters of design and advertising.

Don't get me wrong: every white man should be fit and capable of self-defense. And yes, feminism is still wrong. And no, nobody should *try* to be a wimp. But jock-sniffing is deadly folly. How many of our efforts have been destroyed by drunken brawls, bragging, and indiscretions? How many of our people are dead or in prison because of testosterone, alcohol, or guns, in various combinations? How many of our people are suckers for tough, clean-cut men in uniforms who are, objectively, our enemies? How many of our organizations have been ruined by promoting tough guys and golden boys to positions beyond their competence?

I hold to Jonathan Bowden's ideal of the cultured thug, but we should always err on the side of culture, whereas Pierce and too many others err on the side of thuggery.

The net result of premature populism, kook-coddling, and jock-sniffing, is failure, burnout, and bitterness for all involved.

But what's the hurry? Yes, I know that our population is aging and shrinking. I know that non-whites are demographically swamping us. But in 20, 30, or 40 years—after the lifetimes of many of the people reading this—there will still be hundreds of millions of white people, including millions of tough, angry, macho white men. Indeed, there will be more of them, because although our population in absolute and relative numbers will be smaller and older, white dispossession will have worked its way up to the higher income brackets. The system is manufacturing armies of tough, angry, dispossessed white people for us. They're not going away any time soon.

So we have time to focus on other things. It is too early for politics, so let's take the time to lay solid metapolitical foundations for successful politics when the conditions are right. Metapolitics boils down to two things: propagating ideas and building community.

The basic metapolitical questions are: Who are we? Who are our enemies? What is right? What is possible? We need to answer these questions for ourselves and our people if we are going to lead them successfully. And we need to hone our message and the skills and media necessary to propagate it to all white groups.

Community building means, first and foremost, the creation of a new leadership caste, a guiding intelligence, for our race. This caste will first lead the way to the White Republic. Then it will lead the White Republic. History is made by elites. Racial populist societies will be ruled by elites. Effective racial populist movements will be led by elites. So let us become that elite.

There is no need for premature populism. The people will still be there when we are worthy of leading them and political action can actually make a difference. Thus White Nationalists have the time to get things right. And if there is no time to get it right, then one more repetition of a failed strategy will not save us anyway.

Counter-Currents/North American New Right,
May 3, 2013

ON VIOLENCE

On the question of violence, White Nationalists need to demand both moral strength and intellectual clarity from our leaders.

THE ILLEGITIMATE QUESTION OF VIOLENCE

These reflections on violence were provoked by two events in January of 2011. First, there was the wholly spurious attempt to link *American Renaissance* to the January 8 killing spree of Jared Lee Loughner in Tucson, Arizona. Second, there was the equally baseless attempt to link Harold Covington's Northwest Front to the bomb placed along the Martin Luther King Day parade route in Spokane, Washington on January 17. The bomb was safely defused, and Kevin Harpham, who had no ties with Covington, was eventually arrested and convicted.

Jared Taylor's response to the attack on *American Renaissance* was entirely appropriate. He pointed out that it had no basis in fact and that the characterizations of *American Renaissance* were incorrect. It was also appropriate for Harold Covington to respond to the attempts to smear him.

But I do not think it is appropriate for *other* White Nationalists to respond to such smears by protesting *their own* innocence and posting legalistic disclaimers of violence on their websites.

These White Nationalists condemn violence, of course, because they are aware of the state's awesome power to inflict violence on us. They desire to deflect this violence by telling the state:

> You've got nothing to fear from us. We're cute, harmless little fuzzballs. We're chumps who will scrupulously obey the laws concocted and enforced by the people who seek to exterminate us. We don't think violence will ever be necessary to get our people off the path toward extinction. We think that genocidal anti-white policies are all just a hideous misunderstanding. We're all men of good will

here, our rulers included. We think that the people who put these policies in place will yield power someday if we just get our act together and vote them out. And of course if we ever got power, we would not dream of making them answer for their crimes. We'll just shake their hands, like the good sports we are, and say "Good show old boy. Better luck at the polls next time."

When people in our movement are falsely linked to terrorism, our first instinct should be to defend those who are attacked by pointing out the speciousness or groundlessness of the claims and the blatant anti-white bias in the media and law enforcement.

If, however, one's first instinct is to say "I am against all violence," that smacks of throwing the accused under the bus and covering one's own ass. Protesting your innocence when you have not been accused of anything also smacks of a guilty conscience, which subtly concedes the legitimacy of the attack. That's not leadership.

Rather than getting defensive, leaders should counter-attack.

One should never allow the enemy to control how an event is framed. If you allow the question "Do White Nationalists advocate violence?" to be posed by the enemy, it does not matter what your answer is. We lose either way.

The proper response is to change the question, to reframe the issue, and to put the enemy on trial: "Why do the media and law enforcement have a bias against racially conscious white people, such that they will run unsubstantiated smears linking us to violence committed by Leftists like Loughner or unknown parties like the Spokane bomber?"

Anything less smacks of moral weakness and uncertainty.

THE LEGITIMATE QUESTION OF VIOLENCE

The issue is complicated by the fact that violence is a legitimate topic for political theory and strategy, no matter who raises the question. But in the context of a hostile society, we should be the ones who raise the question and determine the parameters of debate, not axe-grinding middlebrow media demagogues.

As I see it, politics is about power, and power always reduces to violence or the credible threat of violence. Therefore, no credible political movement can renounce violence, for the renunciation of violence is tantamount to the renunciation of politics itself.

This is true even if one aspires merely to participate in a political system that seeks to govern force with law and provides legal procedures like election or impeachment to challenge and replace people in power.

The law may provide for the orderly transfer of power, but what ensures that the people in power will respect the law rather than void elections they do not like and tear up constitutions they find too restrictive? Ultimately, it is fear of legal or extralegal retribution, i.e., violence.

BAD ARGUMENTS AGAINST VIOLENCE

1. Is violence immoral in itself?

Obviously not. Most people recognize circumstances where violence is legitimate, and self-defense against genocide is the best justification of all. Just look at the state of Israel and Jews around the world. Jews pretty much have a moral blank check for bullying and aggression, all in the name of self-defense. Meanwhile, mere verbal advocacy of white interests is automatically branded hate. Why is that? Because Jews have power, which comes down to violence or a credible threat thereof, and we have none.

People may have some sort of innate moral sense, but the moral sense of the public is not independent of power. The people always pretty much adopt the moral judgments preferred by the people who hold the whip. If the power relations were reversed, people's moral sensibilities could be changed as well.

2. Is violence bad because we stand for "the rule of law" against the "barbarism" of power politics?

That is naïve. The people are ruled by law, but the government obviously is not. We are ruled by men, not laws. The men who rule make laws for the rest of us. And the people who rule us now have legislated conditions inimical to the long-term survival of our race.

Law is not independent of power, and power just means violence or the credible threat of violence. Law is a product of power. The people who have power make the laws. The people who don't have power obey them. If White Nationalists gain power, we will make different laws. Until then, we obey their laws because they have more power than we do.

3. Is violence bad because it will turn people against whoever uses it?

Again, this is naïve. Like I said, people may have some innate moral sense, but most of the moral judgments that come out of their mouths and guide their actions are shaped by the people in power.

People are not innately "anti-violence." People condemn violence against non-whites because the television and the newspapers tell them to. They do not lose any sleep over that fact that on an average day in America, 100 white women are being raped by black men, because they are kept unaware of that fact, and if they were aware of it, they would keep their mouths shut and not "go there" for fear of being branded racists.

The moral sensibilities of the public are manufactured by people in power, and power reduces to violence or the credible threat of violence. If White Nationalists had power, we could spin the propaganda dial the other way, and people's moral sensibilities would follow.

4. Is violence a bad idea because it might bring bad publicity?

This is just a variation of point 3 above. Jared Taylor has never advocated violence, publicly or privately. I know this, because I have discussed it with him. Yet that did not stop him from being "linked" by liars to Jared Lee Loughner. Harold Covington writes books filled with revolutionary violence. But publicly and privately, he does not advocate violence under present conditions, and those conditions are likely to attain for a very long time to come. Yet that did not stop him from being "linked" by liars to the Spokane backpack bomb.

Do I really need to spell this out? No matter what we do, no matter how nice we are, we are never going to get good publicity from a media and government controlled by our enemies. Again, good publicity is not independent of power, and we all know what power is. The people in power are capable of telling lies about us and making them stick. Yes, the internet has weakened the control of the establishment somewhat. But do you really think, when push comes to shove, that they are going to allow themselves to be "tweeted" off the stage of history?

Whites will only get good publicity when we have the power to control the media. And we all know what power is.

5. Is violence a bad idea because the state might arrest or kill those who use it?

Should we never use violence because we might get hurt? People who think that way are natural slaves. The people who rule us are of course willing to use violence, even if they might get hurt (or, more often, their underlings might get hurt), because that is how people gain and keep power.

If White Nationalists are serious about gaining and keeping power, then the people who rule us naturally conclude that we too are willing to risk using violence. Our rulers are not going to be fooled by putting legalistic disclaimers on White Nationalist websites.

Furthermore, the government arrests and imprisons dissidents who have not advocated or committed violence. Matt Hale will spend the rest of his life in prison, even though he did not advocate or commit violence. (It was a federal agent who did that.) Edgar Steele did not advocate or commit violence, but he will probably die in jail, even though it is increasingly clear that he was framed by federal agents and informants.

Folks, if this is getting too scary for you, you need to bail out now.

The Lesson So Far

We are pacified by pious illusions about limited government, the rule of law, and fair play. We are doped with religion, sex, and TV. But ultimately we are ruled by violence and the threat of violence.

If you believe that the system needs to be replaced or radically overhauled, or if you merely believe that we need to throw the bastards who are running things out, our rulers will try to stop you, because they know that none of these things will happen except over their dead bodies. They believe that your very thoughts and aspirations, even if entertained merely in the privacy of your own skull, bear the seeds of violence against them.

They will begin with soft measures: mockery, shunning, job discrimination, and the like. But if you persist, and if you constitute a credible threat, then they will work their way up to harsher measures. This has always been the case. America was founded by violence, expanded by violence, held together by violence, ruled by violence, and exports its violence all over the globe. (It is about the only thing we export nowadays.)

Being naïve, or merely pretending to be naïve, about the nature of politics and the people who rule us will not save you. Naïveté will probably just get you in more trouble.

A Credible Repudiation of Violence

Merely verbal disclaimers of violence are silly and pointless. If White Nationalist groups and individuals wish to repudiate violence in a credible way, then they should purge their ranks of mentally ill people, the kind of people who flip out and go on shooting sprees.

White Nationalists, despite our professed elitism, tend to be very, very indulgent of mental illness. Perhaps that is because we know that the establishment paints us all as crazy, so we are loath to make distinctions. But we can and must make distinctions. White Nationalists would be crazy not to get depressed from time to time, given how genuinely depressing our situation is. But no serious movement can afford to depend on people with serious mental illnesses and personality disorders like schizophrenia, manic depression, paranoia, narcissism, etc.

We may feel compassion or affection for such people. They may have talents and money. They may want to do their part for the cause. There is no need to be mean to them. But we can't afford to depend on them, much less place them in positions of trust and responsibility.

Why Violence is a Bad Idea for White Nationalists

My friends will no doubt interpret the following as a mere rationalization for the pathological squeamishness of a grown man who still covers his eyes when something violent happens on the screen. But attend to my arguments. I think they are sound.

1. Violence is futile

Setting aside all considerations of morality and legality and calculating merely in terms of forces and potential outcomes, violence against the system is completely futile. Yes, free men take risks. But only fools pick fights that they can never win.

As I never tire of reminding you, White Nationalists are a tiny, voiceless, powerless, despised minority. We are poorly funded, poorly organized, and poorly led. Our enemies control the greatest instruments of propaganda and coercion in history. We cannot beat them with violence. In fact, they *need* us to commit violence. They *feed* on violence, which is why they *manufacture* violence to blame on us.

Violence is futile, not merely because the enemy can catch and punish the perpetrators, but even more so because they can control how people perceive and react to it. The enemy has the power to assign the meaning and morality to our acts. We will never be seen as freedom fighters or romantic outlaws or heroic martyrs. We will be seen as kooks, sadists, nihilists, and terrorists—and with some justice, unfortunately.

We already have enough martyrs. We do not need any more. And martyrdom accomplishes nothing when the enemy determines its meaning. Yukio Mishima's death meant something in Japan, where the samurai tradition is still strong. Here, he would be branded a kook and a loser, and it would stick.

2. Fortunately, violence is unnecessary

Politics is about power, and power reduces to violence or the threat thereof. But what if it is too early for politics? Specifically, what if it is too late to reform the system and too early to replace it?

Then White Nationalists need to focus on metapolitics, specifically: (1) the intellectual development and cultural propagation of our worldview and (2) building a White Nationalist community — a community that is wealthy, powerful, resilient, and dedicated to the perfection and empowerment of its members; a community that can aspire to be the foundation of a future White Republic.

This approach is valid even if the present system could be expected to remain strong for the foreseeable future. In that case, our community would simply have to become very big and very strong to mount a political challenge to the system.

But fortunately there is every reason to believe that the system is in steep and irreversible decline. Nothing lasts forever, especially a society that violates all the laws of nature. I don't know when the system will fail, but it will almost certainly be within the lifetimes of most of the people reading this. Honestly, is there anything that White Nationalists could do to destroy the system better than its current masters? Frankly, my greatest fear is that the system will collapse *too soon*, long before our community is powerful enough to create a white homeland.

We are few, scattered, voiceless, and powerless. The system is vast and powerful, but it is destroying itself. Time may be short, e.g., we may have only a few decades. So we need to focus our time, energy, and resources not on destroying the system but on creating an alternative. But that requires the discipline not to waste our lives and resources in premature and futile confrontations with the system at full strength.

3. Power isn't everything

Throughout this essay, I have stressed the importance of power. In politics, power is more important than legality, public opinion, or moral sensibilities, because those in power create laws and shape people's opinions, including their moral opinions. They have power and we don't. As long as this condition persists, they will be able to do what they like with us.

But power isn't everything. Truth also matters. There are moral opinions, and there is moral truth. There are the laws of men, and there are the laws of nature. (Although Machiavelli was right to observe that unarmed prophets always fail; only the armed prophets succeed.)

I believe that truth is ultimately the source of power, that truth empowers and lies weaken. A civilization rises when it is in harmony with truth, reality, nature, and the life force. A civilization declines as it strays from them. As Spengler points out, a society, like an individual, gains the greatest external wealth and power once it is over the hill and the life force is dying within it.

We have truth, but no power. They have power, but no truth. But the life force surges in us as it ebbs in them, for they have strayed from nature's way. Our power will wax as their power wanes. Then a day will come when we can revisit the question of violence. But today, that question is closed.

Counter-Currents/*North American New Right*,
January 22 & 27, 2011

INDEX

This index lists all occurrences of proper names plus definitions and discussions of important concepts. Numbers in bold refer to a whole chapter or section devoted to a particular topic.

A

activism, x, 7–8, 74, 151–52, **158–62**, **181–84**, 212
aesthetics, 52–53
altruism (self-sacrifice), 64, 65, 80, 82, 116, 130, 149, 159
Amaudruz, Gaston-Armand, 106
American Nazi Party, 14
American Renaissance, 76, 78, 108, 108 n1, 130, 202, 215
American Third Position, 14
Anti-Defamation League (ADL), 207
apostasy (see also: conversion), **173–80**
aristocracy, 61, 136, 137, 138–40, 140–41, 142, 150–51, 199
Aristotle, 24, 40, 51, 60, 64, 136, 137, Auster, Lawrence, 108 n1

B

Baggins, Frodo, 153
Balfour Declaration, 86
Benoist, Alain de, xvi, 2, 35, 230
Black, Derek, 173, **174–75**, 179
Black, Don, 173, 175
Boas, Franz, ix
Bohannan, Colby, 152
Bolton, Kerry, xvi, 230
Bond, James, 172
bourgeois man, **59–60**, **61–62**, **62–63**, 68, 69, 89, 150, 183, 210
Bowden, Jonathan, vii, xvi, 5, 92, 107, 213, 230
Bradley, Amanda, 131
Breivik, Anders, 8, 9 n4, 113
Brimelow, Peter, 197
British National Party, 204–208,
Buchanan, Patrick, 76, 78, 82, 90, 187, 197, 198, 201, 202, 203
Buckley, William F., 13, 192
Bush, George W., 202

C

Calabro, Lou, 152
Catholic Church, 24, 120, 141, 158
character (moral), 159, 162, 167, 175, **176–78**, 179, 180, 183
Christian, Channon, 77, 150
Christianity, 70, 72, 82, 99, 114, **116–18**, 120–23, **124–27**, 169, 178, 183, 194
Cicero, 62–63
Cleary, Collin, xvi, 230
Cochin, Augustin, 36
Communism, 4, 5, 12, 13, 14, 25, 36, 42, 43, 75, 90, 102–3, 120, 150, **158–62**, 172
conformism, 126, 199–200
conservatism (see also: phony Right), 1, 3, 12–13, 18, 44, 67, 76, 89, 112, 114, 115, 127, 133, 150, 153, 164, 183, **191–96**, 197, 202
conspiracy (see also: occult warfare), 21, 26, 30, 32
conversion, **70–75**, **175–76**
Covington, Harold, 15, 15 n3, 215, 218
Cruddas, Jon, 205
cynicism, **56–58**, **58–59**, 61

D

Dabney, Robert Lewis, 18
Darwinism, 7
democracy, 12, 42, 61, 68, 82, **135–43**, 150, 164
Democratic Party, 13, 154
desire, 40, 59, 60, 61, 62

destiny, 27, 34, 100, 107
Devlin, F. Roger, xvi
Diana, Princess of Wales, 49
Disraeli, Benjamin, 22
Donovan, Jack, xvi
Duke, David, 8, 108 n1
duty (moral), 74
Dylan, Bob, 144

E
education (see also: propaganda), 6, 13, 23, 58, 119, 140–41, 142, 148, 151, 198
elitism, 6, 19–20, 29, 31, 33, 35, 77, **135–43**, 150–53, 170, 172, 183 198–201, 209–14, 220
emasculation, 127, 132
English Array, 30
English Mistery, 30
enmity, **39–40**, 83, 92, 108, 216
Epictetus, 51
epistemology, 52
Epstein, Marcus, 201
equality & inequality, 1–2, 18, 61, 72, 75, 86, 137, 149, 174
ethics (moral philosophy), ix–xi, xiv, 18, 21, 26, 39, 42, **45–55**, **56–69**, 71, 72, 75, 77, 79, 80, 83, 85, 86, 88, 92, 97, 98, **99–100**, **100–101**, 104, 106, 116, 132, 133, 137, 145–46, 149, 156, 159, 161, 163, 169, 171, 173, 175, 176–78, 185, 188, 189, 203, 215, 216, 217, 218, 221, 222
ethnocentrism, 31–32, 72, 80, 105
ethnonationalism, xiv, 3, 65, 89, 93, 105, 109, 110
Evola, Baron Julius, 7, 19–27, 31, 133, 151, 186

F
Fairburn, A. R. D. ("Rex"), 125
fascism, 1–2, 4, 5, 6, 206
Faurisson, Robert, 95, 105
Faye, Guillaume, xvi, 2, 35–37, 108, 108 n1, 109, 113
feminism, 16, 83, 87, **128–34**, 191, 200, 213
"Forrest, N. B." (VNN commenta-
tor), 202
Förster, Gerhard, 106
Francis, Samuel, 19, 197, 201, 202
Franklin, Benjamin, 88
freedom, 12, 13–14, 18, 33, 41, 60, 61, 68, 72, 123, 156, 173, 174, 202
Freemasonry, 26, 27, 32
Fröhlich, Wolfgang, 106
Front National (France), viii, 10, 36, 37, 73
Fukuyama, Francis, 41

G
Gaede, Lamb, 179
Gaede, Lynx, 179
Galileo Galilei, 178
Garaudy, Robert, 95, 105
Gardner, John, 193–96
genocide (see also: race-replacement), vii, 2, 3, 4, 5, 9, 66, 76, 77, 81, 82, 83, 84, 89, 92, 93, 94, 95, 96, 103, 104, 105, 111, 112, 146, 193, 217
Gibson, Mel, 202
Golden Dawn (party), vi
Gottfried, Paul, 201
Graf, Jürgen, 106
Gramsci, Antonio, 35, 36
Griffin, Nick, 113, 208
Guénon, René, 7, 19, 20, 23, 25–31
Gump, Forrest, 51

H
Haider, Jörg, vi
Hale, Matt, 219
Hamsun, Knut, 6
Harpham, Kevin, 215
Hart, Michael, 108, 108 n1, 201
Hegel, G. W. F., 25, 41
hegemony, **10–17**, 115
Heidegger, Martin, 7, 151
hierarchy, vii, 1–2, 5, 33–34, 37, 60, 119, 141, 150, 153
Hinduism, 30
history, 6, 7, 19–20, 22, 24–25, 41, 74, 77, 88, 93–94, 101, 116, 126, 170, 186, 192; Hegel on, 41; Traditionalism on, 7, 19–20, 22, 24–25

Index

Hitler, Adolf, 5-6, 30, 33, 67, **85-91**, 94, 111
holocaust, vii, 78, 85, **92-107**
Hood, Gregory, xvi
Hyde, Douglas, **158-62**

I
individualism, x, 32-33, 43, 61, 64, 72, 81, 156, 163, 173, 199-200
inequality, see: equality & inequality
Irving, David, 90, 106
Islam & Muslims, x, xv, 9, 10, 11, 100, 108, 113-15, 122, 124, 204, 205
Israel (also see: Jews & Jewish problem, Zionism), vi, 74, 82, 86, 103, **108-15**, 145, 217

J
James, William, 70-72
Jeansonne, Glen, 131
Jesus, 70
Jews & Jewish problem (also see: Israel, Zionism), iii-xi, 2, 5, 9, 10, 11, **12-14**, 15, 16, 24-25, 26, 31, 43, 66, 67, 70, 72, 73, 74, **76-84**, 85, 86-87, 88, 89, **92-107**, **108-115**, 116, 117, 121, 132, 145-48, 149, 150, 151, 159, 169, 172, 174, 176, 191, 193-96, **197-203**, 205, 206, 207, 217
"jock-sniffing," 213
Johnson, Casey, 150
Johnson, Greg, iii-xi
judgment, 139

K
Kearney, Denis, 125
King, Rodney, 38
Kissinger, Henry, 195
Kojève, Alexandre, 41,
kooks, 183-84, 212-13, 220-21
Krafft, Charles, 8, 179
Ku Klux Klan, 184
Kurtagić, Alex, 7, 76, 78

L
Left, see: New Left, Old Left
Le Pen, Jean-Marie, 36, 105

Lenin, Vladimir, 102
Leonidas, 68
Levin, Michael, 201
liberalism, 1, 12, 24, 38, 42, **42-43**, 59, 82, 89, 109, 115, 116, 118, 120-23, **124-27**, 145, 152, 158, 163, 173, 176, 191, 194
Limbaugh, Rush, 158
Linder, Alex, 83, 197-203
London, Jack, 125
Loughner, Jared Lee, 215, 216, 218
Ludovici, Anthony M., 30
Lyons, Eugene, 12

M
MacDonald, Kevin, iii-xi, xv, xvi, 13 n2, 75, 148, 194, 197, 202, 205-206
Machiavelli, Niccolò, 112, 137, 222
Maddow, Rachel, 189
Mahler, Horst, 106
mainstreaming, vii, 44, 148, 167-68, 183-84, **185-90**, 191-96, **197-208**
Mao Tse-Tung, 102
mentoring, 182, 186
metaphysics, 7, 25, 52, 53, 56, 126
metapolitics, iii, vii-ix, xiii, xiv, 3, 7-8, 9, 11-12, 15-17, **18-34**, **35-37**, 44, 45, 45 n1, 54, 56, 63, 141-42, 151-52, 189, 213-14, 221-22
Meyer, Frank, 12
Mishima, Yukio, 221
misogyny, 131-33
mixed regime, 136-37, 140-42
monarchy, 136-42, 150-51
morality, see: ethics
Mosley, Oswald, 199
multiculturalism, vi, vii, viii, ix, xi, xiv, xv, 15, 43, 56, 57, 76, 80, 86, 111-12, 113, 128, 131, 176, 191, 194, 206, 207, 208
Muslims, see: Islam
Mussolini, Benito, 5-6

N
Nash, George H., 13 n1
National Alliance, 14, 211-12
National Socialism, vii, 1-9, 30, 67,

72, 85–91, 95–96, 108 n1, 111–12, 184, 205, 206, 208
neoconservatism, 13, 13 n2
networks, 8, 32–34, 37, 141, 170–72, 186, 193, 198
New Left, viii–ix, 4–6, 9, 93
New Right, European, v, xvi, 2, 7, 21, 35–37
New Right, North American, v, xiii, xv, xvi, 1–9, 11, 21, 33, 36–37, 89, 92–93, 105, 141–42, 143
Newsom, Christopher, 77, 150
Nietzsche, Friedrich, 7, 41, 56, 100, 107, 151
Nixon, Richard, 192, 195
North American New Right (journal), xvi, 6, 230

O
Obama, Barack, 8, 155–56
objectivity (moral), **63–64, 65**
Occidental Dissent, 192
Occidental Quarterly, 192–94, 230
Occidental Quarterly Online (*TOQ Online*), 169, 192, 230
occult warfare, **18–34**
O'Meara, James, 230
O'Meara, Michael, xvi, 230
organic society, vii, 2, 5, 153
organizations (see also: occult warfare, party politics, secret societies), 15–17, 23–24, 27, 31–33, 37, 130–31, 141, 158–62, 172, 186, 190, 212, 213

P
paganism & neo-paganism, 7, 24, 121–23, 230
Parrott, Matt, xvi, 197–98
party politics, vii–viii, 7–8, 13–15, 36–37
Paul, Rand, 187
Paul, Ron, 156, 187, 198
philosophy, v, xiv, xv, **45–55**, 68, 73 82, 89, 121
phony Right (see also: conservatism), 1, 18
Pierce, William, 4, 15, 15 n3, 191–92, 196, 209–13
Plantin, Jean, 105
Plath, Sylvia, 150
Plato, 40, 55, 55 n2, 59–60, 62, 63, 64
pluralism, viii–ix, xiii, 4, 16, 17, 34, 43, **65**, 118, 120, 123, 131, 174
polarization, 196, 197–98
Pol Pot, 4, 102
Polignano, Michael, iv, xvi, 10, 100, 230
political activism, see: activism
political philosophy, 52
populism, 1, 6, 14, **135–43, 149–53, 209–14**,
Populist Party, 14
Pound, Ezra, 6
propaganda, xiv, 3, 7–8, 23, 58, 72, 78, 156
Protestantism, 24, 120
Protocols of the Learned Elders of Zion, 22–23, 26, 34
Pythagoras, 62–63

R
race (biological), iii, v–vi, viii, 1, 34, 44, 64, 65, 70, 78, 84, 85, 87, 89, 120, 125, 126, 148, 173–74, 193, 195, 198
race-replacement (see also: genocide), 84, 124, 135, 142, 151, 156
Reagan, Ronald, 192
reciprocity, **65–66**, 72, 105, 121
relativism (moral), 43, 46, **46–47**, **65**
religion, 1, 7, 13, 21, 30, 58–59, 70–72, 89, **116–18, 119–23, 124–27**, 164, 198, 219
Republican Party, 13, 67, 153, 187, 190, 193, 202
resentment, **149–53**, 209
Resistance Records, 211
revisionism (historical), 4, 90–91, 92, **93, 93–94, 94–96**, 96–97, 99, **100–101, 103–104**, 105, **105–106**
Right, see: conservatism, New Right, Old Right, phony Right
Robertson, Wilmot, 30, 166
Roosevelt, Franklin Delano, 82

Rudolf, Germar, 106
Russell, James, 187

S

Sallis, Ted, xvi
Savitri Devi, 30, 133, 186
Schmitt, Carl, **38–44**, 56, 60
Searchlight Institute, 204–208
secret societies, 21–25, 30–33
self-sacrifice, 64, 65, 130, 159
Seneca, Lucius Annaeus, 51
September 11, 2001 (9/11) terrorist attacks, 10, 73, 74
sex roles, **128–34**
Sharpton, Al, 152
skinheads, 205, 208, 209–12
Slaughter, Kevin, xvi
Smith, Bradley, 95
Socrates, 51, 54–55, 55 n2, 59, 61, 68
Southern Poverty Law Center (SPLC), iv, 178, 194, 207
sovereignty, xiv, 2, 3, **40**, 44, 110, 135
Spencer, Richard, 152, 197
Spengler, Oswald, 7, 151, 223
spiritedness (*thumos*), 40–41, 59–60
spite, 109, 114, 145–46
Spotts, Frederic, 90
Stalin, Joseph, 12, 90, 102
status, x, 49, 61, 126, 132, 165, 176, 178, **197–203**
Steele, Edgar, 219
Stevens, Brett, 152
Stoddard, Lothrop, 157
Stoics, 51
Stolfi, R. H. S., 90
Stolz, Sylvia, 106
Strauss, Leo, 55 n2

T

Tanstaafl, 76
Taylor, A. E., 55 n2
Taylor, A. J. P., 90
Taylor, Jared, 108 n1, 197, 201, 215, 218
Tea Party, 187–89, 196, 206
terrorism (see also: violence), vii, 2, 4, 5, 9, 216
thumos (spiritedness), 40–41, 59–60

Tocqueville, Alexis de, 199
tolerance, 118, 121, 123, 174
TOQ Online (*Occidental Quarterly Online*), 169, 192, 230
totalitarianism, vii, 2–5, 9, 12, 58, 65, 75, 89, 93
Traditionalism, 7, 19–33, 59
Trainspotter, xvi
Trotskyites, 13
trust, 31–32, 120

U

universality (moral), x n2, 38, 41–43, **64**, 65, 72, 80, 82, 83, 104–105, 116, 120–23, 125, 145, 173, 196

V

Venice, 141
Vinson, Irmin, 94
violence (see also: terrorism), xiv, 3, 39, 43, 112, 114, 165, 204, 297, **215–23**

W

Walker, Michael, 130
Whitaker, Bob, 105
White Nationalism, iii, vi, x, xiii–xv, **14–15, 15–16**, 17, 19, 26, 31–34, **44**, 56, 57, **63–66**, 66–69, **70–75**, 76, 78, 81, 85, 88–92, 95–96, 105–107, **108–15, 116–18**, 121–23, 124–27, **128–34**, 135, 136, 140–41, 142, 145, 146, 148, **151–223**
Wilders, Geert, 113, 204, 205–6
Williamson, Richard (Bishop), 106
Wilson, Woodrow, 82, 86
Winfrey, Oprah, 189
wisdom, 33, **49–50, 50–51, 51, 51–53**, 54, 63, 137
World War I, 82, 86–87, 103
World War II, vi, 1 n1, 2, 4, 12, 25, 43, 85–91, 93, 94, 96, 97, 102, 113, 205–206

Z

Zimmerman, Dirk, 106
Zionism (see also: Jews & Jewish problem), 26, **108–15**, 117
Zündel, Ernst, 106

ABOUT THE AUTHOR

GREG JOHNSON, Ph.D. is Editor-in-Chief of Counter-Currents Publishing Ltd., as well as Editor of *North American New Right*, its webzine (http://www.counter-currents.com/) and its biannual print journal. From 2007 to 2010 he was Editor of *The Occidental Quarterly*. In 2009, he created *TOQ Online* with Michael J. Polignano and was its Editor for its first year.

He is the author of *Confessions of a Reluctant Hater* (San Francisco: Counter-Currents, 2010) and, under the pen name Trevor Lynch, of *Trevor Lynch's White Nationalist Guide to the Movies* (San Francisco: Counter-Currents, 2012).

He is editor of Alain de Benoist, *On Being a Pagan*, trans. Jon Graham (Atlanta: Ultra, 2004); Michael O'Meara, *Toward the White Republic* (San Francisco: Counter-Currents, 2010); Michael J. Polignano, *Taking Our Own Side* (San Francisco: Counter-Currents, 2010); Collin Cleary, *Summoning the Gods: Essays on Paganism in a God-Forsaken World* (San Francisco: Counter-Currents, 2011); Irmin Vinson, *Some Thoughts on Hitler and Other Essays* (San Francisco: Counter-Currents, 2011); *North American New Right*, vol. 1 (San Francisco: Counter-Currents, 2012); Kerry Bolton, *Artists of the Right: Resisting Decadence* (San Francisco: Counter-Currents, 2012); James J. O'Meara, *The Homo and the Negro: Masculinist Meditations on Politics and Popular Culture* (San Francisco: Counter-Currents, 2012); and Jonathan Bowden, *Pulp Fascism: Right-Wing Themes in Comics, Graphic Novels, and Popular Literature* (San Francisco: Counter-Currents, 2013).